Praise for *Beginning Again*

"In a region historically marred by displacement and stereotypes, the poignant first-person narratives collected in *Beginning Again* reveal a stunning, multidimensional Appalachia, a chosen home that illustrates the power of belonging." —APPALSHOP

"Through intimate, first-person narratives, *Beginning Again* turns a tired stereotype of a monolithic Appalachian history, culture, and timeline on its head. Caringly shepherded by editor Katrina Powell, these stories collectively paint a complex portrait of a region and people steeled in resilience and resistance. Our region has long needed this book—an invitation to those here and beyond to expand our conceptions of who exists, who belongs, and who builds a loving home within these mountains." —RAE GARRINGER, author and editor of *Country Queers*

"*Beginning Again* successfully highlights the global connections that have long been integral to the making of Appalachia. Powell and those who share their life histories broaden the understanding of who is Appalachian and reveal how many seek safety in a place that is often portrayed as toxic. The individual narratives tie displacement in a variety of contexts to processes ubiquitous to capitalism and colonialism. The stories are an approachable calling in, asking us to reckon with the inequalities in our region, but also to hold hope that our communities will provide when political and economic systems fail." —LESLY-MARIE BUER, author of *Rx Appalachia*

"This wonderful book showcases the global, stereotype-busting diversity of Appalachia. It takes us from Rwanda to Staunton, Virginia, from Indigenous Monacan people to newly arrived refugees in Roanoke, offering a brilliant kaleidoscope of stories about migration, deprivation, and transformative human connection." —BARBARA ELLEN SMITH, author of *Digging Our Own Graves*

T0051471

Contributing Editor
Jordan Laney

Translators
Dina Fathi Ali, Leyla Nazhandali, Joseph Scarpaci

Transcribers
Maryam Bledsoe, Eliana Swerdlow, Aileen Thong

Interns
Michelle Kim, Kit Brazas, Jenni Hall

Additional Interviewers
Jordan Laney, Laura Murphy, Katie Randall, Jessica Taylor

Research Assistants
Tarryn Abrahams, Katie Beth Brooks, Kelly Scarff

Curriculum Advisory
Deirdre Hand, Janet Hanks, Babikir Harane

Fact-checking
Reading List Editorial, readinglisteditorial.com

Copyeditor
Cindy Black

Beginning Again

Stories of Movement and Migration in Appalachia

EDITED BY KATRINA M. POWELL

Haymarket Books
Chicago, IL

Published in 2024 by
Haymarket Books
P.O. Box 180165
Chicago, IL 60618
773-583-7884
www.haymarketbooks.org
info@haymarketbooks.org

ISBN: 979-8-88890-101-4

Distributed to the trade in the US through Consortium Book Sales and Distribution (www.cbsd.com) and internationally through Ingram Publisher Services International (www.ingramcontent.com).

This book was published with the generous support of Lannan Foundation, Wallace Action Fund, and Marguerite Casey Foundation. This project was supported in part by the National Endowment for the Arts.

Special discounts are available for bulk purchases by organizations and institutions. Please call 773-583-7884 or email info@haymarketbooks.org for more information.

Cover image of Margo Miller, executive director of the Appalachian Community Fund, at the Knoxville Botanical Garden and Arboretum, 2022, by Jessica Tezak, www.jesstezak.com.

Cover and interior design by Rachel Cohen.

Narrator illustrations by Lacy Hale, www.lacyhale.com.

Printed in Canada by union labor.

Library of Congress Cataloging-in-Publication data is available.

10 9 8 7 6 5 4 3 2 1

CONTENTS

FOREWORD

I will raise my eyes to the mountains; from where will my help come? My help comes from the Lord.

—Psalms 121:1–2

I think that this part of the psalm is the proper introduction to Appalachia because all of the Appalachians, all of the people, came here for comfort.

But let's just take it back a little bit. The rabbits, the ground-hogs, the wolves before we killed them off, all found comfort in Appalachia. The trees, the bushes found comfort in Appalachia. The Indigenous people lived here first *with* Appalachia.

The next group that came were the people that the English kicked out. And the Irish kicked out, because they didn't want to, for lack of a better word, be *bothered* with them. And those settlers began to destroy the trees and the bushes because they wanted to make things. The Black Americans came, mostly as people running from slavery. And as they ran from slavery, they found that they had friends in Appalachia, that Appalachia could offer comfort to those who needed a way to be safe.

During the time of the Underground Railroad, we've been told that Appalachian women made quilts so you could follow a quilted map from Georgia to Maine toward freedom. There would be a quilt laid outside of a cabin, which relayed a message. We think of escaping from slavery as a nighttime run, but you couldn't see a quilt at

night. So fleeing slavery was also definitely a daytime activity, and it
sometimes meant communication between the whites who had been
kicked out of Europe and the Blacks running toward freedom. They,
too, understood what it was like to not have a home. When they
hung lanterns at night to light the way for the enslaved, the people
who chased the enslavers could see the lanterns too. They reached
out to work with them, to move during the day. So we need to look
at the daytime running of the enslaved—there's a story there—of
the white women lynched for their compassion, of people working
together for comfort and home.

We also know—and it's incredibly important—that without
Appalachia speaking up, as it were, for America, the outcome of
the Civil War would have been different. West Virginia decided
it would not remain a part of Virginia and said that we will not
send our sons to die so that the Shenandoah can have slaves. When
West Virginia—with its Kanawha River—pulled away from Virginia, it blocked the Confederacy's access to the Ohio River and
saved the Union. If they hadn't done that, it would have been a
different war. So the United States owes being united in part to
Appalachians. They stood up for that which was right and have
continued to do so.

Parts of Appalachian history will cause some to be embarrassed
and ashamed. But we also know that Appalachians, whether they
were Black or white or Indigenous, have welcomed visitors from other nations, have welcomed other people who are escaping not slavery
but the violence of other nations, and Appalachia has offered them
a home.

These are a great people. And the stories shared in *Beginning
Again: Stories of Movement and Migration in Appalachia* are those
of people who have found comfort in Appalachia and who have
brought their sense of what is right to Appalachia—whether it's
what's right for the people, what's right for the trees and animals,
or what's right for the water. How do we listen to what nature has

given us? We must learn to listen to the lessons of Appalachia. So we are fortunate that this book is bringing the voices, which is to say the heart, of the great people who have chosen Appalachia as our home.

Nikki Giovanni
Tutelo/Monacan land
Blacksburg, Virginia
March 2024

INTRODUCTION

Everyday Existence and Resistance

I grew up in Appalachia, in the rural town of Madison, Virginia. My dad's side of the family has been in Appalachia for generations, migrating from the Scottish Highlands in the mid-nineteenth century. I consider myself to be Appalachian. My grandfather is from Roanoke, and he was assigned to my hometown during World War II, like many physicians at that time. My dad was born and raised here, but I was born in California at Mather Air Force Base, where my dad was stationed when he met my mother. When I was born, my mother and I joined my father at Naha Air Base in Okinawa, where he was stationed during the American War in Vietnam. After the war, we moved back to his hometown in Appalachia—I was four. I have some earlier memories of living elsewhere, but most of my memories are of Madison County, deep in the Blue Ridge Mountains. My relationship with the area and with the mountains was fraught as a girl. In many ways I felt out of place. There wasn't much room for a mouthy, sarcastic tomboy—or at least it seemed that way. I thought I had to leave to find where I belonged. It wasn't until much later that the landscape brought me back.

When I was growing up, we hiked nearly every weekend in Shenandoah National Park, and I was always aware of the history of displacement and resettlement in and around that land. When the park was formed in the 1930s, mostly white settlers were displaced from their homes and relocated to resettlement housing in the surrounding counties. The few African American families that lived there were not afforded resettlement options. And long before that, Monacan and Manahoac communities had been displaced by white settlers. So I was raised in a community where movement, mobility, and forced displacement were routinized and historical. After graduate school, I wrote my first book about the displacement of families from the park, studying handwritten letters written by displaced residents as they were relocated. Reading about their longing to remain in place, their voices jumping off the page, I realized how much a part of me the landscape of Appalachia is and how critical it is to understand it as a complex and varied place.

Fast-forward to 2016—J. D. Vance's book *Hillbilly Elegy* was published, and the damaging stereotypes repeated in that book frustrated me and many of my colleagues at Virginia Tech. This is a deep-seated frustration, as Appalachians are often mischaracterized. In early 2017, the Trump administration put into place a travel ban on people from "Muslim" countries, using racist stereotypes about refugees and migrants. As in many other communities in the US, refugees and migrants were resettling in Virginia from Syria, several countries in Africa, Central America, and other places. Though resettlement in Appalachia wasn't a new phenomenon, news media reports often portrayed the situation as a new "crisis." Doing so tended to place blame on individual families and perpetuated the dominant view of refugees and immigrants as being only victims and a drain on resources.

I knew from living here, from teaching Appalachian students, and from researching displacement narratives that not only were all those negative stereotypes not true—they were harmful. They influenced policymakers as resources were distributed, and they precipitated many human and civil rights violations. I began to imagine *Beginning Again: Stories of Movement and Migration in Appalachia* as a way to collect narratives within Appalachia, from people whose ancestors had lived here for generations and from those who had just arrived, *together*, to highlight the diversity of the region and the long history of movement, migration, and resettlement in Appalachia. The histories of displacement in Appalachia over time, including that experienced by Indigenous and African American communities, often isn't even acknowledged. Furthermore, the exploitation of resources and people in the region, for instance with mountaintop removal and coal mining, is part of that long history and is little understood by the broader public.

***

This project began in 2017, instigated by the official institution of the aforementioned "Muslim ban." At this time, the war in Syria was in full swing, and Amal, one of the project's first narrators, and her family had recently attended an event at Virginia Tech to welcome refugees. Meanwhile, immigration and asylum policies at the Mexico-US border and for-profit detention centers continued to raise deep divisions. Despite this, I witnessed how some local Virginia community members met and welcomed migrants bussed from Texas and Nevada as they resettled in the region. All this occurred against the backdrop of racism, job loss, and poverty—long-standing issues in the region. Local refugee partnerships worried that the travel ban, rooted in xenophobia and fear mongering, would increase hostility and provoke attacks on recently resettled refugees. Volunteers and networks of local, state, and federal agencies worked together to ensure new neighbors would be safe and feel welcome.

Working on the project, I saw how crucial it was to understand this contemporary moment of resettlement in the context of the history of land disputes in colonial Virginia and North Carolina, of forced displacement of Indigenous peoples, and the forced enslavement of Africans. This history matters in setting the contexts of the stories contained in this volume and in understanding the broader narrative of the development of the country. Two narrators who had agreed to be part of the project were unreachable after their

initial interviews; their ankle bracelets, placed on them by US Immigration and Customs Enforcement (ICE) while they awaited their
asylum cases, made visible the way this country tends to criminalize
migrants. Several narrators would only communicate with us via
WhatsApp so that they could not be traced. And a few whose narratives are included in this collection fear for their families in their
home countries as conflicts continue. Despite instances of racism,
violence, nonwelcoming rhetoric, and xenophobia, many are not de-
terred from wanting to stay here, to make their home in Appalachia,
to begin again. There is now and always has been movement within Appalachia—individuals, families, and entire communities have
moved into and out of Appalachia for centuries. An understanding
of Appalachia as a place of movement and mobility expands what
we mean when we say *Appalachia.* In the map shown on page 5, for
instance, the shaded area is an expansion of what the Appalachian
Regional Commission defines as Appalachia, and the crosshatch
shaded area is what is known as the Eastern Siouan language area.[1] Both are included to show the ways that colonialist boundaries/
state-making do not necessarily line up with the areas of communities already living on the land.

The stories in this book reflect an interconnectedness among
multiple groups of people and multiple kinds of displacement. Native peoples such as the Monacan, Manahoac, and Tutelo, among
others, were forcibly removed from their lands during colonization;
Africans were forcibly displaced from their homelands, enslaved, and
brought to the region; coal miners and their families were forced to
relocate after resources were depleted and mines were closed; landowners have lost their lands for public use projects such as a national
park, a pipeline, and highways; the red spruce tree has been depleted

---

1. For more information on the political history of the Appalachian region, see
Stewart Scales, Emily Satterwhite, and Abigail August, "Mapping Appalachia's
Boundaries: Historiographic Overview and Digital Collection," *Journal of Appala-
chian Studies* 24, no. 1 (2018): 89–100.

due to climate change. These and many other migration and resettlement moments in Appalachia highlight the historical and more recent reasons for resettlement.

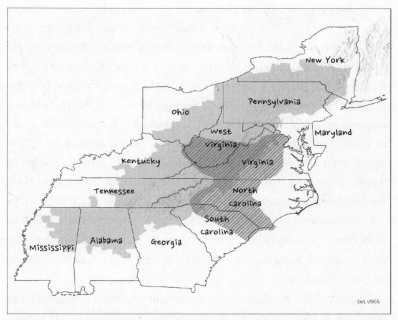

Designed by Stewart Scales, Department of Geography, Virginia Tech, used by permission of the designer. See the "Mapping Appalachia Project" at https://mapappalachia.geography.vt.edu/about-2/.

Mekyah's narrative, for instance, highlights the insidious systemic nature of racism—that it is mundane, pervasive. For instance, rather than focus on a single incident when he was called a derogatory term, it is critical to him that we understand what he calls the "slow burn," the cumulative effect of the bigoted attitudes he and his friends encounter daily. Mekyah's clear sense of his own story rewrites a US narrative and the Appalachian narrative. In refusing to recount a particular incident of bigotry, he counters that it's too easy to identify a particular individual perpetrator. It's bigger than that, it's every day, all the time, not the *n* word but many other words and incidents. He wanted his narrative to focus on what he's *doing*, not what is being imposed upon him.

The narrators in *Beginning Again* do not see themselves as victims. They don't really see themselves as heroes, either. They're just ordinary people—they get to the daily business of living their lives in their communities, even in the face of adversity. Some of their experiences with injustice are related to a singular traumatic event or issue; some are not so clear. As Mekyah suggests, much is best described as a slow burn—systemic failures to ensure equity, both for people whose families have lived in Appalachia for generations and for those newly arrived. Displacement is a shared experience, albeit experienced differently and in inequitable ways by various groups of people. *Beginning Again* holds space for stories of the region, both historical and contemporary, connected by displacement, migration, and resettlement. What the narratives in this volume suggest is that every instance of displacement—and every place in which displacement or resettlement occurs—is layered with issues of access, equity, race, gender, class.

Appalachian Studies scholars, community media, and activists have long worked to dispel simplistic and flattened perceptions of the region and its people. Works such as Beth Macy's *Dopesick*, the podcasts *Country Queers* and *Inside Appalachia*, Elizabeth Catte's *What You Are Getting Wrong about Appalachia*, and Elaine McMillion Sheldon's documentary *King Coal* highlight the diversity in the region and the extractive practices that have decimated resources there. Nonetheless, damaging representations and narratives that degrade the people who live in the area persist. Despite these representations, despite the continued extraction of natural and human resources with devastating effects, and despite the broken promises of and harms caused by big business, people in Appalachia live complicated lives like anyone else.

As a girl growing up in Appalachia, I experienced firsthand some of the effects of negative stereotypes about the region and its people.

Some equated my accent with a lack of intelligence, while others assumed that girls shouldn't pursue higher education. Later, as I studied the history of Shenandoah National Park and interviewed descendants of the families displaced when the park was formed in the 1930s, I heard in their stories a resistance to the stories told *about* them and their ancestors. As a teacher of autobiography and displacement narratives, I wanted to understand the history of eminent domain law in relation to the region, which of course is intricately connected to the history of the founding of the country, the Takings Clause in the US Constitution, the genocide and forced relocation of Native Americans, and the intersections between citizenship for African Americans and Native Americans, especially in relation to displacement and a series of federal laws restricting movement, land ownership, education access, and a number of other rights.

***

During the early planning of this project, I met Dina Fathi Ali, one of the volunteers with the Blacksburg Refugee Partnership (BRP). As an Arabic speaker, she provided a critical service as newly resettled families from Syria adjusted to life in Appalachia. She is tireless in her volunteer work, connecting people to resources and providing translation for them as they navigate doctor visits, register children for school, and open bank accounts. When I asked her about her own experience moving to the region, she said:

> When people ask me, "Where are you from?" I say, "I'm from here." I've been here for twenty years, so I feel like I'm a local of Blacksburg—a native of Egypt but a local of Blacksburg. At first, I felt like, *You're an outsider, a stranger, a visitor, a temporary person.* How do you grow roots in a place and feel like you belong here? When I started volunteering with BRP I felt even more connected to the area. It deepened my sense of belonging. I was helping people who just came from a different part of the world, and I felt like I know this place and I can help the newcomer make a place for themselves.

Dina migrated to Virginia for education in the mid-1980s. Her story is filled with the daily stresses of managing immigration requirements, such as going back to Egypt every six months to extend an education visa. The stress and cost of travel with small children was compounded when she and her husband had to go back to Cairo during the violence and chaos of the Arab Spring. Yet Dina's story reflects what many refugee and immigrant stories do: after having their own experience of navigating US immigration policy, they in turn help others adjust to a new home. Importantly, Dina's experience highlights the ways that a long, slow, steady, and routine readjustment is part of resettling in Appalachia.

The stories in this volume illustrate just a few of the many ways people (re)settle in the region. The narrators relate more expansive possibilities for what it means to be Appalachian. As many mention in their narratives, the physical landscape—the mountains and valleys, the hills and hollers, the lakes and greenery—can evoke both refuge and suffering—refuge in the ways its beauty can provide solace and quiet, and suffering as climate change, mountaintop removal, pipelines, routine flooding, and tornados can upend families and communities. For the narrators in this collection, a sense of identity, and whether they consider themselves to be "an Appalachian," has a lot to do with ancestry and connection to the land. In addition to issues of identity, the narrators in this volume address human and civil rights, access to education, internal migration, family, land rights, racial justice, lack of employment opportunities, longing to return to the homeland, government wrongs, everyday injustices, and community rebuilding.

The narratives that emerged resist and complicate the "overcoming adversity" trope to which refugee stories are often confined. This book highlights how making community can counter simplistic stereotypes of Appalachia as a region. The impacts of displacement are an ongoing, sometimes daily, experience, as waiting in lines, waiting on government aid, waiting for national and international communities to make meaningful changes in policy weigh on residents every day. Like many who have experienced displacement, the narrators in *Beginning Again* exert agency—they find places to have control and push back against those forces that limit them.

The narratives in this collection make clear that there is much to be concerned about in Appalachia. Young people who love living here have difficulty finding decently paid work and are forced to relocate to where they can find good jobs. Several narrators spoke of how their family's expectations and hopes for them, especially around education, weighed heavily on them. As young people with a better grasp of English, they often translated for their parents or helped friends and neighbors, which contributed to their sense that they had to grow up fast. Despite these difficulties and others, many people want to stay—there is a sense of connection to the land that is palpable. The land is tied to Appalachian identity, and when we see the mountains, as narrator Rufus says, many of us feel a sense of home and belonging.

The underlying tension between a love for the region and the reality of inequities is also present in these narratives. Narrators described being welcomed in new communities by some while at the same time experiencing racism and xenophobia from others. Elvir recounts having a connection with his African American peers in high school through common experiences of discrimination—not for his skin color but for his accent. Amal recounts feeling a landlord would not attend to her complaints simply because she was a refugee. Hannah discusses how despite experiencing homophobia, she and her wife maintain their farm and family and make "a difference just by existing."

The narratives in this collection, including those of refugees and migrants, *are* Appalachian narratives, and *Beginning Again* sets them in conversation with one another. With the recent and ongoing crises of displacement and migration in Afghanistan, Ukraine, Gaza, and other regions, and climate change displacement on the rise, movement and mobility in Appalachia will likely increase. The narrators in *Beginning Again* help us discern the issues and challenges of resettlement and (re)building community within the constraints of displacement, inequity, and structural oppression and work toward an Appalachia where more can be embraced and where all can thrive.

Katrina M. Powell
Tutelo/Monacan land
Blacksburg, Virginia

EDITORIAL DIRECTOR'S NOTE

The twelve narratives in this book are the result of oral history interviews conducted over a five-year period between spring 2018 and fall 2023. With every Voice of Witness narrative, we aim for a novelistic level of detail and (whenever possible) a birth-to-now, chronologized scope in order to portray narrators as individuals in all their complexity, rather than as case studies. We do not set out to create comprehensive histories of human rights issues. Rather, our goal is to compile a collection of voices that (1) offers accessible, thought-provoking, and ultimately humanizing perspectives on what can often seem like impenetrable topics; and (2) can meaningfully contribute to the efforts of social justice and human rights movements.

In order to honor our narrators' experiences, Voice of Witness oral histories are crafted with the utmost care. For this project, editors and interviewers were trained in VOW's oral history methodology by then education director Cliff Mayotte and me. Recorded interviews were transcribed, translated if needed, and organized chronologically. Then, the resulting narrative drafts went through multiple rounds of revision and follow-up interviews, to ensure depth and accuracy. The stories themselves remain faithful to the speakers' words (we seek final narrator approval before publishing their narratives) and have been edited for clarity, coherence, and length. In some cases, names and details have been changed to protect the identities of our narrators and their family and acquaintances. All the narratives have been carefully fact-checked and are supported by various supplemental materials—including an essay, a timeline, and a glossary—included in the back of the book that provide context for, and some explanation of, the history of and present-day issues surrounding movement and migration in Appalachia.

We thank all the individuals who courageously, generously, and patiently shared their experiences with us, including those we were unable to include in this book. We also thank all the frontline human rights and social justice advocates working to promote and protect the rights and dignity of people in Appalachia.

Finally, we thank our national community of educators and students who inspire our education program. With each Voice of Witness book, we create a Common Core–aligned curriculum that connects high school students and educators with the stories and issues presented in the book, with particular emphasis on serving marginalized communities. As we continue to amplify a diversity of voices in our book series, we are also committed to developing curricula that directly support students in English Language Learner (ELL) communities. In 2020, about 4.96 million public school students were learning to speak English as a second language. In California alone, ELLs account for about 19 percent of the total public school student population, and these numbers continue to grow. In response to this need in our education networks and beyond, we continue to expand our offerings in this area. Our education program also provides curriculum support, training in ethics-driven storytelling, and site visits to educators in schools and impacted communities.

I invite you to visit voiceofwitness.org for free, downloadable educational resources, behind-the-scenes features on this book and other projects, and information on how you can be part of our work.

In solidarity,
Đào X. Trần
Editorial Director
Voice of Witness

CLAUDINE KATETE

BORN: 1992, Kigali, Rwanda
INTERVIEWED IN: Staunton, Virginia
Social Worker

Claudine's family fled Rwanda in 1994, when she was two, during the civil unrest there.[1] One brother and her father were separated from the family during the confusion as they moved through several camps before arriving in Namibia. Claudine spent twenty years walking to and living in camps, including the Osire Refugee Camp in Namibia, before arriving in the United States in 2014. When the family was finally able

---

1. The population of Rwanda is made up mainly of two ethnic groups, the Hutu and Tutsi. The two groups intermingled, but Hutu political extremists fostered supremacist ideology and encouraged discrimination against the Tutsi. On April 6, 1994, a rocket shot down an airplane carrying the presidents of Burundi and Rwanda. This action sparked massive violent massacres, which led to the deaths of more than 800,000 people.

to move to the US, Claudine had to travel separately from her mother and other siblings. She arrived alone in New York and later reunited with her mother in Virginia.

When we met at a World Refugee Day celebration in 2018, Claudine, her mother, and her sister arrived in dresses of vibrant colors— dresses her mother had made. Claudine was pursuing a degree in social work at Mary Baldwin University in Staunton, Virginia. We later met in the university's library—a beautiful white building on a hill.

THE MOON WAS FALLING

I wasn't even in kindergarten when we left Rwanda. I was around two, just a baby. We left Kigali, and I remember walking in Congo— it was more than sixty miles. I remember it seemed like the moon was falling, and I was scared. My mom tells me the stories of that journey. She said, "You were only carrying your jacket, but you were crying about it." I remember the refugee camps in Zambia and in Angola but not in Congo or Zaire. I remember most clearly the Osire Refugee Camp in Namibia, because that's where I really grew up.[2]

We were part of the group of refugees who flew from Rwanda very early in the war. My sister, two brothers, my mother, and I were separated from my father and my brother Claude during the shooting in Rwanda. The rest of us arrived at a camp in Zaire first, but we didn't stay long because my mom could tell it would not be good— there was no food, no work. So she decided, "We're going to leave." We walked so very much in all those countries. The only place that I

---

2. Osire is located about one hundred miles north of the Namibian capital of Windhoek. Originally built to accommodate refugees from Angola and the Democratic Republic of the Congo in 1992, Rwandan refugees came there during the genocide in 1994. At its largest in 1998, there were approximately twenty thousand people living in Osire. What Claudine referred to as Congo is officially the Republic of the Congo. See "Maps of the World" at www.vidiani .com/large-detailed-political-map-of-africa-with-all-capitals-1996 for additional information.

remember that we actually traveled in a vehicle was when we got to Namibia and the UN took us to the camp. The rest of the journey was only walking.

I was around five when we lived at the refugee camp in Namibia. My first language is Kinyarwanda. I speak five languages: Kinyarwanda, Kirundi, Swahili, Portuguese, and English. Namibia's official language is English, and Portuguese was the first language I learned in school because the Angolans were the ones who were teaching us. In the camp, they were the ones distributing the food and managing shelter, so you really needed to speak Portuguese. We spent ten years without hearing anyone speak our language apart from my mom. We were the first Rwandans in that camp. There were many other people in the camp: Ethiopians, some Sudanese, Congolese, and Burundians too.

Growing up in the camp, I always wanted to further my education. But the camp didn't offer scholarships to students who are from Rwanda. There are so many policies about eligibility, so Rwandans didn't get any scholarships. The camp only offered education up to grade ten. From there, if your parents didn't have any form of income, you had to stop. But my mom worked very hard. She used to sell vegetables that she grew and saved some money. She sent me to grades eleven and twelve at the school in a nearby town.

The school was called Paresis Secondary School. It was in Orwetoveni, a small town in the Otjiwarongo region, about one hundred kilometers from the camp. It was really difficult. I couldn't identify myself as a refugee because there was a lot of stigma and discrimination in the city. I had friends who were from Angola. Angola is very close to Namibia. To avoid stigma, I'd say, "I'm from Angola," and I never really gave my true identity. One day at school, one of the grade eight teachers—I don't know how she found out—said, "So you're a refugee." I said, "Yeah, I'm a refugee." Everybody was looking at me like they were surprised. After that, it made it hard for me to navigate school because they saw me as different.

THAT WOMAN, SHE'S FIERCE

My life in the camp was all based on hope. Namibians worked in the camp with the United Nations High Commissioner on Refugees, but the UNHCR's agreement with the government prevented refugees from working. The UNHCR in the camp provided vocational trainings, so I was certified to work. But I couldn't get a job. They don't employ refugees in the city. If you were a refugee, you couldn't have any relationship with the nationals who worked in the camp. If a national working in the camp had a romantic relationship with a refugee, for example, they were automatically fired and could never get a job with the UNHCR again. We weren't allowed to do any form of business with them, not even buying goods. This set up bad feelings about the refugees.

We were given many things, but there was much more that we needed, such as food and firewood to cook. If you went for firewood near the farms outside the camp and a farmer saw you, you could get shot. So many people were shot because of that. There were a lot of people who died because the farmers didn't like refugees going to their farms. So we didn't go get any firewood outside the camp. When you live in an area without any means, you find ways to support your family, so there were tensions as people tried to survive. We had to compete for food and other rations.

It was difficult not only for us children but for my mom too— she didn't have a husband. She was young, but she didn't get married again. She was still a very strong woman and always defended us in the camp. She didn't speak English or Portuguese well, but people always said, "That woman, she's fierce. You don't want to mess with her." If other kids beat us up, my mom would come and defend us.

In the camp, fetching water was a constant chore and there was lots of fighting over a place in line. To fetch water, you had to leave something behind to save your place, like a stone or a brick, so others would know it's your turn to fetch. The men wanted to be dominant and didn't like my mother fetching, so they would try to take our water container. If someone tried to move our container my mother would fight. Even men used to fight my mom, but she fought back. She didn't give up. She said, "Fetching water was like war."

WHEN THEY SHOT AT US, PEOPLE JUST SPREAD OUT

I don't remember Rwanda because I was so little when we left, but when the fighting started, when they shot at us, people just spread out. At first, we were all together as a family, but when there was shooting, crowds of people ran, pushing into each other. Of us five kids, my mother ended up with just four of us—my brother Claude wasn't with us when we left for the camps.

In the chaos, Claude ended up leaving with a man who knew my mom back in Rwanda. They fled Rwanda together because people were just going anywhere to any country. My brother and the man went to a camp in Uganda. That's where he raised my brother. When Claude was a teenager in secondary school, the man passed away. Then Claude lived with friends in the camp. My mom went really far, to Southern Africa.

Claudine's family didn't know where her brother was for ten years. Then, by chance, they heard about a Rwandan man raising a boy in a camp in Uganda who wasn't his son. Claudine's mother worked with the Red Cross to find out if the boy was Claude. The Red Cross identified Claude, but rather than move him to Namibia, the family decided to add him to their resettlement case so that when they moved to the United States, his case could be processed with his family.

We found my brother after many years, and it was so emotional for my mom, going to the airport to see him. For us siblings, it wasn't as emotional. My mom and Claude were crying when they first saw each other. For us it was like, "Nice to meet you, brother." We were raised by our mom, and he was raised by a man who was a stranger to us. We're totally different people. Even the culture that we grew up with, Namibian culture, it's more like European cultures, like here. They don't have the culture of Uganda or Rwanda. He grew up more in that culture. We had spent more than twenty years apart until Claude came to the United States in 2017.

You don't decide where you are going when you apply for resettlement. The UNHCR said resettlement was being offered to widows, orphans, and families who cannot go back to their home country. My mom was born in Burundi, but moved to Rwanda when she was younger due to the Burundian war and married there. Burundi had war long before Rwanda, and she was an orphan. She doesn't even know whether everyone from her family is alive or not.

To get resettled, you go through interviews with the UNHCR. They interview you, and then, if you qualify, they send you a letter. This process took us five to six years. We actually got accepted for resettlement in Canada at first, but for some reason it didn't work out. Then they transferred our case to the USA. Once everything was approved, US immigration services came in and met with us. They really do a very fierce security check. They ask us many personal and distressing questions, like "Were you abused?" They go back to your village and try to find your family members. It's difficult because you never know your status during the long process. Sometimes they don't even call you back, and they never tell you why they didn't call you back. So it's all just hoping and waiting.

Finally, after eighteen years in the camps, we came to the United States. I arrived in New York alone because we had to travel separately—I don't know why. It was so difficult because we knew when families were separated for travel it could be years before they could reunite. That trauma was too much for my mom. She was very upset, crying; we were all crying. She didn't want to go without me, but the UN told her, "You really need to go. At least you can go with your other children, and we're going to follow up from there."

After my mom and two siblings left, my older brother was still in the camp with his family—his wife and kids. Then the camp officials told my older brother that he was going and I was staying. I was devastated. *Oh, my God. What is this?* I thought. They just said to us, "This is what we got from the International Organization for Migration." The IOM makes all the decisions and people who are in the camp have no authority, no control over what happens. Finally, a few weeks later I was told I would be going. Thank God I was on the list. The airplane was frightening. All of us refugees had little bags with "IOM" printed on them, and they shuttled us through. I arrived in New York and my brother came to get me. The hotel where we stayed had so many refugees that they were sleeping in the corridor. It was so cold in January. My older brother found work in New Hampshire and stayed there. I got on a plane to Virginia where my family picked me up at the airport. I hadn't seen them in a month. My siblings said my mom was really depressed while she was waiting for me to come. She couldn't eat. I was so skinny too. When I was still in Namibia and most of my family had left, I couldn't eat anything because I imagined everything that could happen that would keep me from my family.

A DREAM COME TRUE

When we finally arrived in Virginia it was really like a dream come true for us. It felt so good. At the camp—I have many pictures—it was so dry. Our house was awful. We slept on the sand. If there is any wind, this sand falls on you. It's so windy and it's a desert. Everything is dry. And it's so cold and dry that in the winter our skin would crack. We used to call our dry skin "maps" because it would crack. I used to think that my eyes would never be clean anymore. To shower, which was outside, we put together some blankets, some clothes for privacy. But we had to walk on the sand to get to the showers. By the time we got back to the family tent, our feet were already dirty. We'd have to use a bucket of water at the door to wash our feet again and go inside.

So that was our whole life; that's what we knew. There were so many things in the United States that we didn't even know how to do, like drive or swim. If I was still back in the camp, I wouldn't be able to drive. How could I? I couldn't even have a car. So these small things are a really big deal for us.

It was so cold when I first arrived in the US during the winter, and I thought, *Wow, there's so much firewood here.* It was really amazing to see and know that I was going to have my own bed. I'd never had my own bed. I used to sleep with my sister in this tiny room, and we were always arguing, arguing, arguing over space. Here we still share a room, but at least I have my own bed. And we were like, "Wow." The beds and things are donated—people didn't even want those mattresses—but for us that was really something.

It has been so beautiful being somewhere green like Appalachia. Even though it's windy, you don't feel all the sand like at the camp. Virginia is really beautiful. I actually felt something here. I used to get lost a lot in the city. Because it was so different from the camp, so plentiful, we were just really happy here.

A PROCESS TO ADJUST

There was a time that I had been here maybe eight months or so. I spoke English fluently. I went to see the health specialist person in the resettlement office. She tried to tell me I had a package, and I didn't understand what she was saying. I told her, "Please explain what you mean." She told me, "You've already been here long enough to know, and plus, you speak English." I was offended by that and really pissed. I was like, "It doesn't mean that I don't know how to speak English. Where we come from, we didn't get packages. We didn't receive any mail. You have no idea. When you go to the hospital, you just go, you don't make an appointment." Small things like that were so difficult for us to get used to, and especially if someone doesn't speak English, it's even worse. Just talking on the phone is difficult. And then they just shut you down if they can't understand you. You can't even go back to the office because they're not going to help you. I just want people to know that regardless of whether a person speaks English or not, it's really a process. It takes time for people to get used to everything when they move here.

Even though it's been hard, it's really worth it now because I know that at the end, I'm actually going to have a country. That wasn't how it was in the camp. I had my mom, and we didn't choose that life. That life was imposed on us for reasons that weren't even about us. I can still feel the suffering of hunger, the struggle as a kid, I really didn't understand. We were fine eating whatever my mom prepared, but overall, it was so much struggle. She was like, "I'm just going to dedicate myself to my kids and raise them."

So every time that I go through struggles now, like with my college roommate or difficulties concentrating with my studies, I just remind myself where I came from, how much I wanted this opportunity. So I cry and put myself back together. I have to do it because I know it'll be better. How I deal with it all comes from the experience, the harsh time that I had, and just knowing how my mom made it. She lived in New Hampshire for a while and worked in housekeeping at the university. It was very difficult work, but she still did it. I just compare all the struggles that we're going through and think, *You really have to make it work. Otherwise, you won't come out of it.*

MY PLAN WAS BROKEN

Coming to America, we knew that once we got here, we could further our education. Before arriving here, I already knew what I wanted. I wanted to do some form of social work so that I can come back to the refugee camp and help other people. Refugees in the camps mostly don't get services that would be helpful for schooling and work. I just want to be that resource and pass on information to the people that actually need it.

At Virginia Western Community College, I majored in human services because I want that career. I got an associate degree, and while attending Virginia Western, I did nails for four years. I'm glad I still know how to do them. Virginia Western has a transfer program to Mary Baldwin University or Radford University. The best advice I got from one of my professors was for me to go to Mary Baldwin. She helped me with the transfer process. It was stressful at first because failing is not an option for me.

I finished my courses in the social work program at Mary Baldwin in the fall of 2019. I started my field placement with Roanoke City Department of Social Services in early 2020. It's very practical. You practice all the things you learn and plan for in class. At the agency I worked a regular eight-hour day Monday through Thursday. Then on Fridays we had class and I caught up on assignments. In class we talked about our experiences, about assignments, and about what was going on in our field placement. We listened to our classmates' experiences and learned how to deal with stressful cases.

I was in my field placement for two months, and then in mid-March I found out that everything was cut off. I had to stay home because of COVID-19. All the classes at Mary Baldwin went online. There were so many activities that I was still required to do for field placement, like attending advocacy community meetings. But I was unable to because those meetings were no longer happening. So I worried if I could still graduate. Luckily our program director adjusted our requirements so we could graduate and still meet our professional requirements. I continued to do my work remotely and did research to cover the hours. It's not the same though. I worked with Adult Protective Services at the agency, and we did a lot of home visits. After the shutdown I didn't have direct contact with clients. I had two clients of my own that I was working with, and before I left, my cases were closed.

I was very disappointed about the graduation ceremony from Mary Baldwin—it was canceled. I had planned a big celebration. Family and friends were coming from across the country. Even family in Rwanda that my mom reconnected with were coming to celebrate. My graduation was a reason for all of us to get together. But my plan was broken. I was going to wear the cap and gown. We couldn't take the photographs with all our family and friends. My mother was going to see me walk across the stage. She worked so hard to get me here. My brothers couldn't travel from New Hampshire. I know they're all proud, but it wasn't the same.

Since my field placement was going to be in Roanoke, I moved out of my dormitory and into an apartment in January and drove to class on Fridays in Staunton—an hour's drive. My mother moved back to Roanoke from New Hampshire. She was helping my brothers there, but now we live together in Roanoke. When my sister's classes at Radford University moved online, she moved in with us. It was really hard. I was the only one working during the pandemic. I worked at the *Roanoke Times* delivering newspapers to pay the rent on the apartment. I worked from midnight to 4 a.m., driving and taking papers from house to house. I made about $1,400 a month, but the rent is more than half of that. It was really good to be together though. Mom has a plot at the community garden. So she grows vegetables and that helps us. We all love being with her. She takes care of us.

Before my field placement was canceled, I didn't sleep. I'd come home and get ready to go to the agency for work. I was worried about being able to find a job in social work because most of the places where I looked for a job were closed. I have student loans.

I was able to go to graduate school at Radford and earned a master's in social work. Then I applied for a job as a social worker in northern Virginia. It's the first time I've lived away from my mother in a while.

I LEARNED THAT LIVING IN THE CAMPS

Since I was younger, I've wanted to open my own agency, a place for social work but with high school students wanting to pursue education—like who I was when I was getting ready to go to college. I want to work with immigrants and refugees, and I want to work with students directly. After high school, there are many who rush to go into the workforce. Some are pressured by their parents, and I know from personal experience that some parents have cultural beliefs and traditions that keep their kids from college, especially girls. Some girls, their fathers pressure them to get married. Also, this is a new country for them, and they might not have access to information. There's so much more that we can achieve if we go to college.

I really miss college because I lived on campus with friends and shared experiences with them. We would get together at the library and talk about our classes and our problems. I liked going downtown to the coffee shop with my friends too.

I haven't seen my brothers in New Hampshire in a long time, but because of COVID-19 I couldn't see my brother who lives here in Roanoke either. His wife was pregnant, and my nephew was small, so we were very careful. We did a Zoom chat for his birthday. I didn't see my boyfriend for two months. He lives in Maryland. We Zoom chatted a lot during that time. I hope things get back to normal soon. Sometimes when I think about it, you know the saying, "It is what it is." You live with it. When you don't have control over something, what can you do? Stressing won't help you. I learned that living in the camps.

As of 2023, Claudine is living in Falls Church, Virginia, and works as a clinical social worker. After finishing her master's degree in 2021, she found it difficult to find related work because of the pandemic. Now, though, she's able to do the work she'd hoped to, helping families navigate social assistance programs, including resettlement.

ELVIR BERBIĆ

BORN: 1981, Derventa, Bosnia and Herzegovina
INTERVIEWED IN: Roanoke, Virginia
Student Affairs Manager

Elvir Berbić came to Roanoke, Virginia, with his family when he was fourteen years old in 1995, after living for three years in refugee camps in Croatia. A student affairs professional in higher education for the Virginia Tech Carilion School of Medicine, he also volunteers working with teenage boys through a local soccer enrichment program. We first met Elvir at a local coffee shop during a joint meeting of service providers and volunteers for refugees in the New River Valley. In his role as a volunteer soccer coach and mentor for refugee youth, he shared insights into the perspectives of families as they transition to a new landscape and culture.

Elvir is known throughout his community, serving on a variety of boards, including the Blue Ridge Literacy Center. Always with a smile, Elvir is quick to offer insights and solutions. Here he recounts his story, including vivid scenes of being a teenage refugee himself and the challenges of navigating a new culture.

THE WHOLE WAR WAS SURPRISING

My name is Elvir Berbić—obviously, that pronunciation is Americanized. The way you'd say my first name is not "Elvir"; it's "El-veer." My last name would not be pronounced "Bear-bick"; it would be "Bear-bish." My family and I moved to Roanoke on August 29, 1995, as refugees from Bosnia. I'm from a town called Derventa, in northern Bosnia, about thirty kilometers away from the border with Croatia.

When I was about five years old, around 1986, we moved into an apartment building in Derventa. It was a new development in the eighties, and my father was able to secure an apartment for us. Our neighbors were from different religious backgrounds. We lived in a very secular environment, so the whole war was surprising. When I was ten, the war started happening across the Croatian border, and it was coming into our side of the country, the northern side.

During the first week of the fighting, my father and other neighbors would rotate shifts to guard the entrance of the building. They had an AK-47 and a pistol. I would come downstairs and visit them and see what they were doing. I never really knew what was happening. I just wanted to hold a gun. I thought it was a toy because it looked like a toy, which I knew it wasn't once I held it. I remember asking my father if I could hold the AK or the pistol. I specifically remember my dad taking off whatever holds the bullets, emptying the shells (including the one that was in the chamber), putting the safety on, and handing me the gun. And this was about ten o'clock at night because they were keeping guard throughout the night. I put the pistol in a holster around my waist, put the AK around my shoulders, and I held it, and it was really, really heavy. It was cold metal. It was like, *This doesn't feel like a toy. It feels like I'm holding a bunch of bricks.* I was a skinny ten-year-old; I didn't weigh much. Then I handed it back.

People started to leave the apartment buildings because they were easy targets. They went into basements to hide. But we left the country. It was like, *We're not going to anybody's house; we're just going to leave the country.* When we were leaving, I saw military people positioning themselves in certain areas holding the same weapon I had been holding a couple of nights back. And I had seen and heard the sound of an AK from a distance. On our TVs at that time, they would show very gruesome things, not only people lying on the ground, but people being executed with the same kind of weapon that I had been holding in my hand.

My mom and brother and I left, but Dad stayed back to defend the neighborhood. After that, I wouldn't say I'm anti-gun, but I don't want to hold one. I really don't have any desire to own one, to go to gun ranges, to hear a weapon go off. I just don't like hearing it because it reminds me of that time.

AFRAID TO GO OUTSIDE

When my mother, my brother, and I left with some other family members, we were in three vehicles. My aunt's father-in-law drove the truck he owned, a delivery truck for juices and sweet teas in cartons. So he would use those goods to pay off the guards at each checkpoint to let us through. There were two more vehicles behind us with my grandma and three other family members from my aunt's side.

Right before crossing the border, there were these small villages, and the houses were blown up, just burned or shot up. There were farms, and the animals were dead on the ground. Nobody was doing anything with them, because when a mortar hits, it just plows down everything that's alive. So there were dogs and cats and livestock on the road. They couldn't hide. I remember us going really fast down this one road, because there was nothing—literally nothing—as we went through the town. We were driving on the road, trying to avoid potholes that were created by mortar shells, as many as you can imagine.

So basically, there's just one guy shooting the mortars, and he just keeps filling the launcher. He fills it, adjusts it, fills it. They didn't expect anybody to be coming through this wide-open area. So we were just flying through, and the mortar hit way behind us, just as we made that connection with the border. We crossed another guarded area, gave some of our goods to the guards, and they let us pass through.

I didn't know what the heck was happening. It was so fast. Yes, there was a level of fear; I just can't describe my emotions and what we were going through at that moment. It was so foreign to me. It was just like a dream, like all of a sudden, we were picking up all our stuff and leaving. I know about what happened at Virginia Tech in 2007—it's that but times a thousand.[1] Fighter jets flying by, knocking out the windows due to the sound barrier being broken, and having to board up the windows and stay away from them, and being afraid to go outside, all these things.

After two or three years of war, there weren't any trees. Not only because of the firefights, but because we didn't have any heat and needed to cut them for wood to build fires. When you don't have trees, there are no birds. People see war on TV, but they don't smell it, they don't hear it, they don't feel the impact of a bomb. We may see it, but it's so different when you are there, and you constantly have this fear. Thankfully, we were able to get out in time. Many people did not, of course.

---

1. Here Elvir is referring to the shootings at Virginia Tech that occurred on April 16, 2007. Thirty-two students and faculty were killed by a lone gunman, and the event had a devastating impact on the university and the surrounding communities.

I've had conversations with people who told me that when they were young men, in their early twenties, they had to be out there with a gun not really knowing what the heck they were doing. And you hear stories of alcoholism and a lot of people taking drugs because they just couldn't deal with the memories. So they have PTSD and then on top of PTSD, there's drug addiction, because they're dealing with the trauma.[2] So this is why in graduate school I paid so much attention to the history of war, particularly because of this country's foreign policy across the world, to try to understand it, and I still try to understand it. War is not pretty at all. No sane person can come out of it. And I don't know how people can readily say, "Yes, I'll do it," or "I'll vote for it."

A CAMP WITHIN THE CITY FOR REFUGEES

When we left Bosnia in 1992, we went to the most familiar place that we knew at that time, the city of Pula.[3] My aunt had moved to Pula long before the war, in 1979, and we had visited her every year for summer vacations since I was one year old. Every summer we celebrated my July birthday there. So at first it felt more like summer vacation, because we'd been doing it every year. But my aunt's apartment was a one bedroom. We were there with her family, her two kids, two of my cousins, and their husbands and kids, and then my mom, my brother, and I show up. My dad was able to escape later with his sister and his mom. And then also my mom's brother and her sister-in-law also escaped with their two children, one of whom was a newborn, and they also went to that apartment. So we're talking at least fourteen people. People were sleeping everywhere. We had to find another place to stay.

---

2. PTSD is post-traumatic stress disorder.

3. Pula is a seafront city on the southern tip of Croatia's Istrian Peninsula. Known for its harbor, beaches, and Roman ruins such as the Pula Arena constructed between 27 BC and AD 68, it also has several naval bases and ports, including the Pula Naval Base and the Katarina Naval Base.

Later on, the city opened up a camp within the city for refugees and we decided we had to go there, because we could not live in that city on our own and they had resources for refugees, like meals. Actually, my dad could not stay in the camp because males of fighting age, or military age, could not stay in the camps unless they were injured. So my dad slept in our car outside the camp for like five months. I think he got mugged twice. He was working there illegally as well to earn some money for food while in Croatia. My mom, my brother, my grandma, my aunt, and I went into the camp. We stayed in a big room with other people. The first camp we went to was an abandoned military base. It had been abandoned pretty quickly and was in relatively good condition. During the summer it was okay, but in the winter, there was no heat, there was nothing, so we just had to bear it. After a year we moved to another camp not too far away. It was also a former military location, a small base. And that was a little better. They had bunk beds, but still, privacy did not exist.

In a room, about twelve by eighteen feet, they fit in three families of three to four individuals each. You don't have a kitchen. Of course, we didn't have anything in there other than sleeping bags. There were three families living there, so we created our own space. We put some sheets up on a string to create a little more privacy. It's not really privacy, but that was our life for about three years.

The city put us in the fifth grade when we entered Croatia, and that fifth grade was strange because they put all the refugees in one class, and the locals went to their regular morning classes, and we would go in the afternoon. It was a room designed for maybe thirty students, and we had about forty-five—we would just pile in there. The majority of my teachers were also refugees from Bosnia. They were teaching what they usually taught in Bosnia.

We were learning in our separate system until seventh grade, when we got integrated. That's a big word in the United States, too, *integration*. So we got integrated into the Croatian system. Croatian is a slightly different language than Bosnian, with different emphasis on certain things.[4] My papers would be graded, and I was corrected here and there. So it was a little bit harder, but we were able to go to school and get some education, even learn English.

The refugees in the camps were not all Muslim; there were a lot of Catholics too. So even though most Croatians are Catholic, they couldn't just pull the Catholics out of the refugee camp and put them in the city's schools. That would've caused a riot. So they just put everybody together and said, "All kids of a certain age, just sign them up for school." About 60 percent were Muslim; the rest were mostly Catholics.

A good thing for my brother and me is neither of us have fully Muslim names. So it was hard for the locals to distinguish us other than our accents. "Elvir" is a newer name that came into use in the seventies. It started out being given to Muslim boys usually. But because in the seventies we had this communist society, it was given to a bunch of people. And it was really never seen as a Muslim-only name. It was just a new name that could be given to any boys. "Elvira" existed here in the US too. So the name doesn't reveal a person's religion or ethnic background.

My brother's name is Edi. It's short for Edward. It's a semi-common name around. It's not popular. My mom wanted to call him Edi, spelled E-D-I, which is Eddie here. But I remember him signing his name "Eddie" to let people know this is how it's pronounced. So when we got here, people didn't know where to place him—a boy with a seemingly American name and an accent.

For a time at the refugee camp, there were of volunteers from various countries who came to the camp, lived with us, entertained us, taught us things. They had a little space for us where we could

---

4. When Yugoslavia existed, Serbo-Croatian was the country's official language. After the conflicts of the 1990s, Yugoslavia was divided up into several new nations, which each established their own official languages. Serbo-Croatian was divided up into three languages: Bosnian, Croatian, and Serbian. Serbian still uses both the Cyrillic and Latin alphabets, while Bosnian and Croatian are written in Latin script.

just be kids. The volunteers all spoke English, but they were from all different countries. They didn't speak our language. There were some local volunteers, so that was easier, but we had to learn English. That is the first time I saw volunteers or heard the word "volunteer." This is at age twelve. That stayed with me.

My brother and I were usually okay, but we did face discrimination from some of the Muslim boys who were in the camp because we would eat pork. I didn't know at that time that Muslims were not supposed to eat pork. I never really had these conversations with my family because they ate it. My grandparents did not, because they were religious. So we never really found ourselves belonging in this or that group. I was always very much of an outsider, I guess. So I have a different view of things.

JUST TRYING TO STAY SAFE

My first experience with discrimination was as a refugee in Croatia. When I became a refugee and moved to another country, particularly to a country that was in conflict with mine, I was treated as a second-class citizen. Most of the time, I stayed in groups of people from the camp when we would travel to different areas of the city. I always watched my back. We would hear a lot of instances of things happening to people from the camp, in alleys and in buses. What distinguished a refugee from a local at this time in Croatia wasn't how we dressed or anything like that—it wasn't a physical thing. It was our accents.

We were in a region of Croatia that's far away from Bosnia. It was closer to Slovenia, and the farther you go toward Slovenia and Italy, the accent changes. If I can compare it to the US, it's probably the difference between accents in New York versus Louisiana. People definitely knew who wasn't from Pula. And on top of that, we were in a conflict and there was a level of nationalism that really plagued some people, kids maybe a little bit older than we were. I was in a camp for kids between the ages of eleven and fourteen. We'd have to watch out for older teenagers who were looking for trouble, just trying to stay safe when we were outside of the camp limits.

We got mugged one time. Two of my friends and I went into a historical building, an old, beautiful arena, like the Colosseum in Rome but miniature. We jumped a fence and roamed around. We weren't skipping class exactly. The locals had to take Italian and we took English. So when they had Italian, we would just leave and return in an hour.

The three of us went up to this huge platform, and there were three guys there. We decided not to stick around when I realized they didn't have backpacks, and we did. And as we were coming down the stairs, talking, they were following us and spitting down on us because they heard our accents. And as we approached the ground level, they yelled at us to stop. One of my friends said, "Let's just see what they want." And they came down and asked who we were. One of the first questions was, "Do you have any money on you?" And we didn't—we never did. So one of them pulled out a knife. He wasn't close to me, and he decided to kick my oldest, biggest friend, but my friend didn't respond to that. My friend told him who we were. And then he was like, "Oh, I didn't realize you guys are from the camp." These guys were from one of the orphanages near the camp.

In Pula, the orphan kids were considered Gypsies.[5] So we're both outside of this war thing, right? The majority of refugees found friendships with the Gypsies because they're seen as second-class citizens too. And some of them also experienced discrimination. Croatia is a Catholic country and the majority of the Gypsies have integrated Islam into their religious beliefs. And since the majority of the refugees at that time were Muslim, they felt connected.

---

5. Here Elvir refers to the Romanis. The Romanis were a minority group in Croatia and the schools in the city established education programs for both refugees and Romanis during the war.

Gypsies in the orphanage were usually in a lot of conflict through gangs. But that day they left us alone pretty quickly when they realized we didn't have any money. Since some refugees were allied with the Gypsies, they left us alone. Later our other friends confronted the Gypsies because my friend pointed them out. Of course, there was a fight in camp. There was no parental supervision in the camps at all. It was a bunch of fourteen- to eighteen-year-olds just doing really bad things, and my friends and I would find ourselves in the middle sometimes.

There were fights in class too. We were studying Islam in the Ottoman Empire. When we were quizzed, a teacher would call us up to stand in front of the class and answer questions. So when the Ottoman Empire came up, my friends already knew a lot of the history. One of my friends' family had lived as refugees in the mosque. His father was working there and studied Islam and the Koran, and he taught my friend. So my friend was picked to answer some of these questions about the Ottoman Empire specifically related to religious beliefs of the sultans. My friend didn't have to even memorize these things. He already knew them. He didn't have to read them in a book. When he walked back to his desk, one of the locals said, "That's not fair. He's Muslim, right? Those are not fair questions." At the next class, that kid disrespected Allah by cursing him, and there was a huge brawl right in the middle of the classroom. So what was happening outside of Croatia and within Bosnia was inserting itself inside this classroom—I won't say frequently, but the tension was there. I tried to stay away from trouble, but I witnessed it.

When I came here, I understood what it is to be a second-class citizen. I had a connection with the African Americans in my high school because of this. William Fleming High School had just started seeing an immigrant population come in. My classmates saw that, yes, I'm a Caucasian person, I'm a white person, with this really thick accent. They didn't see me as a regular white kid who was born in the region. To them I was different, but I never felt discriminated against by them. I was a minority; I was the only one in terms of my immigrant status and my skin color too. But I never felt like a complete outsider because I was with outsiders. I thought my high school was the norm. I never really knew that other parts of Roanoke existed because I didn't have a car. So when I went to college, that was a significant difference for me. In high school it was mostly African American, and in college it was majority white. There was a big disparity there. That was the second cultural shock that I experienced. Also, I was living in an area where the majority of immigrants and people of color live, because we didn't have money. So race and class had a lot to do with where we were placed when we came to the US.

I WAS THE ADULT IN THE FAMILY

We lived in a less prosperous area. I went to public schools. I was fourteen years old when we came here, and at that point in my life, I was the adult in the family because I was the oldest son and because I was the most knowledgeable in English. I served as translator those first years, really throughout my time here with my parents.

Both my brother and I witnessed our parents struggling, not only with language but to advance in their work and to have more money despite their lack of education and lack of language skills. Their social life was impacted too. They were limited, and they couldn't really engage in a community. They knew that there were resources out there, but they never really strayed far from what they knew. There was security and safety within certain limits, and that's why I don't think they fully realized themselves here in the US. They were just about work, work, work. My parents were never happy here; they never really learned the language. My father went back to Derventa in 2010.[6] But my mom cannot go back there. She left last year to live in Croatia with her family.

---

6. "In November 2016, Open Democracy highlighted that more than one million refugees were choosing to return home after twenty years of life abroad." See the

My brother and I both saw this, and we learned from it. My parents, especially my father, would always say, "You don't want to end up doing things I do," meaning, being a physical laborer all your life. When I saw that my parents were continuously having to do physical labor, I also thought, *I can't do that for the rest of my life.*

In 2006, I was still living at home while I was going to Virginia Western Community College and working full time at the Home Shopping Network in the mail order warehouse. I decided to ask my father—it was not a decision that I just made—if it would be okay for me to quit working full time and pursue a degree. They were fine with that and even kind of happy about it. They saw me as a quiet kid who never took initiative. So when I went to college, they were happy.

But before that my role, and my brother's role, was always to help them and others in the community with questions like, "How do I use a credit card? How do I pay my bills and get a driver's license or secure a loan?" All these things that my brother and I had to help with. I'm the older brother, so I always had to protect and watch out for him too. I was always in a protective, watchful, supportive role, making sure that nothing bad happens to Edi.

When I experienced discrimination, it was primarily related to language, because I didn't have a great understanding of English, and I had a really thick accent. When I came here, I remember being made fun of for what I was wearing. In the refugee camp in Croatia, we didn't have many clothes or shoes, so we tended to wear the same shirt for several days, as long as it wasn't dirty or smelly. And that was a normal thing because we didn't have washing machines. We quickly figured out, in the United States, people change clothes every day. I also remember kids talking behind my back and laughing, and I didn't know what was going on, but as I started getting to know the language, they began asking

---

Borgen Project's "Ten Facts about Bosnia and Herzegovina Refugees" at https://borgenproject.org/10-facts-about-bosnia-and-herzegovina-refugees.

me questions, like "How do you say this, or how do you say that?" And it was usually curse words because they wanted to say something inappropriate that nobody would know. I did well in math in middle school, but all the other classes were horrible. I just didn't do that well, because I didn't understand the language, and everything was really fast moving. The discrimination I knew about happened to our parents at work.

For me to go from being a teenager, translating and helping my parents, to where I am right now, volunteering, partially has to do with what I've always done—translating, speaking for others, being their voice. I was translating for the neighbors and others too. At around age sixteen I figured out how the DMV works, what it takes to shop for car insurance, and so on. I would sit with my parents and an insurance agent. The agent would talk to me like I was an adult as I translated for my parents. So not only did I translate for my parents but also for the many Bosnian community members who started coming between 1995 and about 2000. Among my parents' neighbors and friends, word of mouth spread. I was the designated DMV guy, or insurance guy, or whatever guy. I became that person—the liaison. The whole time I helped others, and it became a part of me.

I was always an adult in that situation. And I realized that the kids that I work with now are also in a similar position. They want to be kids, they are kids essentially, but at the same time, they are also adults, and they're striving for something greater. They're trying to support their family, they're trying to do what their parents want them to do, and at the same time, they understand why that pressure is on them.

We got to where we are right now through determination, resilience, and focusing on the reasons we're here. My parents came here simply for the future of my younger brother and me. We did struggle, primarily me, but we took full advantage of the educational system. Both my brother and I went to college. I went for my undergraduate studies at Radford University; my brother went to George

Mason, in Fairfax. Then he went to VCOM to become a physician in 2012, and now he practices in New Jersey.[7]

My brother was the initiative taker, the risk taker. I tended not to do that because I carried the weight of taking care of my parents and brother. But when I decided to pursue my degree at Radford, my brother was in Fairfax, and my parents were okay without me. I was a little older than the other students, so we found a one-bedroom apartment, and my mom and dad paid rent for that apartment and their own apartment in Roanoke. Mind you, they were still working for basically a minimum wage at Home Shopping Network, ten or eleven dollars an hour, paying for my brother's studies at George Mason and mine at Radford. So it was a big deal that both sons left. They still needed me, but we all were a little more flexible. I still made frequent trips to Roanoke over the weekends.

I socialized some, but it was hard to connect with some of my classmates. They were younger, and there were not many foreigners in our program. I was part of an international student group, and I would go to hear guest speakers do presentations on certain parts of Europe, for example. One year they were doing Eastern Europe, particularly the Balkans, and that was good. It felt like the university was really open to this sort of inclusivity. It's a learning environment, and we're learning about certain subjects in books, but also learning about ourselves, about folks around us. I felt good at Radford, and it was close to home. Those things bridged it for me.

Most of the work that I did for my undergraduate and graduate degrees was related to war or conflict. Everything had to do with human interaction and its contexts, particularly conflict and war. College is where I grew. I came out of my shell during the years while I was at Radford. My undergraduate degree is in public relations. I was always interested in persuasive elements of communication, organizational development. While I was in the master's program,

---

7. VCOM is the Edward Via College of Osteopathic Medicine, located in Blacksburg, Virginia.

most of my research had to do with propaganda. I wanted to know what created this distance and this way of thinking; how do we approach wars? I felt we had a very nonchalant way of thinking to press a button and launch a bomb somewhere. I would research why people were complicit or why they weren't angry about it. I solely focused on the media, and then, of course, how we process media messages. I began researching rumors and how they permeate an organization, and how they are found to be valid or credible, and how it makes people feel, and how they operate within the environment of false information.

I WAS THAT PERSON

After I finished my master's degree and got married, my mother-in-law, who is from Mexico, introduced me to a gentleman from her church who had a soccer program for refugee kids. He had a vision for this program for refugee boys from a variety of places and saw me as someone who could relate to the boys. There are no guiding principles exactly, but it's founded on Christian principles of helping. I come from a secular background, and my parents and their parents come from Muslim backgrounds, so I don't have a lot of experience with Christianity, but we all want to help these kids, so it really doesn't matter what background you come from.

I volunteer with the youth because I realized there are so many things happening for them at that age, specifically after leaving high school, so many uncertainties, and I feel for them. I was thinking, *Oh my God, they have so many things to deal with.* I'm sure there's a lot of anxiety right now specifically for those about to leave high school, because they don't know what they want to do exactly, and they're stuck between two different cultures, an American culture and their own.

Now our organization includes Danny, who was a soccer coach for years. He reaches out to colleges and coaches he knows for opportunities for scholarships through sports, and I focus on the academic side of things. We talk about who has injured themselves, who is possibly having a surgery, or who needs some help in certain areas. We are constantly keeping up with them. Danny focuses on coaching, and I focus on their well-being. I don't ask them how soccer is going; I ask them about their grades and their families. I want them to see that I care about that a lot more than them kicking a ball around, which is obviously significant too. But my priority is in their development.

I work with these young men because I was that person. I want to help them focus on getting educated and helping their families and communities. So we are their liaison to the community, their mentors and teachers. I give back this way because I remember those years, and I never had anybody to guide me. I feel like this is something that is needed specifically in the complex systems the boys are in right now. I help them with documentation, who to ask for this, where to go for that, and keep them focused. I've learned from them that they don't really need pushing in a direction but just opening doors.

For example, I talk to them about how to build a résumé, how to interview, all these things, for those that may be interested in just getting a job after graduating from high school. They don't all necessarily choose to go to college. It's small things, like handshakes, like introducing yourself. And all these things that they may not realize are so important—from healthy eating, making good choices about what you're putting into your body—are valuable to young men to know.

When we give them rides to practice, we pick them up from their homes and take them to the fields. We have been working closely with Landon Moore, who owns an indoor soccer facility, and he allows us to play in there for free, so they love that place. And we have transportation as well through one of the churches. We pick them up and, on these rides, we talk about how things are going. It's really about relationship building more than anything. And over these last several years, I've gotten to know the young men pretty well. We talk about networking and getting to know your community. This really helps them see possibilities for themselves.

We help them find a league to play in. I'm helping one of the kids who doesn't have parents apply to a community college in Nashville. Just today I received the news that one of our kids has been accepted to the Hispanic College Institute at Virginia Tech. I helped him apply recently. I picked him up, I brought a laptop, and we sat down and put together an application. The application process for them is a shock. It's very demanding and intimidating at the same time. To fill out some sort of application, not even related to a college, it's a learning opportunity. They might completely mess up how they fill out that application, but if you come back, we'll learn how to do this. We try to challenge them outside of soccer in many ways.

Fundamentally, there are a lot of similarities between what I experienced when I arrived and what the boys go through now, like learning a new language, securing a job, and dealing with the paperwork necessary to obtain certain things, like health insurance, car insurance, a license. Their families receive roughly three to four months of financial aid from ORR, and then after that, you're on your own.[8]

When my family came in 1995, there were only eight to ten Bosnian families here. We had to integrate into the community quickly because most of the people we communicated with spoke English. But today, there are more people from various communities, like Nepalis or Burundis. More Afghans are coming. Folks tend to stay within their community and talk within their community, and that's understandable, but the process of learning a language is a little slower as a result. The elephant in the room is racism, and this is something that we have to pay attention to. It's a different experience here for someone who's a white European than somebody who is of African, Middle Eastern, or Asian descent.

---

8. The Office of Refugee Resettlement, which is part of the US Department of Health and Human Services.

When I came here, I experienced some discrimination, but I cannot imagine how that goes for somebody who is not white. It's common in the US for teenagers to go to college somewhere out of state or outside of the city. But with refugee communities, that's not necessarily the case. They tend to stay with each other to help each other out. That part I completely understand. Our mindset was almost exactly the same; hence, I didn't leave the community when my brother did because somebody had to stick around to help the parents.

Roanoke and southwest Virginia do have problems with discrimination. When I'm taking the boys to practice and I ask them, "How'd the game go?" In one conversation they told me that they don't get name-calling much from the players, but it usually comes from the parents, on the sidelines. And I thought, *Wow, that's significant; that's important to note and sad at the same time.* The boys told me that they don't pay much attention to it. They brush it off, so I'm glad that they can do that and not take it to heart. The African kids are experiencing it on a different level, and their conversations are a little bit different. On Facebook they express some of these things by posting quotes or sayings or videos expressing the complexities of race in this country.

Sometimes our conversations will pull out a memory. Something reminds them of something, and they will talk about getting disciplined in school in their home country and how different it is here. One kid told me he didn't wear shoes before coming here and that somebody made fun of him because he had dirty shoes. He said he never even had shoes until he came to the United States. I said, "How did that make you feel?" He said he doesn't care, but he wanted to talk about it. I think it takes someone to just to listen, to understand where they're coming from, and ask them, "What do you need?" I never pressure them to do anything in particular. For instance, I tell them, "Going to college, for me, it was essential; for you, it may not be." But I advise them to get some sort of skill to help them and that will help their family in the future. I lived part of my life in a refugee camp, but some of these kids were born in camps. So their stories come out in little spurts. I don't sit down with them and say, "Tell me a story." I'm with them, week after week, year after year, and those little tidbits, you can only hear them if you're with them multiple times over a few years.

I think the boys see my role now and what I do as significant, that I care about them and that they're important to me. I say to them, "Hey, I was in the same shoes as you." I also say to them, "This is my family. This is the support group that I have. Always remember that most of the things you do and will accomplish don't just come from your own efforts, you really have to have some sort of a support group, and you know you do with our group." We all post pictures on our Facebook group, and many of their pictures are with their family members. I tell them our group is exactly the same thing. I posted a picture from when I was playing soccer for William Fleming High School, and I told them, "Hey, we didn't even have a field. None of these things existed, so see what you have right now." One of the kids joked about my picture, "Wow, you look so different." I said, "Well, it's been eighteen years, you'll look different in eighteen years." He said, "We'll see about that." We have fun with all that. I'm going to be seeing them at graduation on Saturday, and I already have things in mind to say to them. They're not going far away, but I want them to think about their futures and the importance of education. This is why I created a scholarship for refugees at Virginia Western Community College, because I know most of the boys I work with will go there. I think education is so important, and that's why I'm working with the kids, because I know they have amazing stories.

A few weeks after the interview in 2018, we worked with several service organizations and Elvir's group to host a World Refugee Day event in Landon Moore's soccer facility. The younger kids had a game on one of the indoor fields, while the young men in Elvir's youth group played an intense and fast-moving match. Families shared meals, participated in a workshop, and watched the World Cup on a big screen.

In 2022, Elvir traveled back to Derventa to visit the town where he'd lived. He said seeing his town was a very emotional experience and reminded him how important it is to remember that time.

MEKYAH DAVIS

BORN: 1996, Big Stone Gap, Virginia
INTERVIEWED IN: Big Stone Gap, Virginia
Activist and Nonprofit Coordinator

Mekyah (pronounced meh-kai-yah) Davis lives in a small town in the southwest mountains of Virginia near the Tennessee and Kentucky borders. His love of Appalachia and his family's place in the region is reflected in his reverence for the landscape and his dedication to his work. He is the co-coordinator of Black Appalachian Young & Rising (BAYR, pronounced "bear"), an initiative of the STAY Project, a grassroots effort whose mission is to make their communities places for Appalachian youth to stay.[1] Mekyah's commitment to STAY is fueled by his desire to live in Appalachia, but, like many young people, he finds decent employment opportunities scarce.

---

1. For more on the STAY Project, see www.thestayproject.net.

Mekyah spoke of his childhood with affection, describing his family and living in the mountains in detail. In speaking about his friends who moved away to find work, he mentioned that some people assumed he wouldn't want to stay in Big Stone Gap. He gestured toward the mountains behind his house, and asked, "Who wouldn't want to live here?"

EIGHT GENERATIONS

I went to Powell Valley High School until it was consolidated with Appalachia High School during my sophomore year.[2] Like in a lot of communities in Appalachia, Powell Valley's high school building was old and needed repair. There wasn't enough money to build a new one, so they merged the two high schools to save money. It was a huge change for our community and meant a longer drive for many students.

My mom grew up here. The Mitchell family actually goes back eight generations here in Big Stone Gap. Some of my aunts and uncles relocated to Maryland, Detroit, and Atlanta, but my mom stayed here. My dad is from Birmingham, Alabama, and they met during their first year at Berea College, in Kentucky.[3] When they got married, they came back here.

I think it was a lot for my dad, moving to a place like this, after being at a college that was focused on social justice and in an atmosphere that was welcoming. My mom's family is here, but in Birmingham my dad grew up around a lot more Black folks. He never did like it in Big Stone Gap. It was a culture shock to him living in a town of mostly white people.

---

2. The town of Appalachia, Virginia, where Appalachia High School was originally located, is about five miles from the town of Big Stone Gap, but the route to get there is over the Cumberland Mountain range.

3. Berea College, located in Berea, Kentucky, and founded in 1855, is a small liberal arts college known for its abolitionist efforts, being tuition free for students, and having a social justice focus on Appalachia.

When Wallens Ridge State Prison opened, my dad got a job there, but he was one of fewer than twenty Black prison guards.[4] The corrections officers were known to be awful to the prisoners, and my dad couldn't do much about it as a Black person. It's not something he talked about much, but prisoners were beaten, and it was not good. It was a struggle for him, being a young Black man working in a prison where Black folks were behind bars, and he was the only one outside.

ALWAYS MUSIC PLAYING

I have really fond memories of being a little kid in Big Stone Gap. We lived near my grandmother, and we played outside all the time. My parents were eighteen when they had my twin brother and me. They were both encouraging and loving. I had several friends and we played football together. I met my best friend Cameron playing football. Cameron, my friend Fonseca, and my brother Noah were always together and having fun. My family talked about race at home, in the sense of being aware of what it is to be a Black person in this country, but we didn't talk about it a lot. We didn't talk about police brutality; it was more about navigating the world around us. Whenever we would run around with friends, my parents would say to us, "Y'all ain't your little white friends." They meant we had to watch the way we would interact with authority figures, like our teachers or the police.

At home we had a good time. My dad loved music, so there was always music playing, like Outkast, Kanye West, older John Legend.

---

4. The controversial Wallens Ridge State Prison was built in 1999. At that time, only 5 percent of the prison guards were Black. For more information, see Edward Fitzpatrick, "State Inmates Call Virginia's Wallens Ridge 'Hell,'" *Hartford Courant*, June 19, 2000, www.courant.com/news/connecticut/hc-xpm-2000-06-19-0006190028-story.html and Craig Timberg, "At VA's Toughest Prison, Tight Controls," *Washington Post*, April 18, 1999, www.washingtonpost.com/wp-srv/local/daily/april99/supermax18.htm.

The *Get Lifted* album is seared into my brain. My dad took us fishing a lot too. Noah liked to fish sometimes, too, but fishing was how me and my dad bonded—it was our thing. We also watched sports together. He was an avid fan of the Lakers and the Cowboys. I liked Notre Dame. He played video games with me and my brother.

He really likes to cook, too, so we'd have wings and chili while watching football. He's a great cook, though he uses lots of garlic. He makes these great drumsticks with pepper and garlic—a recipe I've been trying to replicate lately. When he made chili beans, he burnt the bottom of the beans, just a little bit, making a really delicious and unique chili. Once, when I was seven, he made us lamb. He put it in front of us and we asked what it was, and he said, "Just eat it." We said it was good. And then he told us it was lamb, and we were mortified. But it was funny too. There was a lot of laughter during those days.

We really didn't see him much, though. He mostly worked the night shift at the prison. Every once in a while, he would come home during what was his lunch break, but it would be midnight. If I was up too late, I would see him during those times, wearing his black, black boots and his dark navy correctional officer uniform. There was a little yellow patch on the shoulder with a state of Virginia emblem with the state flag on it. He also had a big black belt that held a metal chain, a bunch of gadgets, and his gun. He and my mom would sit at the table while he ate. He also wore his National Guard uniform when he went over to Mooresville, North Carolina, for training once a month. So we were used to seeing him in a uniform.

He was thoughtful and quiet, really intelligent. He didn't really express any emotions. So when he had to leave for Iraq in 2002, we didn't really know what to think, he just said he had to go. The lead-up to him leaving all seemed mundane. There were other guys in our community going, too, and everybody acted like it was normal. Mr. Renfro, who was later my fifth-grade math teacher, went to Iraq too.

I was obsessed with my dad's Desert Storm uniform. It was different than his regular army uniform. The desert sand uniforms have browns and grays instead of dark greens and black. And he had different boots—light brown, not black. My brother and I watched him trying it on and packing it. He left his normal army uniform here when he got called up. It hung on the inside of the closet door in my mom's room while he was deployed.

When it was time for him to go, we all took him to Fort Eustis near Newport News. My mom, Noah, and my baby sister, Tierra, all went to take him there. It was a big trip and we all just stood there, mom holding the baby in one arm, holding my brother's hand with the other. We hugged, but it wasn't emotional, not there. Once we got in the car to leave, we all cried. My mom got a speeding ticket, and the cop didn't know what to think with all of us crying.

Noah and I were seven and Tierra was three, so it was a lot of chaos during that time while my dad was away, and Mom was taking care of us alone. I got into football, Noah got into music, and Mom took care of the baby.

NO OTHER JOB BUT THE PRISON

I remember being super happy when we knew he was coming home two years later. He kept mixing up me and Noah. He couldn't tell us apart for a while when he first got home. It makes sense because everything was chaotic—he was adjusting to being back. In terms of work, there wasn't anything for him, no other job but the prison.

When he got back from Iraq, he didn't talk anything about the war. My mom told me later that there was a meeting for spouses that she and other people went to, and the officers told them not to ask the soldiers about what they'd been through or what they'd seen. "Don't try to force anything out of them," they told her. There weren't any tools for any of us, especially for my dad. He didn't know how to navigate the trauma of the war. And in the Black community especially, taking care of our mental health is not something we talk about. Here was this brilliant, sensitive man, now not functioning—an alcoholic—and I wonder if it would have been different if there were services for him or just a way for him to talk about it. We didn't know—we were just kids. We expected him to integrate back into life, into our family life. But it didn't get better.

He was twenty-seven when he got back. He had to work at the prison again. But he came back changed, and there wasn't anything for him to help him cope. The war affected him. He was gone from the time I was in second grade to fourth grade. When he came back it was really hard, and my parents fought a lot. Then, in February of my sixth-grade year, his mom—my grandmother—died. Then it got really bad. He started drinking more and he never stopped. My parents got divorced right before my ninth-grade year and then we went nine years without really seeing him. He moved to Hazlehurst, Mississippi, near where he was from in Alabama.

After my parents got divorced and he moved, I remember feeling different. I thought, *Why can't he be there?* I knew he loved to watch me play football in the eighth grade, and now he wasn't there to watch me play in high school. But you learn to not worry about it; you have to, or else it's too hard.

Right before they got divorced, he went on his two-week National Guard trip. I knew he wasn't coming back after that. We were getting ready to play a game—it was August, so it was really hot. Our field is down in a little valley. We were warming up, and I just so happened to look up toward the hill, and I saw him. He was in his uniform, and he was just standing there. We'd been working out so hard. I was breathing hard and sweating and the coach was calling me back, but I was so excited to see him there, looking down at us. He didn't get to watch me play after that, but my mom was at every game.

So I played football, which kept my mind off things. I was athletic and competitive, but I was also good in school. Looking back, I think football was a means of survival and fitting in. It's how I found my friend group. The first friend I ever made was in football. We're still best friends. I found an identity in football, and it was how I navigated some of the hard stuff in school.

IN THE HEART OF APPALACHIA

There were some tense moments in high school and on the football field. Nothing blatant, just constant racist jokes and threatening behavior. I just wanted to survive in high school and to fit in. I had to learn how to navigate the environment, but I wanted to stay true to myself. I was supposed to be a tough football player, but I felt like I had to put up with all that really toxic and harmful behavior because I was a young Black person. I was exposed to people who were blatantly racist, but mostly it was them telling jokes using Black stereotypes. I had to play along. It felt like we were not always allowed to react because of where we were, in the heart of Appalachia.

Honestly, a lot of my favorite memories are from playing football. Friday nights were electrifying and chilling—there's no other way to describe the atmosphere. There's three thousand people in the stands, cheering for you and your team. There's no other feeling like that. Despite those really hard times with my family and racist teammates, I still remember those football game nights.

It was my friends who got me through. Fonseca was one of my best friends growing up, Robert Anthony Wade Fonseca. He played football, too, and we liked to hang out and have fun. His dad was a doctor and was always gone, and his mom had some health problems, so she wasn't super mobile. We could hang out at Fonseca's house and do pretty much what we wanted. It was basically a party house, but it was also a refuge for us.

One night we were playing at Richlands High School, a school we play every year—big rivalry. The year before we had *barely* lost, so we were really wanting to beat them. It was a close game and with just seconds left we were losing by three points. On the very last play of the night, our quarterback couldn't pass it, so he ran it himself. He almost fell, but then he ran it back for a touchdown. It was like a scene from a movie. We finally beat Richlands. Everybody cheered and jumped on top of each other to celebrate. I was at the bottom and felt like I was going to suffocate. There was this guy on my team who said something racist to me in the pile. That was typical.

But winning was so amazing. Then, as we were leaving the field, our mascot got punched in the face by someone from the other team. Then another kid got stabbed. We were happy that we won and yet scared to death. When we left on the bus, we passed a building in the middle of town that the other team set fire to. That was my childhood—these great moments with really hard moments.

When we got back, Cameron, my cousin Des, and I spent the night at Fonseca's. We just laid in this giant bed together, replaying the game, laughing and talking loud about beating Richlands. My cousin danced around us while we bounced around on the bed. We were laughing and having a great time. The three of us—white, Black, and Brown boys—together laughing and joking around. But all this heavy stuff was around us. Shit we'd seen, knowing there wasn't any way we could stay here after graduation even though we wanted to. We made fun of each other, we laughed at each other, but there was also tenderness in those moments.

Fonseca was really sweet and caring, looking out for us all, making sure we were all having fun. He was really sensitive. Once when we were riding the bus to a game, I'd fallen asleep but woke up hearing him sniffling. He told me he was having problems with his girlfriend. To make him feel better, I told him, "We're going to play this game!" He laughed, and yelled, "Yeah!" but he had a faraway look in his eyes too. He was a softy, a sweet dude with a really big heart.

I FELT FREE THEN

I feel the natural beauty now that it's fall, when we go from summer to cool fall air. It's a season of change, when the leaves turn colors and the temperature is cool, I remember those football nights. I felt free then, in a way I don't feel now.

So football is basically what got me through school. I mean, I didn't have the terminology for it at the time, the racism in school. It wasn't until I read *The Souls of Black Folk* in college that I could look at it this way. Dr. W. E. B. Du Bois uses the term *double consciousness* to describe the experience of being Black in America, and that was my experience growing up in Big Stone Gap. When I was younger, I felt that I had a Black experience of Appalachian identity and culture. My family was Black; I didn't want to assimilate, but I felt I was Appalachian.

I think back on how damaging the racism was to me, to the psyche of young Black folks like me. All the harmful, internalized stuff I heard throughout the school year—it's a lot. There were probably ten Black kids in my high school class out of 152. We didn't know how to deal with it except to survive, go along. We couldn't voice how we felt.

I didn't ever feel fearful going to school, but I think that's just because of the reputation I built for myself—I had comfort and a safety net. When I was playing sports, I was playing a violent sport, and on top of that there were people shouting racial slurs and actively trying to cause me more bodily harm at the bottom of the dogpile. So I don't think I was fearful for my life, but, you know, it's funny. Well, it's not funny, actually; it's sickening. I went to school with people I *knew* were racist, and they went on to become like a sheriff's deputy in the county.

WE WANT TO STAY HERE

This house that I just moved into is the house my mom moved out of when she temporarily moved to Johnson City where at the time, her children, sister, mother, and other family lived. She grew up here, her mom grew up in this house, her granny and great-granny too. Everybody on my mom's side of the family has been on this piece of property. I didn't appreciate this land when I was younger. But there's a rich legacy to this place. You know, Big Stone Gap is not perfect, and when I was younger, I remember talking to my friends and they'd all say, "We can't wait to leave," but I'd say, "I love it here!" I love the mountains. I love being able to go outside to just sniff the air and have an almost overwhelming sense of nostalgia for how this place has shaped me to be who I am. Big Stone Gap is not perfect, and it has its issues, but if we all leave, it's never going to get better. It's never going to be the community that we want to see. One day I plan on starting a family and I want to at least have the option to build my family here, to raise my family here. And then they raise their kids here if they want to. They should at least have that option. But we won't have that option if we don't have safe, inclusive communities. If we don't have the infrastructure to try to clean up the years of damage from extractive industries—that left no clean drinking water, for example. There's so many issues that we need to fix. But it ain't gonna happen if all the young people leave. If we all just decided that Appalachia is irredeemable and can't be safe, then who's going to fix it while we're all away?

In fact, I don't know anyone who *wants* to leave. Well, I know there are some people who want to live someplace bigger and that's fine. But I know a lot of people who are perfectly content to go traveling and then come right back here to live, to be nestled in this quietness and slow life that Big Stone Gap has to offer. A lot of my friends aren't here right now, even though they want to be, because they went to college and haven't come back yet, but we all *want* to be here. The lack of a robust economy, and access to education or work, is what's preventing folks from being here. For work, the only options here are service work, retail, call centers, and prisons. There's not much else. We don't value our arts and cultural workers the way we need to. And that's one of the next logical steps for us as we think of ways to use arts and culture to build economic sustainability throughout our communities and our region.

We know that whatever we do can't be something that replicates extraction in a different way, whether it be of the land or the people. It's gotta be something that is sustainable for the environment and that gives people dignity and pride and joy in what we do. So that we're able to not just survive but thrive. I don't have all the answers, but I know that what we have been doing ain't working. We can't re-create another extractive system in disguise, 'cause that ain't what we need either.

EVERYBODY IS A TEACHER

I graduated from high school in 2014 and attended UVA Wise for a year.[5] I took some time off and then I went to the local community college where I took a sociology class with Dr. Ken Tucker. That's when I read *The Souls of Black Folk*. But I wasn't really sure what I wanted to do with my life. Near that time, I got involved with the STAY Project.

I have a friend, Olivia, who was on the steering committee for STAY. They're from Big Stone Gap too—that's how I know them. They reached out to me and said, "Hey, I got this organization that I think you might find interesting." So they put me in contact with Lou Murrey, who was the solo coordinator at the time and is co-coordinator with me now. Lou came to Big Stone Gap, and we had coffee at the Huddle House, and they told me about STAY and its commitment to finding ways for Appalachian youth to stay in the region. I talked about the possibility of having some type of Black youth engagement event in the future. Later that year Lou suggested I go to the STAY Summer Institute. It's the largest in-person

---

5. University of Virginia's College at Wise.

gathering of the year for the STAY Project. It's a weekend-long event where young people from throughout the Appalachian region come to engage in peer-led workshops.

Lou reminded me to register for the conference. "We really want you to come," they said. "We'll pay for you to come; we'll make sure you get there and back." So I went, and it was a beautiful experience. It was my first time being in a space like that. It was truly liberatory, engaging in an education style with the understanding that everybody is a teacher and everybody is a learner. STAY brings everyone together to learn and to realize our collective knowledge and power. If Lou hadn't followed up with me, I might not have gone. That weekend changed me, and so after that I applied to be on the steering committee of STAY. I got selected in December 2018. Around that same time, I attended a Call to Action for Racial Equality conference up in Charleston, West Virginia. And then the next week, STAY had a strategic planning meeting to see what its role could be in uplifting and supporting Black youth and youth leadership within the organization in the region.

I started serving my first term on the steering committee in January 2019, and by March I had also attended the Alliance for Appalachia meeting. It was then that I said to Lou, "Hey, you know there ain't no other young Black folks in positions of leadership in any of the spaces we've been in." Lou said, "We have resources. Would you be interested in holding some type of gathering to bring together Black youth throughout the region?" So I put together a five-person advisory committee and started Black Appalachian Young & Rising. Also we hired Charice Starr, a popular educator at the Highlander Research and Education Center, as a consultant. She was an invaluable source of wisdom on planning this gathering. The Highlander Center is our fiscal sponsor. The purpose of the gathering was to bring folks together, celebrate the joy of being together, and talk about overcoming both the physical and psychological isolation that young Black folks all too often face in this region. Second, we wanted to examine what it means to be a Black person in Appalachia. What does the Appalachian identity even mean to us? Third, we wanted to address the critical lack of Black youth leadership and representation in the spaces and organizations in our region.

In November 2019 approximately forty Black youth and five elders from across the region came together at the Pine Mountain Settlement School in Kentucky, and it was beautiful. On our first night we had an opening grounding session where we learned the history of the STAY Project, that it was started by a multiracial group of youth from West Virginia, East Tennessee, and Kentucky. There's been barriers to being able to live up to the mission of uplifting and supporting Black youth, so we talked about this, the specific history of Black folks in the region.

Our leaders included Charice Starr; Joe Tolbert, who is one of the founding members of STAY; and also Elandria Williams, another popular activist who passed away recently. We also had Dr. William Turner and Ron Carson with the Appalachian African-American Cultural Center down in Pennington Gap, who were able to tell us about the history and legacy of Black folks in the region.[6] That was the opening session, exploring issues of identity, setting up the container for learning and growth. When we held our closing session, I was crying tears of joy, just so happy to be able to bring youth together to affirm our place here. Since then, COVID has put a wrench in our in-person gatherings. But for now, we're in the process of building up the infrastructure to hold more events and to support youth and to make the program transformative. We had the first ever Appalachian Love Fest, a music festival in Harlan County.[7] But then COVID hit, and we didn't have an in-person gathering for a while, until we did a socially distanced camping trip in Mountain City, Tennessee.

---

6. See www.aaaculturalcenter.org for additional information about the work of the center.

7. For additional information about the music festival and other activities of the STAY Project, see www.thestayproject.net.

At the BAYR meeting we had youth from Alabama, Kentucky, West Virginia, Tennessee, and southwest Virginia—from all over the region. We came together over the course of the weekend, and by the end they opened up, came out of their shells, and were a little bit vulnerable with one another. I think I was overwhelmed in the moment, thinking about the legacy of the event. It was the first gathering of its kind. There was a pure joy of being surrounded by other young Black folks, and I realized, after not knowing about college and what I wanted to do, that this work is my destiny; this is what I'm meant to be doing in my life.

A WHOLE LOT MORE COMPLEX

I've not always identified as Appalachian because of the narrative that is pushed upon us. Appalachian is mostly thought of as being homogeneously white, poor, working-class coal miners—and there's not a lot of variations. Appalachia is a whole lot more complex than that. Some of what we talked about was the complicated relationship with the land and the people, being in touch with nature and the outdoors, but also realizing that some folks, whether they're from Birmingham, Knoxville, or Charleston, don't have access to that nature. What does that lack of access do to people? We also talked about resiliency. We can't ignore that the South has the largest population of Black folks in the country. We have to understand that Black folks have an array of different life experiences, including LGBTQIA ones. So we can't leave anybody out of the conversation when we're talking about identity or Appalachian identity. And I see now that since we've been talking about embracing Appalachian identity, there's a new sense of urgency about it, about letting folks know who we are: that we're here and what our experiences are. We have lots of folks in their early twenties, but we have more people from ages fourteen to eighteen, who are talking about being politically conscious and aware. We want them to know how impactful their thoughts are and that their voice matters.

A lot of Black folks don't identify as Appalachian, but Appalachia has a rich cultural history of Black folks. There was an influx of Black folks from the deep South right after the legal end of slavery, and there are generations of Black miners in the region. That being said, with the layoffs in the mines, people had to move and find other jobs, just like white folks. But it's important to remember the violent incidents that occurred and that there was an exodus of Black folks from the area, incidents like those in Corbin, Kentucky, or Erwin, Tennessee.[8] So if there's an impression that there aren't Black folks in Appalachia, understanding that legacy is important, that it ties into the more recent white supremacy and anti-Black sentiment going on in the region and the country. We'd be doing a great disservice to the youth we meet if we didn't mention that history because it's not like Black folks just aren't here for no reason or that they don't want to be here. Knowing about "sundown towns," places where Black folks couldn't or can't go after dark, we have to know about it.

A SLOW BURN

My typical day usually involves meeting with the STAY steering committee, and we're also involved in a couple governing structures for similar organizations, like the Southern Movement Assembly, a collective of people in southern states from West Virginia to Florida and Texas that respond to crises or disasters.[9] With COVID, my week has a lot of calls and planning. We're building up the

---

8. In 1918, several events led to the forced exodus of the whole Black population in Erwin, Tennessee. Similarly, in 1919, a white mob forced the two hundred Black residents of Corbin, Kentucky, onto a freight train out of town and enforced a sundown policy.

9. For additional information about the work of the Southern Movement Assembly, see www.southtosouth.org.

infrastructure and visibility for the BAYR program, so we have lots of promotional and educational materials ready when we can have in-person events again. I spend a lot of time cold-calling potential members—just like Lou did for me—telling them about BAYR and seeing how they're doing. I want to share with them how valuable it was to me to be able to have a network across the state and the region of like-minded young people who are working toward a common goal. I want other youth to know that they are a part of that story too. It's important for young Black folks to have spaces to gather and to be known to each other. It's hard to find points of connection on your own. So we have to be intentional about how we're doing outreach and how we're getting the word to people.

I do all this because of watching my dad and because of Fonseca. In 2016, I got a phone call from one of our friends that Fonseca had died. He overdosed. Fonseca's not an isolated case. There's an opioid epidemic here. A young person who faces isolation and sadness here has nothing. There are no avenues for help. I think about how he could've used someone to help him. Look, they're really killing us: no jobs, no health care, no mental health care. So many people I know are walking around deeply traumatized and don't have a language for it and will never be able to pay for the resources to cope with it. That's why many of us go into the military in the first place. It's a place to have work. Or the prison; it's the only kind of employment. The military is one of the few ways we can make a life, and then they send us to war and don't do anything for us when we get back. We need jobs so we can stay here. Not just any jobs but ones with a living wage, where you have dignity and benefits like health care.

For Fonseca and my dad too—what if things were different? Would they still be here? Fonseca's story, his experiences influence the work I do. I was talking to my dear friend Nina—she's also on the steering committee for STAY down in Birmingham, Alabama. We were talking about all the BAYR program needs and what it's like for people now, and for our parents and grandparents. It's a slow burn, you hear me? It's day to day, at work, in town, in government. Having a space for Black youth to be able to come together, to be safe and feel cared for. It's a revolution of spirit and mind to respond to overwhelming despair. It's a revolution to care for myself, you hear me?

In our communities, whether it be gun violence or looming climate crisis, having access to health care, specifically mental health care—we need spaces to not feel the weight of all of it. All I can think is, *What if Fonseca had a network like this?*

When Fonseca and I were around each other, we were allowed to be ourselves, fully ourselves, to each other. We had a brotherly bond. It's crazy that it's been six years now since he died. I wonder what he would think of me now. I think he'd be really proud of who I have become. When he was alive, I was humorous and lighthearted. When he died, I was lost for a couple years. I think he knew I cared about him, knew I loved him. I think I'm good at making the youth I work with feel heard and seen. I'm joyous, and even though the work we're doing is serious, we try to have fun.

We are young people and deserve to have lives outside of work. We shouldn't be developing chronic illnesses or stress-related conditions from our employment. So at STAY we reduced our work hours. A lot of social justice work creates burnout for people because they're so committed. And then there's usually not enough people to go around. So I'm really glad there's an intentional way of planning for people to have jobs in Appalachia and have good lives.

I'm still deciding if I want to go to graduate school, in either sociology or in education. I have a vision for the things I want. I want to have a happy little family with a garden; I want to be able to look at my mountains and be joyous.

AMAL

BORN: 1993, Homs, Syria
INTERVIEWED IN: Blacksburg, Virginia
Homemaker

Interviewed with Katie Randall

We first met Amal at a gathering to welcome newcomers at a community garden. At the event, Amal's enthusiasm to get to know people was infectious. In between running after her six children, one of whom wanted to be in the pond with the ducks, Amal wanted to have her picture taken with many people. When a small group of us went to Amal's home for the interview in 2017, she made Turkish coffee and spent a good bit of time explaining the significance of sharing a good cup with family and friends.

Amal arrived with her husband and six children in Roanoke, Virginia, in 2015, after a year in refugee housing in Lebanon. They had fled Syria the year before because the bombings destroyed most of Homs and the nearby town al-Qaryatayn, where they originally fled after the massacre in their neighborhood, Karm al-Zeitoun, in 2012. The civil war in Syria, which began in 2011, has caused more than seven million people to be internally displaced and more than five million to flee to neighboring countries. Neither Amal nor her husband knew English when they arrived in the United States, and they struggled at first to navigate the many organizations and volunteers assisting them.

"Amal" is a pseudonym, used to protect her, her family, and her relatives who remain in Syria.

A HAPPY, BEAUTIFUL FAMILY

My life was really sweet and good in Syria. I went to school. Contrary to the rest of the society or the community, my dad was supportive of my education. When I was twelve, I lost my dad to a stroke. Our life kind of continued in a stable way, but our culture does not necessarily encourage girls to continue studying after a certain age. The family thought that I should discontinue my education. The teachers were preparing my class to move on to the next step and they were taking pictures of my class and I told them, "I don't think you should include me because I won't be able to continue my education." The teachers knew my dad and our situation, and they were very supportive. They said, "If it's an issue of money, then we'll try to come up with the money for your education." They knew I wanted to go on with my education. But I had to leave. Even though I left school, home was another kind of schooling where I learned a lot of good things. What I learned at home, from my mother and my siblings, it still helps me now in my life. I learned about being a good wife, mother, and daughter.

Before I got married, I was living in my family's home, and when I married, we moved to our new home in 2002. They're both my home. When I first got married, I was kind of sad to leave my family's home. After a while and after having children, it all changed. Growing up in my family, we were six girls and three boys. We were a happy, beautiful family, and we never thought that we'd be separated from each other. Every Eid and every occasion, we'd gather and give presents to the children and make wonderful food.[1] Our neighborhood was Karm al-Zeitoun, which means "the olive grove." It's been a long time since I've said, "Karm al-Zeitoun."

OUR ACCESS TO SUPPLIES WERE CUT

Before the war, my oldest son was in second grade. The teacher used to like him very much, and he was her favorite student. We had to take him out of school midyear, because he was facing problems from the teacher. She started to hit him on his knuckles. When the war began, she told him, "You have to tell us if your dad has any weapons." The teacher belonged to the Alawites, al-Assad's faction, and the school was in an area under their control.[2] After the first bombings, if somebody had any grudges against somebody who was from the Sunni faction, they would write a report to the police and get back at them and be vengeful. And the Sunnis couldn't do anything

---

1. Eid al-Fitr is a celebratory time marking the end of Ramadan. Ramadan is a time of fasting in Islam. Muslim's fast from sunset to sundown for a month, and the end is celebrated with feasts and presents.

2. Sunnis and Alawites are two sects of Islam within the Muslim community in Syria, with a long, complicated history. As a minority, the Alawites have a history of being oppressed. However, with the rise of minority Alawite rule since the 1960s, the government is more sectarian and intolerant of political dissent. Bashar al-Assad's government imposes restrictions on the Sunni sect, which has led to increased tension. An overall context of political repression, economic hardship for the majority, and lack of political freedoms led eventually to the civil war, which began in 2011 and continues to the present. This history and the factors leading to the war are much more complicated than this brief summation allows. For more context, see Zachary Laub's "Syria's Civil War: The Descent into Horror" at www.cfr.org/article/syrias-civil-war.

at the time. So I couldn't do anything to the teacher who hit my son, and I had to pull him out of the school. We also had to pull my other son out of daycare, because kidnappings were very, very common.

The Alawites rule, but they are also the minority, so the easiest thing for them was to just kill anyone opposing them. After that month, everything was very tense, and things were just not working—no food or supplies were available, and people who were friends became enemies. To get relief, the Sunnis used to call for emergency supplies and help over the speakers in the mosque. People in the nearby neighborhood would start calling for help and all the rescue and emergency workers and security forces would go to that area, giving the Sunnis a break from the patrols. Once we were told that al-Assad's military was poisoning the water and we were not able to drink it. Because most of the shops belonged to the Alawites, our access to supplies were cut. We are Sunni, but we were neither supporters of the war nor in opposition to the war. We got word from the Alawites, through people we know, "Either you leave the house or we're going to harm you." The neighborhood where we lived had been kind of deserted by others. My husband, the kids, my husband's brother and sister, her husband and children, and I all lived in the same house. There was always shooting. If we needed to get any food or supplies, we would have to go out very early in the morning. The Alawites started robbing people's homes. Our house was very close to the main road that separates the two neighborhoods. When we were threatened, we moved to another street right in the middle of the Sunni area.

Sometime after, we were away for a few days at my family's home. Because we lived in the city, we didn't need to drive—we walked everywhere or had a driver. After the bombings, we only had someone trusted drive us. While we were going back, our driver's brother called and said, "Another family in the neighborhood was killed, so don't bring them back." So we didn't go back. Then we went to my brother's house for six days. We had four children then.

That was when the well-known massacre in Karm al-Zeitoun happened.[3] I know people who still have family there, and they sometimes go to my family's homesite and send us pictures and videos. Nothing is left there, not even the walls.

While we lived at my brother's, when we went to get food, we would cross intersections and roads, all of us huddled together because there were a lot of snipers. There were young men who would stand in those intersections to secure the way. It was just a matter of fifteen minutes but it felt very treacherous.

NO WARNING

We decided to flee to the countryside. We didn't have a car, so we had to go to a bus station. My brother accompanied us, and we kept telling him, "Don't come with us. Don't risk your life. You don't have to come with us." At the bus station, most of the other young men who were there belonged to the Alawite faction, the regime faction. During the massacre it was known there were a few young men who slaughtered kids. So when we saw the young Alawite men at the bus station, they were talking about killing kids. When they saw us, one of them was kind of feeling sorry about the murder of the young children. The other guy told him, "No, don't feel sorry." And he looked at us and started insulting us. And when I saw how he was talking and how he didn't feel any remorse, I was very afraid.

I remember that moment. Thank god we were able to leave after a while. We reached a safer place, a place called al-Qaryatayn, which means "the two villages."[4] There were people who gave us a room, and I stayed there with my kids and husband. There are two arches

---

3. There have been several massacres reported in Syria during the war, including the one in the Karm al-Zeitoun neighborhood of Homs in March 2012.

4. Al-Qaryatayn is located in the Syrian Desert about 125 kilometers northeast of Damascus. Villagers and townspeople from Homs took refuge here during the early part of the Syrian war.

when you enter the town, and from our room we could see the army before they entered the town. So when all the tanks and army vehicles came, we saw them. There was no warning before the bombing started. There were a lot of bombs, and I was certain that we were going to get hit because our house was out in the open. There was no way for me to escape with my kids—it was nighttime. And they were throwing flares to see if anybody was trying to escape, so the snipers could shoot them. We stayed put and said our prayers and our goodbyes to each other.

Then in the morning, the helicopters flew over, and they were just shooting directly on people. There were fires burning and a lot of people were killed. During the Friday prayer, the army would have a lot of presence there. Like a hundred people just standing in front of the mosque. So if the army saw more than five people gathered, they would say, "This is an unlawful gathering." All of this wasn't enforced by police. It was army personnel who were controlling the area. This remained the case for nine months when we were there.

WE DECIDED TO GO TO LEBANON

We didn't reach a decision all at once to leave Syria altogether. We tried all these things first, but things just kept getting worse and worse. Then my husband said, "Let's go to Lebanon." While we were still in Homs, the distance between me and the family was not that far, but I couldn't see them because of the bombings. Then when we went to al-Qaryatayn my family was about an hour away, and still I couldn't see them. I told my husband, "I can't go to Lebanon. It's too far away from my family." Even though we went to al-Qaryatayn to be safe, we still experienced killing and fires and kidnappings all around us. Leaving Syria was the last resort. We couldn't go anywhere else in Syria, so we decided to go to Lebanon, and it was very difficult. We left only with the clothes that we had on. When the kids got hungry on the road, we didn't have anything to give them.

On the way to the border, we had to go right through the regime's center in Damascus, the capital. The drive was beautiful, we
could see the horizon and the mountaintops. But we would also
see the army presence everywhere. In that part of the country, the
Alawites and Sunnis live together, but at that time, the bombing was
targeting the Sunnis. We went right through the middle where there
was intense bombing. When we went through the blockades on the
road, there were thugs known as *shabiha*, who are part of the regime.
They're not officials, they don't have a rank, but they work with the
government. And they had blockades made with ribbons with the
whole road lined up with military. The thugs were going through
and searching every car. So there was a huge backup of traffic. When
they talked to us, they asked, "Are you trying to flee?" We said, "No,
we're trying to go find work." Then the bombing started, so they
started letting people go. How we were able to flee to Lebanon with
all that chaos, I don't know. My kids were crying. My husband and
I were too. When the bombing started and we were going through
those blockades, we said goodbye to each other again. I always replay
those moments in my head. I remember it on my own, but sometimes it's better to let it out with other people.

EVERYTHING WAS DIFFERENT

Some of my husband's family members had fled to Lebanon before
us, so we knew somebody there. When we got there, they found us a
place. You can't really call it a house, because it's very expensive to have
a house there. So we stayed in a rented garage. My husband worked a
little bit, but it wasn't his kind of work. Our situation before the war
was kind of easy. He didn't really have to do any hard labor to earn a
living. But in Lebanon, everything was different. Everything was com-
pulsory. There were a lot of people, very few jobs, and the whole society
there was not really accepting or loving. Most of Lebanese society, the
way they looked at refugees or received them was not very favorable.

Over the months we lived there, we had many difficulties. For instance, the Lebanese do not want to have Syrians be considered as Lebanese citizens, so there's no integration. Syrians there demanded citizenship because of the situation that we were in, and we weren't sure we were going to go back to our country. But there was a push-back not only from the government but from the society there. There are good people there, but a lot of people are not.

In the past, the father of the current Syrian president, Hafez al-Assad, had troops and control over part of Lebanon. He had a lot of say in what went on in the Lebanese Civil War, and he was responsible for a lot of atrocities in Lebanon, and maybe this was the reason the Lebanese would not accept the Syrians. So when my babies were born, the birth certificate specifies that the parents are Syrian. It doesn't guarantee them Lebanese citizenship. It says date of birth and the nationality of the parents—that's it. I've lived in both situations—the war in Syria and as a refugee in Lebanon, and I feel that it's better live in war conditions in Syria rather than be a refugee in a place like Lebanon. Either I survive or I die. There are no other options; we have no other choices.

My husband had to do any job, anything that he was offered, so he started working in construction. Not like here in Blacksburg though. In Lebanon, it's more difficult. It's more labor-intensive. Like he would have to carry buckets of gravel. He would have to carry lots of bricks. The kind of stuff that is not necessarily done here manually. What the Lebanese laborers wouldn't do, my husband had to do. One day workers brought him home early because he could not move. He had injured his back. He was given some painkillers until he was able to just sit up. We went to a physician, a doctor who would see refugees. He had to get some kind of scan that would cost around $300. We didn't have a single dollar. It was really bad. Some people helped us, and he was able to get that scan. They said that he had fractures in his spine. Third to the fourth, fourth to the fifth, and then the bottom one. The most important one. The doctor said, "You cannot work for six months." He said, "Not even to lift a kilo." The medication he prescribed cost $400 a month. Without the medicine, my husband was either going to be paralyzed or had to have an operation. Four hundred dollars in Lebanon is a lot of money. One of my husband's friends said there was a Saudi man who said, "I want to help any Syrian refugees." In Islam, it's important to help people anonymously, so this man did not want to be known. My husband's friend told him, "Give me the prescription," and the Saudi man, whom we never met, paid for the medication. In one week, my husband was better, and he went back to work. The same kind of work. Nobody expected that. I saw him when he was down, and when I heard the doctor—I was with him the whole time—after one week, I was really surprised. I was praying that by the time they bring him back he wouldn't be paralyzed or something worse. But it all went well, and I have a lot of faith; I put my trust in God. It was a really difficult situation.

When we were in Lebanon, our oldest son went to play outside on his bicycle. He'd just gone out, and his dad was working nearby. So I told him, "I'll make some tea, and you can take it to your dad." And so he told me, "I'll bring my brother too." When he went outside, a car came suddenly and hit my son, injuring his leg. So instead of my oldest coming back to get the tea, my youngest one came and said, "Brother fell and injured himself." But my youngest was always exaggerating, so I really didn't take him seriously. But when I looked at his face, I knew there was something serious. I couldn't believe it. It had been just five minutes that they'd left.

My son's bone was broken, and his foot was bent to the other side, and there was blood everywhere. I couldn't believe it. I just covered my eyes and said, "I hope this is just a dream." People who gathered said, "Don't move him until an ambulance comes." The ambulance took him to the hospital, and the hospital staff demanded some kind of investigation or report. When they heard the story, they said, "You have to make a report. You have to say whose car hit your son." And this was like a public hospital. They don't take money. That's why my husband took him there. But my husband said, "I don't want to press any charges against anybody." They told him, "You can get a lot of compensation, money, if you say that." He said, "I'm not going to press charges, because my son is fine. And it's my son's fault that he was playing in the street." Finally my husband took my son to a different hospital because he was tired of arguing. It took a long time for my son to recover. He had to have three operations before he was okay.

In Lebanon, it was as if we were dying every day. There were times we didn't have food. The whole environment in the garage where we were living was not good. And so the kids were sick most of the time. Every now and then, one of them would have to go to the hospital. Because we were registered with the United Nations, it would cover some costs. The UN covered 75 percent, and we had to cover 25 percent. My youngest, he would get sick all of a sudden. He would get an asthma attack. He had to go to a hospital and get an inhaler. I had some friends, and I would always keep in mind that as long as my husband is working, I can borrow something from them to pay back later. Because usually it happened at night that he got his asthma attacks, and I would have to find a way to take him to the hospital. Once for a whole week, I couldn't take my youngest to the doctor because I didn't have money. And then I borrowed money, and I took him to the doctor. The doctors told us not to cook in the house because the air quality is bad. It's humid. And it affects his breathing and his respiratory system. Then when it was difficult to get food for the kids, I would say to them, "We can't have any cooked food because of your brother." So it was an excuse to say, "We can't have cooked food, so that your brother doesn't get sick." It was very difficult in Lebanon, but we were patient at that time, because we heard about the possibility of coming here to the United States.

The process to come to the United States took two years for Amal and her family. After many interviews and documentation processes and delays, Amal and her family arrived. By this time, she had two additional children. They first arrived in Roanoke and were placed in housing that was questionable. Amal describes her struggles negotiating her housing situation while not knowing English. Like all refugees entering this country, Amal was navigating a variety of different federal, state, and local organizations including Catholic Charities, International Refugee Rescue, the Office of Refugee Resettlement, the Department of Public Welfare, the landlord, and so on. When she described her situation, it was difficult to determine who was telling her what information and who had decision-making power to help her. As she tried to navigate these various agencies, she became increasingly frustrated and depressed, unsure if she would be able to change her family's situation.

FOUR MONTHS OF PURE MISERY

Through the UN office in Lebanon, we were told that we were going to be in a good home. We'd been happy when we were told we were going to the United States in spite of our sadness about leaving our family in Syria. When we first arrived in Roanoke, we could see the mountains and we were reminded of home. Some parts of Syria are brown and dry, but we have green too, and patches of land for farms. We were unsure but glad to be in the United States. When they brought us to the house in Roanoke, I started crying, and I said, "You cannot be serious bringing us here. You don't think we're human?" It was so dirty. The whole house had stairs going up and down. It was difficult for my son, who'd hurt his leg in Lebanon. Sometimes he had to sit on the steps and slide to come downstairs. And he wouldn't step on that foot when he was going up. It was difficult for him. We told our caseworker about this problem, but it didn't make any difference. And every day we would discover something major in the house.

The place wasn't secure. It wasn't clean. We'd only eat crackers and packaged food; we couldn't cook. There were mice and cockroaches there, and nobody wanted to eat anything. It was so bad we would go sit outside in some small park or something, and then at the end of the day, we would go back. We couldn't stay in the house much. When we told our caseworker about all the problems at the house, he said, "This is much better than where you were, so be grateful."

We went to the caseworker many times. I told him, "When we heard that we're coming to the United States, we were happy, because we know that in America, there is care for the animals. What about the human beings who are coming from war-torn places?" Sometimes the agency staff wouldn't see us. But then we told them the children were depressed, they would sometimes receive us in the office. We would just tell them, "We just want two bedrooms that are decent for anybody to stay in." They would tell us, "You're a big family of eight. You cannot live in a two-bedroom house. These are the laws." And yet we were in a terrible three-bedroom house. It was very, very bad treatment, and four months of pure misery.

Our bedroom was on the middle floor, and the kids' bedroom was on the top floor, and the kids were afraid. So I put four of them in one bedroom, and me and my husband and the two girls stayed in another bedroom, and we didn't use the downstairs at all. We would hear the children screaming, because the mice would be scurrying around, and they would burrow in their walls. And we would wake up in the middle of the night with them screaming. We had to turn everything upside down to find the mice.

And the caseworkers wouldn't believe us until one day when we were sleeping, I heard a noise in the bedroom. And the two girls were with me. I didn't even remove the plastic wrap from the mattresses because I was hoping to go to a clean house. So I just left them wrapped like that. The mice were just chewing through the plastic. We woke up, turned on the lights, and the mice were with us in the room! My husband blocked the door, and he was running after them, and I was taking videos of how he was trying to get them, because they wouldn't believe us. We took two videos of how they were eating our stuff. Rice and flour and bulgur—all that stuff, the mice would get into it, and we'd have to just dump everything. It was just disgusting. Two sofas. We found more mice. When we said, "We want something to be able to sit on," they said there was nothing for us. We just put the dining room chairs out in the living room, we would just sit there, and that's where we would receive people.

We would always go to the office. The baby was about two months old, and we'd beg them, because of the horrible living conditions—and the food that we'd try to cook we always had to dump because of the infestation. Then they said, "You have to sign the lease." We'd talk and talk and then they'd say, "But it's important that you sign the lease. Once you sign, we're going to come and fix everything. Anything that's broken or torn, we'll fix it. We'll take care of everything." After we signed, we didn't see anybody come to take care of the problems. We'd go to their office and ask for the caseworker who was responsible for us. And we knew that he was there, we could see him, and they'd tell us that he wasn't there.

I told him that we didn't like the house and we wanted to go back to Lebanon, or he needed to find us another place to live. He responded that we had paid a deposit for electricity from the money that the government gives to refugees and that "if you leave before the lease term, you lose everything. You lose all that money."

I said, "I don't care. We just want proper housing that we can live in." When we were unable to get anywhere with them, we took pictures of the mice. We went to the police because the person we worked with had left the organization—we didn't know where to turn. They told us when we first came that you can't take what's rightfully yours by force. You're going to have to go through the police to settle any dispute. So we went to the police. After a few days, we got an eviction notice in the mail.

So I went to try to talk to them. Nobody would receive us. I spoke with a friend of mine who's an interpreter. I took a picture of the eviction notice and I sent it to my friend. She said, "This eviction notice takes effect in twenty days." So we asked why. I felt like the organization abandoned us.

When I was finally able to talk to the representative, he was very cunning with us. He said, "Do you want to know what you received in the mail?" I told him, "I know what's in that letter. A notice that we need to leave the house." I was very calm and smiling. He was really surprised. He said, "Are you happy that this is what's happening? You have to think of a solution." I said, "I'm not going to leave the house." He said, "No, you have to leave in twenty days. You have to find a house." I said, "I'm not going to leave the house. It's your responsibility. You have to find me an alternative." He told me, "You cannot do that." So I said, "I've repeatedly come and tried to work this out, to tell you about our situation, but you refused to work with us, so we had to go to the police. And as a result, you conspired with the landlord to get us evicted. I'm going to go to the airport. I'm going to call the media. And I know a lawyer, and I'm going to tell him to contact the media."

Of course, I didn't have a lawyer or anything, but while I'm talking, I can see how scared he's getting. He said, "Who's your lawyer so we can contact him?" I said, "Don't worry about who he is. I'm dealing with him. He's going to handle our case. I'm going to pay him. It's none of your business. You were the one who told me that if you leave the house, you're going to lose all your rights to any deposit. So I'm not going to leave the house. Because you're the ones who are evicting me. Then you should give me back the deposit." He said, "No, none of that is going to happen."

So I told him, "You're the caseworker. You're handling this whole thing. How can you tell me that if I leave early, I'm going to lose it, and now you're the one who's driving me out?" I told him, "I'm waiting for the day when we're going to be thrown out on the street." He said, "How come?" I said, "If we get thrown out on the street, the police will come. I have the lease and I'll tell them my story." Really, they hadn't done anything good for us during those four months that we were in Roanoke.

OUR SOLACE IN THIS WORLD
IS THAT WE'RE TOGETHER

That time was really difficult for me. When you go about your day-to-day life, you just forget about what happens. But then when we had to deal with the mice and the eviction, those things reminded me of how difficult the whole situation was. Despite all the misery in Syria and all the sadness in Lebanon and when we first came here, it was really not important as long as we were together. We were going to get through this. We knew another family that had lost a husband and some kids. I saw a lot of difficult things. Our solace in this world is that we're together.

My parting from my extended family was very difficult, because we were very close. In Syria I tried every day to visit. And all of a sudden, now for seven years, I don't see them. I would be there seven days a week, and now it has been seven years. Sometimes I try to tell myself that this is typically what happens. You know, when a woman gets married, she leaves her family's home and moves away. And a lot of women got married and leave with their husbands. So I think, *Okay, I'm in the same situation with people who get married and have to move away from their childhood home.*

After living in squalid conditions for a few months and facing eviction, Amal met some people from Blacksburg, Virginia, who were organizing to form a partnership to sponsor resettled families there. The Blacksburg Refugee Partnership (BRP) was forming in the summer of 2016 and had started communicating with Catholic Charities about bringing families to Blacksburg. They offered to help the most threatened people. Usually families come directly from other countries, but because Amal's family was facing eviction, and because her new family liaison, Dina, now a part of the BRP, knew the graduate student who had met Amal's family, they offered to help Amal's family move to Blacksburg.

We met a Syrian family when we first arrived in Roanoke, and they helped us celebrate Eid after Ramadan had ended. This family greeted us and gave us money for the kids for Eid—that is typically what Muslims do. About two months later the family visited us in the house. When they arrived, I was standing on the chair, screaming. We were trying to chase the mice out. The family came in, and we apologized for the mess and chaos. So they asked about our conditions, and they were appalled at what we told them. We didn't have the language to tell the caseworkers, and no one was being responsive to us. This family brought with them a Palestinian who's a graduate student at Virginia Tech and worked with the Blacksburg Refugee Partnership. He went back to Blacksburg and told them about us, and they decided to help us. So later they asked us if we wanted to move to Blacksburg. My husband asked me, "What do you think? We have no idea what we're going to get ourselves into." When word got out that we were moving to Blacksburg, we got phone calls from other Arab people in the area, in Roanoke, advising us not to go. But I told my husband that I felt good and optimistic about this opportunity and that we should not lose that chance. And thank God, we found something that surpassed our expectations by coming here.

The four months that we were in Roanoke, the way people looked at us, we felt like we're not even human. Every way you look at it, it's much better here in Blacksburg. And when my kids go to school, I feel like they're with me. I don't feel like I'm sending them away and fearful for them. I feel safe and my kids are safe. The people and the treatment are better here. The volunteers celebrate Ramadan with us.

THE LANDSCAPE HERE IS VERY SIMILAR TO SYRIA

In our faith, we have acceptance for whatever you go through, whether it's good or bad. We say Allah has destined or has decreed that, and his will shall prevail. I can read a person from just a look. And if my heart feels that I can trust them, then that's it. I told my husband, "There's nothing that's going to be worse than what we face in Roanoke. Anything will be better than this." After a year of living in Blacksburg, I trust people here. I don't feel like I'm being tricked. And there are friendships and loving relationships that have developed with the people here, from their interactions with us. Not just with BRP but also the people, the community in Blacksburg. We turned a new page. We came to a new life. We don't forget the past, but we live in our present and we think of the future. We're making a home in Blacksburg now.

The landscape in Blacksburg is similar to my home in Syria. We have very similar things there like mountains and trees, so much greenery. The only difference is that I miss having my family here. Before the war, a lot of tourists came to Syria for the beautiful outdoors. Homs and Damascus used to be very popular destinations for people to go shopping in the markets. Here in Virginia, we can go outside with our family. It's a treat to have meetings with all the families, especially when we're outside.

During our last visit, we all had lunch together, and the children told us lots of stories. The children asked their mother to play videos from her phone on their television screen. As they ate stuffed grape leaves and falafel sandwiches, they explained the context of the videos of themselves dancing in Lebanon. They are happy and smiling, dancing in the small garage space where they lived, awaiting word from the UN about traveling to the United States. As the children watched themselves, they told story after story about what they were doing at that time, how old they were, how they love to dance as a family, and how their tastes in music now include some American songs in addition to the traditional Syrian songs in the videos.

When we're alone as a family, we go on outings. We make tea and coffee in our thermoses, and we buy things for the kids to eat on the road. We turn on the music, sing, clap, and make videos. We choose a nice spot by the New River, where the train tracks are, and we have a picnic. Even if we only go to Oasis, the international grocery store, we turn on the music, and it's like we're going someplace different. We visited Radford the other day, near the river. We went for a picnic there. We played music and danced with the children. Even when we were in Lebanon, when we were in a small garage, and my husband didn't even know how to drive, we always had fun. We put on music, put on the TV, and the kids are dancing. I made a video of them dancing. I keep those videos for them to watch themselves when they were little, dancing and having fun.

RUFUS ELLIOTT

BORN: Amherst, Virginia
INTERVIEWED IN: Blacksburg, Virginia
Monacan Tribal Citizen, Housing Director

Interviewed by Jessica Taylor

*Rufus Elliott is a tribal leader in the Monacan Indian Nation, a fed-
erally recognized American Indian tribe with members in Virginia,
Maryland, West Virginia, and Tennessee. Rufus lives in Williamsburg,
Virginia, but his extended family and other community members live in
Amherst, Virginia, in the foothills of the Blue Ridge Mountains, where
he was born.[1] With a long history of forced removals and displacement*

---

1. "We heard that you were a people from under the world, to take our world from
us." —Amorolek, Manahoac/Monacan, 1607. Though one of the oldest Indigenous
communities in the country, the Monacan Nation only became a state-registered

of Indigenous peoples in the region, which resulted in lack of access to education for the Monacan community, Rufus's graduation from college was celebrated as a great accomplishment by the entire community.

In his role as a tribal leader, he attends many events to play traditional music and provide Monacan blessings. During a celebration event in 2022, Rufus played a traditional drum. The crowd, mostly non-Native people, sitting in a large banquet hall, was quietly chatting. Rufus walked up to the microphone and suddenly the small drum made a booming noise across the room. Rufus sang and drummed, preparing the place for the gathering. Once the opening song was finished, he explained that Monacans come from the "connection of two words: Ahkon, which means "meadows," and Shuq, which means "hills" or "mountains." So in our understanding, we call this place the land of meadows and mountains." Rufus says that to know one Monacan, we have to know the history of the Monacan people. During this celebration, his uncle, Chief Kenneth Branham, described Rufus as a great historian of the Monacan tribe.

Like many Monacans, Rufus lives in a multigenerational community, where storytelling and celebrations occur often. His memories of his grandmother and great-uncles sharing their history inspired him to become a historian of his tribe as well.

OUR HOMELAND

As a kid I was funny and good-natured, I guess. A lot of close friends who have known me since childhood would tell you that there is a certain intensity to me, behind my smiling face. Although I accomplished some things, a lot of that didn't come easily. I did not grow

---

corporation in 1988, was officially recognized by the Virginia General Assembly in 1989, and gained federal recognition in 2018. The Monacan Indian Nation owns a 110-acre property on Bear Mountain, where there is a community garden, held in trust for the Monacan Nation's future generations, and where the Bear Mountain Indian Mission School still stands.

up in the easiest of circumstances, but I grew up in a loving extended family. We like to laugh. There's a flip side to that, a certain drive and intensity to break the generational obstacles my elders faced.

I grew up in a very rural area, in a small village of twenty-eight little houses near the Blue Ridge Mountains. It was a community established as low-income housing for Monacan families in the 1940s, and when I was a kid in the seventies, Monacans lived in the majority of those homes. My mom and I lived in one house, and I lived next door to my grandmother, Lacie Johns Branham, and my great-grandmother, Cammie Johns, lived three houses up the street. My great-grandmother put me on and off the school bus as a kid.

The Blue Ridge area of the Virginia mountains is what most Monacans would consider our homeland. Our ancestors passed on a love for the Blue Ridge Mountains. They were from the mountains, and that's the way they would describe our heritage. If you asked, "Where are you from?" they would say, "Well, we're from the mountains of Virginia." When I was growing up, every Monacan I knew talked about feeling better when we're on our land, when we see the mountains. On very rare occasions when we could get my grandmother out of Amherst County, I remember she'd always say that she felt like she was home when we would turn a corner and she could see the mountains. That's the way we talk about being home.

WITH THE ELDERS ON THEIR PORCHES

My earliest memories are of being a small boy running up the street to my great-grandmother's house or running across the street to my great-uncle's house. I spent a lot of my childhood with the elders on their porches, and there were a lot of days spent with the old guys playing checkers. I have cousins my age who grew up on the same street, and we did the typical small child things like playing games. But my really vivid childhood memories are of times I spent with the elders telling stories.

One of my favorite elders was Uncle Lucian. He was my great-grandmother's brother. He lived across the street from me, and one of his sons, Gene, lived with him too. I spent a lot of time over at their house. I'm sure sometimes I was bugging them. But they taught me a lot, not only about our history as Monacans but also other things, like gardening and drumming, that I see now are a big part of my personal interests.

My elders were avid gardeners. As a boy I spent a lot of time with them learning how they gardened by the moon cycles. When we gardened together, they told me stories and history, but it wasn't a formal conversation where I'd say, "Hey, can you teach me about being Indian?" or "Can you teach me about being Monacan?" What they taught me emerged over time.

I gardened with my grandmother too. In my community, almost everyone had a garden. We used our gardens to support each other. Some folks were known to grow good tomatoes. Other folks could grow good green beans. When we had more than we could use, we would share and trade. I probably got on their nerves as a little boy—I was in everybody's gardens. I went from one to another. Monacans were always really dependent on their gardens, but in my time, gardens were used to supplement what you could get at the grocery store. We grew corn, beans, succotash beans, squash, tomatoes, peppers, cucumbers. Everyone had a garden that was about a quarter of an acre behind their house, but multiply that by twenty gardens in the entire community, and it's a lot, and everybody shared.

If I close my eyes and imagine time spent in the garden as a young boy, there are two places my mind goes: the warm summer evenings where I could hear all the birds and the tree frogs and the evening crickets. The other is hearing my grandmother and other elders hum while they worked in their gardens. We laughed and joked. There was a lot of laughter, a lot of quiet humming.

Our culture really revolves around the four seasons, and our tribal ceremonies follow the lunar calendars and these seasons. Planting and harvesting had their own ceremonies and dances. It's something that was taken away from Indigenous people in this country: ceremonies and dances were discouraged or banned. It was illegal for people to get together and have these ceremonies. Those laws really affected Monacans—my great-grandparents and my grandmother—all Monacans. They couldn't call what they did "ceremonies," so they called them "corn shuckings" for a long time. Then during my mom's generation, they could call them ceremonies again.

That's some of the work I do now as a tribal leader—I tie the more modern tradition of corn shucking back to the older ceremonies. I also manage a Monacan tribal garden for my home community. It's filled with the laughter of children rather than elders. Now that I'm a tribal leader, we make sure that we participate the best we can in traditional harvesting songs and dances. Working the gardens is a bridge between our elders and our community today.

When I would hang around Great-Uncle Lucian, he would talk about what he remembered as a boy. He would say, "You know, I remember when there was nothing but Indians up in these hills." He would go on about what that was like then and the things that changed as other people settled into the foothills of the Blue Ridge and Amherst. He really lived through lots of changes. He lived to be nearly 102 years old, so he would have been a boy at the turn of the century. I got to spend time with him in his later years as he reflected on his life. When I went over there, I knew I was going to get a history lesson.

Because I lived in a multigenerational Monacan community, my elders told me many stories about what life was like for them and their ancestors. My mother helped with the Elders Luncheon—she drove a van around to pick up older folks and bring them out to lunch. I went with them because I wanted to go out to eat. I spent entire afternoons with Monacans who were of my grandparents' and great-grandparents' generation listening to them reminiscing while we ate. My mother also did an oral history project where she used an old-school video recorder with the tape on the side. I got to witness all those interviews and hear their stories too.

One important story we tell is about why the Blue Ridge Mountains are so important to us. When William Byrd mapped the areas of Virginia and North Carolina, he hired a Saponi Indian named Ned Bearskin.[2] Along their travels, he asked Ned Bearskin about our spiritual understanding of the afterlife. Ned Bearskin explained to him that when a person dies, their soul would be guided along the path of spiritual ancestors until they reached the foot of the mountains. Then the group would be split into two. If you lived a good life, if you were brave, courageous, honest—all the characteristics of a good person—then you were able to move forward into meadows with plenty of squash from the ground. There were plentiful deer, elk, turkey, and so forth—an easy life. If, at the foot of the mountains, you were judged to have been a bad person—greedy, not caring for others—then you were forced along the path that was rocky. It was cold, barren—nothing grew there. Ice hung from the trees, and the brain had tormented days, until you were seen as having enough time in that land and you were sent back here to try again. We connect what we call this land—the land of meadows and mountains—to our spirituality. Even at the end of our life, we are about mountains and meadows.

THEY LEFT BEING MONACAN BEHIND

Several of my family and many Monacan elders were forced to go to the Bear Mountain Indian Mission School built in 1868 by the Episcopal Church.[3] Monacans were not allowed to go to public school

2. The Eastern Siouan nations are made up of several groups, including the Saponi and the Tutelo-speaking Monacans. They were a part of the Monacan confederacy, whose capital was Rassawek.

3. See the Department of Historic Resources' entry on Bear Mountain Indian School at www.dhr.virginia.gov/historic-registers/005-0230. Mission schools for

until the 1960s and were only allowed to go up to seventh grade with a correspondence course option for another year. It wasn't until 1964 when the first Monacan cohort went to public school in Amherst County. Even then, my mother and uncles had their shirts lifted up at the door, and the light-skinned Monacans were allowed to go to the public school, while the darker Monacans were held back a year and remained at the Indian mission school. They went in pairs to the public school so that they could be safe together.

My grandmother, when she was at the Bear Mountain Indian Mission School, was forced to cook and clean. My grandmother's family all only had a third-, fourth-, fifth-grade education at best. That's why there's this generational gap in wealth and education, no access to the "American Dream." All of that has roots in the "racial integrity" laws.

Rufus's explanation of his grandmother's and uncle's experiences at Bear Mountain Indian Mission School is his response to the question "What was life like for you as a boy?" He responded to most questions asked about him with stories about his community. To understand why he was the first to graduate from college, it is important to know the story of forced removal and forced schooling that his family experienced. The way Rufus tells his story through the stories of his parents, grandparents, and great-grandparents reveals who he is: storyteller and historian.

When I would sit on Uncle Lucian's porch or work with him in the garden, he talked a lot about what it was like to live through the racial integrity era. My grandparents and great-grandparents lived through the time of the Virginia Racial Integrity Act, a law that

---

American Indians have a fraught history in both the United States and Canada. Many children were forced to go, separated from their families, forced to learn English, and punished for speaking in their tribal language. There is much evidence of psychological, cultural, physical, and sexual abuse, and recent efforts toward redress and reparations have made the telling of these histories an important social justice project in many communities.

was passed in 1924 to keep Black and white people from marrying and having biracial kids. This law required that Virginians had to register as either white or "Negro" on their birth certificates. Even though Virginia Indians were neither, they were forced to register as Black. And people born before 1924 had their records changed without their consent. This created a paper genocide of the Virginia Indian community—there was no third category of being Native American or Indigenous. So, on paper, that meant a person's tribal identity was erased.

My grandparents were both from Amherst County and both Monacan. To avoid this Virginia law, they drove to Maryland to get their marriage license because they did not want to put "Negro" on their marriage license; they wanted to put "Native American." That was common. In truth, a lot of Monacans left Virginia entirely to avoid these racist practices.

The racial integrity laws put Virginia Indians in an unidentifiable third category in which there was nothing for us. There was no school program for us. There were already schools for Blacks at the time. There were Black doctors, Black hospitals. These places were not equal by any means, and they were segregated, but they were there. For Monacans, there was nowhere to go. They were labeled "Negro" on their birth certificates, but they couldn't go to the Black schools. So that's when the church stepped in and created the Indian mission schools. But the Indian mission schools only went to the seventh grade.

If you wanted to escape this terrible treatment, it meant leaving the area, leaving family and the community. A lot of Monacans moved to the surrounding states. Some moved to the suburbs outside of Baltimore for work.[4] People there wouldn't know who they were so there wasn't the same kind of discrimination. They could self-identify as Black or white, or in some cases Indian, depending

---

4. Amherst County, Virginia, is about a four-hour drive northeast to Baltimore, Maryland, and Johnson City, Tennessee, is about four hours to the southwest.

on the state, and they could get work. Johnson City, Tennessee, was another area they could go for work. There was a nonstop train from Amherst back then that went directly to Johnson City. My grandfather told stories of jumping trains, basically like sleeping on the trains to go down to Johnson City to work for a while, get some money, and come home. To this day there are sizable Monacan communities in Tennessee, West Virginia, and Maryland. It's from the exodus out of Amherst, Virginia, during the twenties, thirties, and forties.

Although the Racial Integrity Act and racism pushed a lot of Monacans out of Amherst County, most of my own family stayed in Amherst. A lot of Monacans who stayed worked as sharecroppers and tenant farmers in orchards in Amherst until the 1970s. My grandparents and great-grandparents worked in the fruit orchards. The land that I grew up on had actually been a fruit orchard from the 1920s to the 1960s, and as the orchards declined, that land was built up into housing. But because of that, most people also had peach, cherry, or apple trees in their yards. So I grew up around fruit trees too.

Uncle Lucian was actually a foreman at one of the four main orchards, High Peak Apple Farm, during that time. The structure in the orchards was that the white workers had their boss, their white foreman. There were some African American workers, and they had an African American foreman. Then there were Indian workers, and they had their Indian foreman. A lot of the leadership and our community came out of two places: out of the church and out of the orchards. People who were foremen in the orchard also tended to be community leaders when they weren't at work.

Some Monacans, whose families left to escape racism and poverty, were born and raised outside of Baltimore and have now moved back to Amherst. And that's good to see, that they are repopulating part of our original homeland. There's definitely some social anxiety on both sides, I think. Those of us who are from families that stayed wear it like a badge of honor, that we stayed despite social pressure or racism. Because I grew up with three generations of my family, I had direct contact with the culture at all times through my childhood. But for the people who moved away, in some cases, they can have a little bit less comfort in their Indian identity.

Often when Monacans left, they left being Monacan behind, too, for survival. Sometimes they stayed within communities, but not always, and so sometimes you get folks moving back here who are very strong in their sense of identity—their parents and grandparents who moved away did a really good job of making sure of that. And then sometimes you get people who move back here who were really cut off from their Monacan identity. I think sometimes they have imposter syndrome or worry that they're not the same as the people who stayed here. I think it's really incumbent on the people who stayed, like my family, to make them feel comfortable. I think more often than not, it works out over time, and it's different for every person who moves away and moves back. There's just a process of being reintegrated into the community. For some people it's quick and easy, and for others it's more difficult. That's why I do so much work in the tribe now.

With so many who stayed being forced to go to mission schools and with only a few high school graduates, that I went to college was a miracle. I'm one of the first Monacans to graduate from a four-year university, in 2007. That being relatively recent has its roots in segregation and the racial integrity laws that didn't give Monacans access to health care, education, basic rights, and privileges and that offered limited job options. The injustices that Virginia Indians have endured have impacted education and access, similar to African Americans. That's why these "firsts" happened so recently.

LIKE A GAME OF *SURVIVOR*

I give my family credit for my early school years and me doing well in school. My mom was very strict about my grades; however, we never discussed college. My mom never said I had to get good grades because of college. It was more like she thought, *You're intelligent enough to get these grades, so you better get these grades.* We really didn't talk about college, and I didn't have any role models, someone else in my immediate community who had gone to college.

I'm sure there were Monacans who were displaced and moved away from Amherst who had college educations. But in my small community of Amherst, no one graduated from college before me. I didn't know anybody who had ever gone to school outside of Amherst. When I was a teenager, a professor, Sam Cook, was researching and working closely with the Monacan community in Amherst. He took a personal interest in me and helped guide me through applying to college. So it was really Dr. Cook saying, "Hey, you should take the SAT. You should come visit Virginia Tech." That was when the seeds were being planted for the American Indian Studies program at Virginia Tech. The university would have events, pre-college gateway events for American Indians. So we would come down to campus as a community. We would perform Native American powwow dances and sing at these events and shows, and that was my introduction to college.

One weekend, I came down to an event with an envelope folded up in my pocket. I'm probably the last person to ever submit a paper college application. I don't remember who I handed it to, but it was on a Thursday. And then on Saturday afternoon before I left to go home, I was handed another envelope. In it was an acceptance letter. I didn't apply to any other college. I didn't go through the normal college visits and the anxiety.

When I got to college, it was certainly an adjustment. It was different. I hadn't been exposed to so many different kinds of people. I thought Blacksburg was like New York City. It's no coincidence, though, that I felt some comfort going to school at Virginia Tech—it's in the mountains just like my hometown.

The campus is this big place. The buildings look like castles, big, with gray stone.[5] It was eye-opening. I came from a small community where I knew everybody, and everyone knew me. That's good and bad. It's good in the sense that there's comfort in knowing you're likely to see someone you're related to. As a kid, whenever we wrecked our bikes, got skinned up, somebody would pick us up, carry us home. There's a comfort in that extending into adulthood. In a place like that, every car that breaks down on the side of the road, someone's gonna stop and get you. They'll recognize your car and you. But when I came to college, it wasn't that way for me. It seemed like a game of *Survivor*, where everybody's got their own thing they're gonna do. I felt like you're either working toward helping them survive, or you're in the way. The sense of community that I have now at Virginia Tech I didn't have early on, so it was a big adjustment for me. I spent a lot of time the first couple of years going home on the weekends.

My hometown is only two and a half hours away, but you'd have thought I had moved to China. My elders were incredibly proud but also nervous. Few leave our small Indian communities even now—and if they did, they went to Hampton when it was an Indian school.[6] We had Monacans go there, and none of those students came home. So there's that memory, too, where families felt like they'd lose their young. There was a point in our history when a Cherokee in North Carolina offered to educate and host students at the Indian mission school, but no one went because that was right after people went to Hampton and did not come home. We have this

---

5. Hokie Stone is the famous limestone that is quarried in Blacksburg, Virginia. The gray stone is cut for use in the buildings on Virginia Tech's campus, which are largely built in a neo-Gothic architectural style.

6. The Hampton Normal and Agricultural Institute was the original name of what is now Hampton University, a historically Black university founded in 1868. More than 1,400 American Indians were educated there, not all by choice, between 1878 and 1923.

long history of people rarely leaving, and when they do, of not coming home. So while there was totally a sense of pride for the accomplishment of me getting into college, there was also a nervousness about how I might be treated when I got there and whether I would ever come home. That community anxiety is deep.

Rufus's graduation from Virginia Tech (VT) was not only significant to his community and family, but to VT as well—he was the first Monacan to graduate from VT. As a land grant university, VT is part of a group of colleges and universities founded through the Morrill Act, which forcibly took land from Indigenous populations to create universities for the public. Rufus, together with Chief Branham, his mother Sue, and tribal elder Victoria Ferguson, graciously opened the event with Monacan prayers and music, honoring their ancestors and the land on which VT stands. Chief Branham said, "Virginia Tech is built on our home. . . . It is your responsibility to make sure our people have the opportunity to be educated. Today is my grandmother's—Rufus's great-grandmother's—birthday. And you don't think she's here? She's looking down, smiling. She's so proud of what this family and this young man have done."

My grandmother never drove. She never had a driver's license or a vehicle. My mom drove, but there are very rare occasions when she drove outside a forty-five-minute radius from home. Even though it was only a two-and-a-half-hour drive to my campus, the idea that they would get on the interstate and drive down here seemed monstrous. They came down to help me move in, but they never came back down here except for graduation.

My whole Monacan community was important when I went to college. When you grow up in a place like this, it's not just your immediate family. I have second cousins, uncles, great-uncles, all my extended family who supported me, and they all knew what was going on. That was always burdensome: if it didn't work out here, for whatever reasons, I wasn't just letting myself down or my mom down. There was an entire community of people that I felt like I would be letting down. All that anxiety grows exponentially with every person you're dealing with, with a Monacan community and extended family of six to seven hundred people. It was definitely pressure packed sometimes.

My roommate was African American, and I knew him from high school in Amherst. We would've been friends wherever we ended up. We roomed together our freshman year and that made adjusting to college easier. Move-in day was super exhausting and hectic, and I remember thinking my mom would never leave. She kept hanging around, and she was a sobbing mess the whole time. I made sure to not show my anxiety, but the second they left I was anxious too.

I met some other people from the American Indian student organization, but I'll be honest, I didn't recognize the people there as being the same as me. Indian identity is very complicated. It's a real thing, being raised in the Indian community or being raised outside of it but having genealogy ties to it. I'm not saying people who were in the Indian student organization didn't have hereditary ties to a community, but I just didn't really connect with them either. It was hard to find each other on campus.

One of the things I'm happiest about is that my grandmother lived long enough to come to graduation. It wasn't easy for me to get to graduation, but when it finally happened, there was definitely a sense of pride and relief for myself, and then having the family down for it was really cool. My grandmother was there, my mom, my uncle, my sister, a couple of my aunts. Even though Virginia Tech is really big, the separate department graduations are fairly small, so the room we were in was small. Monacans use conch shells in celebrations. We cut off one end and blow them in celebration. My uncle smuggled a conch shell into graduation somehow, and when I walked across the stage and they announced my name, he blew the shell—it was super loud and scared half the people in the room to death. I thought it was hilarious at the time, but I think that was his way of indigenizing the space and the graduation. He was marking the occasion and the accomplishment of a Monacan. It wasn't just his nephew and somebody he cared about; it was also the accomplishment of the community.

BACK HOME TO FIND WORK

When I first graduated, I was very homeward looking. I went back home to find work. But what I wanted to do professionally I couldn't accomplish in my very small rural hometown. That's not just an Indian experience and not just in Virginia, that's all across the country. All of rural America is experiencing the same thing. Indians are getting degrees and job training, but then we can't translate that to doing something for our own community, so we have to move somewhere else, away from our families. That reality didn't hit me until about a year after graduation when I realized, *I can't stay here unless I do something that has no relevance to my education.*

I ended up going to NC State University for the NC TEACH program, to work toward getting certified to teach.[7] I worked at a restaurant part time and then I realized that I could make more money managing a restaurant than I could teaching. I finished the program, but I never taught. Instead I managed a restaurant chain for a while, and then moved back to Virginia and started working for a property management company in Charlottesville. I did that for a few years.

Then the federal government finally recognized six tribes in Virginia in 2018.[8] That meant that our communities were eligible for some federal housing funding. I realized I could finally work and

---

7. NC TEACH is a teacher licensure program. See https://ced.ncsu.edu/nc-teach for additional information.

8. See information about the Thomasina E. Jordan Indian Tribes of Virginia Federal Recognition Act of 2017, at www.congress.gov/bill/115th-congress/house-bill/984.

live in my community, and so I've been working in Indian housing ever since.

There are still gaps in access to good health care, education, jobs. That lack of access has been a long-time burden, and there are deep wounds that marginalized communities like the Virginia Indian communities bear. There's a high rate of suicide today in Virginia Indigenous communities. Lack of access to all these things has had a trickle-down effect to everyone in the household, even to young people who have not lived during the time of the outright racism of the racial integrity laws. Social mobility within the region didn't exist for my elders. When they went to work and thought, *I'm going to go work without rest to give my children a better life*, it became clear that even if they could work a good-paying job, they weren't going to be able to provide that mobility for their children because it didn't exist, due to the lasting impacts of racial inequities in Virginia. That included access to housing.

I work with Native people who live in multigenerational households that would be considered overcrowded. This can vary across different tribes, but many people don't know how the systems surrounding homeownership work. A lot of the work that needs to be done is in financial education. An education leads to a job, leads to money, but if you don't have a parent or grandparent who owned a home, you don't know how to go about it. Specifically in the Monacan community, it's not unusual to work with someone in their thirties who is the first homeowner in their family or community. I hold their hand and step-by-step help them deal with the process. Another part of my job is helping elders who need home repairs. Part of the reason they don't have the finances to take care of repairs is a result of the injustices of the last hundred years.

I'm currently the housing director for the Chickahominy Indian tribe and, like the other recognized Virginia Indian tribes, it receives annual funds from the US Department of Housing and Urban Development (HUD). We can use these HUD funds to enact any number of programs for our tribal citizens. It's like a rental assistance program, very similar to Section 8 for housing. It covers things like rehabilitation and weatherizing houses, energy efficiency, roofing, those types of things. The main goal is to put people in better housing and increase home ownership among tribal communities. I manage HUD funding for a different tribe than my own. I do this work because of the history of mistreatment of Virginia Indians and how that's affected the community today.

My typical day right now is a lot of policy and compliance work. Federal funds have strings attached. We have to set up our procedures and policies to stay compliant. A lot of what I am doing is figuring out who in the community is eligible for these programs. I've got to administer these programs, to determine how to prioritize who gets the funds. There's a lot of paperwork, and soon we'll roll out some really awesome programs, like funding green homes.

Amherst is situated between Lynchburg and Charlottesville, both of which have developed and grown. There are a lot of people who commute to either city. There are lots of large subdivisions, most often in rural areas, that did not exist when I was a kid. But luckily, the largest parts of the mountain areas haven't changed, and I think one of the comforting things about mountains is that they don't change.

The recent federal recognition of Virginian tribes will open so many doors for the community. It was an incredible thing to see people who lived through the racial injustice of the Racial Integrity Act, and being told their entire lives that they were *not* Indian, have the federal government finally recognize them as exactly that. I'm glad and I wish it would've happened sooner. There were so many elders who didn't live to see that recognition. I wish they had because it is *for them* that so much of the work has been done. We talk about that a lot when we say, as a tribe, the work we do is for seven generations behind us and seven generations into the future. It's not for ourselves. The work that it took to get federal recognition was for people who are no longer here and for people who aren't here yet. So much of the work we do now will be to preserve, to the best of our ability, our history and our culture. This cultural preservation is important for us moving forward. Another big part of this is about improving the lives of our young people and setting them up for success. That starts with housing programs like the one I manage.

The other thing that I really hope happens is that we increase the number of people whose ancestors are from here to come back to the mountains. I want to build ways for people to do that. Also, for the people whose parents and grandparents who were displaced during the racial integrity era to be able to find work. Before, they could see only sentimental and spiritual reasons to come home. But hopefully now they can see financial and career-driven reasons to come home—that the tribe can offer that infrastructure and ability to have a family-supporting job. We hope to grow the community here in Appalachia.

A CARDBOARD BOX OF BONES

Rufus is committed to connecting Monacans to tribal traditions and assisting the community with equitable housing access. He spends time not only performing tribal music and organizing powwows but also being involved in the national movement to protect sacred burial grounds and ancestor remains.

I'm married, and I have two beautiful little girls, ages six and four. I'm a very proud girl dad. My wife is Pakistani and Filipino. We're a multicultural family, and we raise our girls that way, to know all of who they are, not just bits and pieces. That certainly includes their Monacan ancestry.

When I'm not working, I'm very much involved in broader Monacan and Virginia Indian initiatives. I continue to work on the Monacan tribal garden that we harvest to supplement the Monacan food bank. We use the garden to teach language, songs, dance, and ceremony to young people.

I'm also on the NAGPRA committee for the Monacan Indian Tribe.[9] We review development and construction projects that may impact cultural heritage sites, especially burial grounds. New projects in the worst case impact the human remains of our ancestors. We also work on initiatives to repatriate cultural artifacts or remains that have been distributed in the past to museums or universities. I'm also part of a group that organizes and performs the repatriation ceremonies. We've had to repatriate remains before, and we do these things properly, in the way our ancestors would have been buried originally.

Once, the workers handed us cardboard boxes that contained remains that had been improperly removed. When I opened the cardboard box of bones that belonged to my ancestors, I looked inside and saw a child's skull. There is a lasting cost for my community on an emotional level to have to continue to do these things, long after the original wrong. It's part of the reason we fight to keep sites like Rassawek, our historic capital, undisturbed.[10] For us, financial

---

9. NAGPRA is the Native American Graves Protection and Repatriation Act. "Since 1990, Federal law has provided for the repatriation and disposition of certain Native American human remains, funerary objects, sacred objects, and objects of cultural patrimony. . . . With this law, Congress sought to encourage a continuing dialogue between museums and Indian Tribes and Native Hawaiian organizations and to promote a greater understanding between the groups while at the same time recognizing the important function museums serve in society by preserving the past." See the National Park Service's entry about the Native American Graves Protection and Repatriation Act at www.nps.gov/subjects/nagpra/index.htm for additional information.

10. When the James River Water Authority announced that it was going to build a pump station at Rassawek, tribal members protested to protect the area. As of September 2020, the National Trust for Historic Preservation and Preservation Virginia had named Rassawek an endangered historic site. Building on this site and the potential disturbance of burial grounds are injustices that Native tribes continue to redress.

reparation is not really up for a discussion—it should be a given. We're talking about respecting Monacan history and respecting that no one wants their ancestors taken out of the ground and delivered to them in a cardboard box.

It's why I do all this community work. I currently have a fellowship, working on preserving and digitizing Monacan oral histories and song and ceremony recordings. I want all Monacans to have access to their own history and culture and for that history and culture to be available to Monacan citizens anywhere in the world. The deep history of colonization and long-held cultural practices are important for knowing your own identity as Monacan.

I was born and raised and spent most of my life in the Appalachian Mountains, so I guess technically I'm Appalachian. But truthfully, I view "Appalachian" as a label for a community of which I'm not a part. I consider myself Monacan, period. No one's ever asked me whether I'm Appalachian. The scope and breadth of the traditional Monacan territory is from the fault line in Richmond all the way to the New River, as far north as the Fredericksburg area, and down just past the North Carolina border. That's the ancestral territory. Most Monacans I grew up with in the older generation never put a boundary on it, no county or state lines.

Monacan identity is separate and different from Appalachian identity. However, Indian identity in the Appalachians heavily influenced Appalachian culture, non-Indian Appalachian culture, to the point that sometimes they're actually indistinguishable. There are things in the non-Indian Appalachian communities like folk stories, home remedies, gardening, hot raising.[11] Those things are heavily influenced by Native Americans in the region, and some people don't necessarily realize that we're several generations into this. They do something because that's the way their daddy did it and so on and so forth. Some don't know the origins of lots of practices from the

11. Hot raising includes using raised beds with a layer of manure under the soil to create heat for early spring planting.

Monacan culture. But I see the parallels very clearly. I think the reverse is also true. When I was growing up, I remember the Appalachian bluegrass music that my grandparents and great-grandparents loved and played, more than Indian music. So they definitely complemented and shared with each other.

Most of our villages were historically set along the James River from the Blue Ridge to the falls at Richmond. I enjoy spending time on the river in Monacan territory and kayaking on the James River, going from one village to another. It's something that connects me to my distant ancestors, knowing that they traveled on the same river in the same way.

HANNAH MARTIN

BORN: 1975, Garfield, Washington
INTERVIEWED IN: Elk Creek, Virginia
Potter

Hannah Martin has been a helicopter mechanic in the US Marine Corps, a surface warfare officer in the US Navy, and a theatrical stage manager in Portland, Oregon, and New York City. Hannah lives on a thirty-acre farm in southwest Virginia with her wife, Emi, and their young sons, Rowan and Davis, where they grow produce and bake bread to sell at the local farmer's market.

During our first conversation via Zoom, Hannah worked on waxing the bottoms of pottery to prep them for firing later. Hannah's studio, Heart Moss Pottery, is located in downtown Independence, Virginia, and is where she makes ceramic mugs, plates, and bowls. After enlisting in the marines, attending the US Naval Academy, serving as a lieutenant in the US Navy, and being stationed in Okinawa, Japan, she earned an MA in theater arts from Portland State University and an MFA in dramatic writing at New York University. She met Emi there and after they married in 2011, they moved to a farm in Elk Creek, Virginia, in 2012.

HOMEMADE BREAD

I was born in Eastern Washington in a little town called Garfield. My mother and biological father were nature hippies. They met at a party and then ended up buying several properties in the Northwest. My mother had me at home and her chiropractor was her unofficial midwife. When I was six months old, they bought a little piece of property in northeast Washington, where they built a cabin with their own hands. They used old-style methods like cutting down trees with chainsaws and using those giant knives to scrape the bark off. We didn't have any running water or electricity. My mom hauled water from the creek to the cabin to heat on the woodstove. We boiled that water to cook with and for washing laundry too. She baked homemade bread, and they were very focused on the garden. We grew lots of vegetables, like tomatoes, beans, cucumbers, and there were also certain plants that I was told to conceal. My parents said, "If a police officer shows up, don't tell them these plants are here."

When I was three, my parents broke up. Mom and I were on our own for a little while. We stayed in the cabin, and when I was five, Mom decided that we were going to take a road trip. We packed everything that we owned into our Datsun station wagon and drove to California. For a while we slept in the car, and I guess we were homeless, though I didn't realize that until years later.

I have wonderful memories of that time. Like once during a foggy, foggy morning, we woke up to a woman knocking on our car window. And she says, "Oh, why don't you come in and have breakfast with us?" They lived in a little single-wide trailer, and we had

Cheerios. They were wonderful, lovely people. Once we were staying with some friends on the coast somewhere and they had a kid who was near my age. He and I went out to play on the beach, and I had all my little Matchbox cars on the beach. There was a sneaker wave, and it nearly took us away, but the biggest problem for me was that I lost all my Matchbox cars. Another time we got into a little rowboat at night and rowed out in the waves. We ended up rowing alongside a giant tanker—I think it was dangerous!

Mom knew people to stay with along the way as we were heading down the coast from Washington to California. We stopped to visit somebody she had met at a party, and he suggested asking someone else if we could stay on their land. We stayed in a little place in the desert, in the middle of nowhere. We showed up, and ten days later, she and the man I came to call my dad got married. He was very strict, and he was Christian, so the rules and religion were huge changes for me.

At first, we lived in a one-room cabin in the middle of nowhere in the desert, near Lake Isabella. Then a year later, they got the opportunity to move to a little town—Mojave, California—to run a nonprofit street ministry called the Dove's Nest.

A lot of my actual growing up was in Mojave, first through sixth grades. I would hang out at Dove's Nest after school and do my homework and meet all different kinds of people. We called people traveling through "train tramps" because there was a train line going through town. Various folks would give me things like little broken lockets when I was hanging out there. I still have them in my jewelry container.

When I was in sixth grade, my parents got an offer to work in Berkeley, California, doing social services for the Salvation Army. Berkeley was a big change, of course, moving to the big city. After we were there for three years, we moved to Reno for a while and then back to the Bay Area outside of Oakland, where I finally graduated from high school.

VERY STRICT RULES

When my mom married my stepdad, it was a huge change. It went suddenly from being me and my mom and her rules to my stepdad's very strict rules. One of the rules had to do with food—I had to eat everything on my plate at every single meal. That wasn't something I was used to, obviously, and if I didn't eat it, then it would be saved for me to eat cold at the next meal. Scrambled eggs that I rejected for breakfast were served still cold for dinner. My stepdad took a lot of offense to me saying things like "yuck" to my mom's food. He believed in corporal punishment. When I said "yuck" to dinner, I would just jump up and run because I knew he was going to get me, and I was going to get spanked. So that was very, very different than the kind of laid-back atmosphere I had been in before Mom remarried.

I think my mom really appreciated somebody who was willing to accept her and love her as a single mom and bring her child into his household. He just died several years ago, and she misses him terribly. She loved him very much. The change was hard for her as well. But I think that she really appreciated structure, rules, and limits. We had been pretty nomadic up to that point, with no stability. She converted to Christianity when they got married, and she's still very religious. It provides stability for her. When I was a kid, we moved a lot and even when we were in one place, we still moved houses from one end of town to the other. The longest I'd ever lived in one place in my entire life, before Elk Creek, was when I went to the Naval Academy, and I was in the same dormitory for four years.

My stepdad had a son who was five years older than me. When he was in fourth grade, he got in trouble and his mom said, "Go live with your dad." He had visited before, so I knew him. Later I found out that he had been sexually abused by one of his older stepsisters' boyfriends, and he decided to pass it on to me. When I was twelve to thirteen, he sexually abused me. Later, when I was in high school, I spent quite a bit of time coming to terms with that abuse. I was

really unsettled. I was questioning my religion because of the shame
and the guilt that I thought would be associated with me for being
abused. I would get in my Ford F150 truck, with three on a tree, you
know, and I would just drive for hours and think.[1]

After I graduated from high school, I went to Purdue in West
Lafayette, Indiana. My grandfather went there, and I wanted to
get as far away from home as possible. It was two thousand miles
away, and I was glad to go. But when I got there, I had a hard time.
With the removal of that structure—a certain bedtime and the re-
strictive religious environment—without rules like no makeup and
no pierced ears, no secular music, I couldn't handle it at Purdue. I
lost all the structure, and I just never went to class. I was dealing
with trauma and rebelling against the restrictions. I was depressed,
I think, from the abuse, and I didn't know how to find my own
balance. I came back to the West Coast after a year and went to
community college.

But it's not like anything changed. I just continued to skip half
my classes in community college, and my friend and I would hang
out. I was half in love with her, but I wasn't out to myself at that
point. So we were hanging out, and she said, "Let's join the navy."
But my stepbrother was in the navy, so we joined the Marine Corps
instead. I was living with my parents and signed up while they were
away at a conference. It was the hardest thing I've done to them,
making a big decision like that. I was at work when they came home,
and I just left the Marine Corps paperwork sitting on the table so
they would find it. They were upset, but it was too late.

In 1995, when I was twenty-two, I went to boot camp and injured my ankle pretty badly, though I still made it through and
became a helicopter mechanic in the marines. It was interesting and
fun, and they had just opened up that field for women. While I was
in boot camp, they opened up a bunch of different fields for women.

---

1. "Three on a tree" refers to the gearshift on the steering column in a truck.

So it was me and one other woman in our shop of eighty guys. My commander discovered that I was really good at organization. In addition to fixing the helicopters, I also managed all the training records for the shop. Once I proved that I was good at that, they put me in charge of the general shop operation, managing tasks and communications. Around that time, I got the news that I had gotten into the Naval Academy. I got promoted to sergeant two weeks before I went to the Naval Academy Preparatory School.

I was always kind of restless and tended to be looking for the next thing. So while I was in the Marine Corps, I took a psychology class and started thinking about college again. One of my dad's friends sponsored me, and an admiral friend of his wrote a letter of recommendation for me. I went to the Naval Academy Preparatory School in Rhode Island for a year first. One of the joys of that program was that I could start fresh and create a new academic path. I discovered I really liked the structure of the Naval Academy—you can't skip classes there or you get charged with demerits.

I finally came to terms with the fact that I am a lesbian when I was at the prep school, and it was my final break with Christianity as well. I had been told that I had to accept all of it or none of it. And I thought, *If I'm going to accept myself, then I can't accept Christianity at all.* I went on a whole journey of researching all sorts of different religions and trying to figure out which one fit me. This was during Don't Ask, Don't Tell, and I was being very careful.[2] I am a rule-oriented person because of the way that I was raised, and I was conscious of the image I was projecting. But at the same time, I discovered that there was a whole LGBTQ family there. Some of those people are still my best friends, and I really appreciate that we had each other's backs.

---

2. This policy went into effect in 1994. Known as Don't Ask, Don't Tell, the legislation that dictated that gay military personnel could serve in the military but were not allowed to reveal their identities. It was overturned in 2011. See the Human Rights Campaign's blog post, "Repeal of Don't Ask, Don't Tell," at www.hrc.org/our-work/stories/repeal-of-dont-ask-dont-tell.

My parents didn't find out about the abuse until I was in the military. I was twenty years old, and I had just been stationed in Okinawa when the one person I had confided in told my parents. It was hard because I couldn't give them a hug when they found out what had happened. My mom blamed herself a lot and still carries a lot of guilt, even though it's not her fault. It was hard because I had gotten to a certain point with it and then I kind of had to regurgitate it again for them. I got out of the navy in 2002, and I'm officially a disabled veteran because of my ankle injury in boot camp.

WE STOOD IN THE LONG LINE AND GOT MARRIED

After I got out of the navy, I went to New York University for dramatic writing. I had been to New York while I was at the Naval Academy and loved it. I met Emi in grad school—she was working on her MFA in creative writing. We got married in 2011. As soon as it was legal in New York, we went to the courthouse, stood in the long line, and got married. While we were dating, she told me that her family had property in Virginia that's perfect for a writing retreat. We visited it a few times. I was dealing with misogyny in the writing world and thought about dropping out. Then I graduated and was teaching as an adjunct at multiple colleges, doing impossible commutes. We just decided that we didn't have to live that way, and I said, "Let's go."

At about that time, her uncle offered us a caretaking spot at the family property. So on the last day of January in 2012, we put everything that we could fit in the Subaru and drove down here. It was going to be a temporary move, but we knew each other's hopes and dreams for the future. Emi had done all this research on sheep farming for a novel she's going to write about sheep farming in Eastern Oregon in the 1950s. She's researching all this stuff, and she says, "I don't want to write about this; I want to *do* this." So when we arrived at the family farm we said, "Okay, let's see if we like doing things like going to the farmer's market and raising chickens." I started baking bread, which we sold at the farmer's market. Back then, it was a little bitty farmer's market, and we started making friends. There was this wonderful, wonderful community of people here. We knew about the local food movement, which was just getting started here in its own way. We were at the leading edge of that here, which was exciting.

We loved living in the community so much that we bought our own four acres and a little two-bedroom, one-bath brick ranch that needed massive renovation, but we got all of that for $72,000, which is unheard of out west. When we talked about whether we would stay or not, the final clincher was that we couldn't replicate the community anywhere else. We live near a wonderful group of people. We know them; we like them. So we stayed. My family out west wishes we lived closer. My dad is in Portland, and now we have small children, so that's really, really hard for him not to see us more.

We have had some hard moments. About a year after we moved here, I became a substitute teacher at a local school about forty-five minutes away. They hired me to be a long-term, temporary substitute for fourth, fifth, sixth, and seventh grades. I had to stay closeted for that job. But one of my students was the son of a friend of a friend, and he knew. He ended up telling all his friends, and then the school administration figured it out. Since it was a long drive anyway, I told them I was ready to leave, and the board was like, "Good, you need to go." It was an interesting kind of moment, because they never said anything, but I knew that they had just found out and that there was more work. But they were like, "How about we just take a break?" And I said, "Well, what about the after-school program I'm running?" And they're like, "How about we take a break with that after-school program?" And I said, "Yeah, okay." And so that was the end. I've run into some of the other teachers since then. They get very weird around me in the Walmart. I think one of the problems with that really was being closeted in the first place and allowing it to happen, allowing the secrecy.

Another difficult time was when I had just set up my new pottery studio, which is located on the main drag of town, very much in the public eye. I pulled up on a Sunday afternoon, and this guy pulls up in his truck next to me. He goes to my mom's church, so I knew who he was. This happens all the time in a small town. Somebody sees something new going on, they strike up a conversation. So he comes up to sell me some tomatoes and peaches from down off the mountain. He says, "Oh, where are you from?" I said, "Portland, Oregon." And he says, "There's some troubles going on there." And I said, "I know, if only the police would stop beating people up, it'd be great."[3] From there it went south really, really fast.

My mom moved here after my stepfather died, and she found a church to go to. The church itself is not deeply problematic, but some of the people in the church are. It kind of came to a head a couple months ago. The same guy who had shown up at my studio stood up and talked about how George Floyd was a criminal and a bad guy. My mom just stands up and says, "God is love and we should be loving each other." Then she never went back.

My mom put up a Biden 2020 sign in front of her house, and she started to keep a log of who was shouting at her from their car or truck. But then the shouting stopped because some of her neighbors knew who was doing it, and they said to them, "Hey, you need to stop doing that." But for a little while there, it was bad. Our politics here is like politics in the rest of the country. As far as us being lesbians in the community, that hasn't been a problem. Now part of it is because we're white. If we were women of color, it would be different. When Emi and I got pregnant, my mom went to her pastor and asked, "What do you think about this?" The pastor said, "This is a beautiful child being born into the world. We should love it and cherish it." And Mom said, "Could you please tell other people that?"

---

3. Protests in Portland and across the country in 2020 were centered around the Black Lives Matter movement and against police brutality.

We love living here, and that hasn't changed, but it has been hard since COVID-19, especially with different thinking about vaccines. We have our wonderful neighbors. One set of wonderful neighbors confessed to us in whispers that they got the shot because they knew that we would support that. But then we've got our other neighbors who are very reasonable people who are not vaccinated, and they're not going to get vaccinated. We disagree with them, but we still hang out with them—they are our neighbors, and we get along with them. They're kind to us. There are things that are wonderful about the local culture that we value and some things that we have to think about, like education and opportunities.

MY WIFE IS THE FARMER

We love our farm. But let me be clear, my wife is the farmer. She's the one who does most everything on the farm. Sometimes I help with feeding the pigs and sheep and various projects like mending fences. I take care of the kids while she goes out and does certain other projects. My mom has Rowan in the mornings, and that's when I go to the studio to make pottery. When we get up in the morning, we make breakfast and have our own chickens' eggs. Rowan helps me gather the eggs. If I go to the studio, I work with my assistant. She works on the main floor, making travel mugs and filling orders, and I'm in the basement wheel throwing. Then I pick up Rowan at noon and hopefully he'll fall asleep on the way home and I can just put him down for his afternoon nap. I try to help Emi get work done while he's sleeping.

She straps Davis, the baby, in a sling and cares for the animals. Like today she moved the sheep to the backyard for a couple of days so she can set up the garden. She set up electric fencing in the backyard and walked the sheep into the yard—with the baby strapped to her, which is always so impressive to me. She often takes Rowan to help with milking the sheep in the morning and in the evening.

When we work together in the field and Rowan is with us, he takes his wagon and uses it as his home base as he explores while we're working. Rowan likes to feed the pigs too. He likes doing "chores," and one of his jobs is feeding the dog in the morning.

During COVID I helped out a lot more on the farm because my business nearly went under. I lost over $10,000 in orders in the space of ten days in March 2020. I had one order from a big company that included three hundred travel mugs. The mugs were all made, and we had started packing them up to ship. And the morning that we were finishing up all the packing, I got an email saying they had to postpone their order indefinitely. And that was just one of the many, many orders that got canceled within the space of a week. So that definitely changed our lives. At that point we didn't know anything about pandemic employment support, especially for artists. All that kind of stuff was really up in the air. Emi worked at the Creamery for a while, and I stayed home with Rowan.[4] I experimented making sheep's cheese and we made different kinds of bread. Eventually the farmer's market came back, and that's how we made a living for a while.

Then everything came back. With the farmer's market, we all started COVID-friendly pickups that were outside and timed in place. We didn't have a lot to sell, but we were selling and then I could add some pottery. Then in September 2020, everyone realized they could order stuff online again and so the pottery business went crazy. I was able to make up basically what I had lost during those first six months of dead time with COVID.

We're the only out lesbians in the county. Everybody knows us. Everybody knows when something happens. When I go to the Elk Creek store someone will say, "Hey, are you missing a dog?" because our dogs had gotten out. When I tell other people I live here, sometimes they assume a stereotype about me or about people from here. People who don't live here make fun of Appalachians. Or assume

---

4. Here Hannah is referring to the Meadow Creek Dairy Farm, which is locally known as the Creamery.

something mystic or spiritual about them. Portrayals in movies are not usually three-dimensional—local people are often portrayed as inbred with bad teeth or bad acne—is it any wonder that these people who have been born and raised here for three, four, or five generations hold on to every little smidgen of their culture they possibly can? Just because you have a drawl doesn't mean you're stupid, right? It doesn't mean you're uneducated. Forty-four percent of families with children under the age of five in my county, Grayson County, are living below the poverty level. I think we should try to understand why people vote against their own interests. It has to do with this deep-seated anger and resentment. Anyway, that's all to say that I'm safer as a lesbian in my county than a Black person. My child is not going to experience the same kind of violence that he might experience in the big city for being the child of lesbians because everybody knows us. Everybody knows who he is, and they're like, "Yeah, we got high hopes for you, Rowan."

Here in our local community, it's about knowing the individual. So our neighbor, for instance, had land around him that came up for sale. It was land that his family used to own. There are large spaces of land that used to be owned by one family, and then it gets parceled out little by little. Some of it gets sold off to people outside the family until suddenly, the original family is on this little piece surrounded by all these other people. So our neighbor had thirty acres around them, and a business wanted to come in and start a Christmas tree farm. Nobody likes that because there's a lot of really nasty stuff that they fly over and spray on the trees. So Emi's mom bought those thirty acres to add to the bit we have. So now that particular neighbor doesn't have to have Christmas trees surrounding them on three sides. And we're farming it with livestock, sheep, and cattle. We fenced it and didn't ask the neighbor to pay, and it created some good blood there, you know. So this neighbor came up to us one day, after knowing us for years, and says that, after years and years of thinking about it, he's realized that we aren't going to go to hell.

Because how was his sin any different from our sin? Just the fact of our living here got him thinking.

There's another neighbor who lives behind us. And he is an amazing world-class fiddle player. He delivers mail. They raise a lot of animals, and his wife is extremely knowledgeable about everything to do with animals and livestock. When we see them, it's "Let's talk about farming." Suddenly there's hours of conversation that doesn't involve politics, or religion, or any of those things. Emi has created those bonds with our neighbors. The neighbor's wife called recently and said, "Hey, we got a mama cow who's going into labor, and do you want to come over?" It was just a wonderful experience to watch them pull the calf and have it be healthy. We learned a lot that helped us later in our first lambing season.

Another piece of property nearby was purchased by a young couple from Pennsylvania, and we've become friends with them. They used to come down on the weekends, and we decided to build a fence between our properties together so we could get to know each other. One day we worked on the fence all day and then it was dark by the time we were done. After we went out back with our dinner, and it happened to be the same night that our other neighbor, the fiddler, had a bunch of friends over, and they were out on their back porch playing music. That group of people were jamming, the fireflies were out and blinking, and it was dark otherwise. We were eating a delicious meal after a hard day of work. Just listening to that. Where else but here could that happen?

I'M FINALLY SETTLED

This is the longest time I've lived in one place by a long shot. You could argue I'm finally settled. But I don't think I have the right to claim being Appalachian. I think that Rowan might be Appalachian, if he wants to be. But I'm not. That would be an honor, and I try to learn to speak the local language out of respect for my neighbors and the local culture. But I wasn't raised here. I will never know gut level what it is to be Appalachian.

I do love this place, though. There's a draw. I mean, it is the most gorgeous place on the planet. I can look out here and know, *If we're going to be poor, wherever we live, we should live someplace gorgeous.* A lot of it really does come down to the fact that Emi is at home here in a very powerful way. She grew up in Chicago, but her family for generations back were unionized coal miners in West Virginia. When we moved here from New York, she became settled in a very, very powerful way.

If we were to ever move from Grayson County, I don't think we could ever move out of Appalachia, because Emi is so connected spiritually to the land here. I'm more transient. I could pick up my roots and go anywhere, but I love feeling like we do make a difference just by existing here. I love the fact that because we're in a "red" county, our vote will probably count significantly. And I love the fact that we can grow our own food, and make cheese, make pottery.

BABIKIR HARANE

BORN: 1989, Gadir, Sudan
INTERVIEWED IN: Roanoke, Virginia
Educator, Student

Interviewed with Laura Murphy

Babikir is known in his community as enthusiastic and committed to education. His tutor in English describes him as "unwavering" in his dedication to his studies. During one visit, when he told us about being admitted to the University of Virginia, we celebrated, and his resolve to finish his degree remains steadfast.

After fleeing Sudan with his mother and siblings in 1999, Babikir relocated to the Farchana Refugee Camp in Chad in 2004. He worked as an educator in the camps, teaching math and science. Just before his family was approved for resettlement in the United States, he married

Maimouna in June 2015. A few months later, he had to leave his preg-
nant wife behind, as her family's resettlement process started after his.
Babikir managed his long separation from his family by studying En-
glish and seeking additional education. He graduated with an associate
degree from the local community college and in January 2023 began as
a transfer student at University of Virginia.

BURNED INTO MY MEMORY

I was born in Sudan, in a village named Gadir of about a hundred huts or houses. I speak Massalit, Arabic, and English. I came to Roanoke with my mother and siblings in 2015. My two older brothers, one brother's wife, and their daughter were already here. I was forced to be separated from my new wife at that time. In 2021, I was finally able to reunite with my wife and child in France for a visit, where her family was resettled. It has been very difficult for us—being resettled to different countries. Right now, I drive for Uber. Before that I worked full time at a furniture factory. It was difficult work, but we had to repay the resettlement costs that weren't covered by charities.

In Sudan, we have more than one culture. The main language is Arabic—like English in the United States. Everybody speaks Arabic in Sudan, but the Sudanese population has many tribes. Each tribe has its own language, and our tribe and its language are both called Massalit, which both I and my mother speak. I think it is the biggest tribe of Western Sudan, and we own ancestorial land called Dar-Massalit, which means land of Massalit in the Darfur region.

The main city, Al Geneina, was near my small village. In Dar-Massalit about 80 percent of the population speaks Massalit. But when we went to Al Geneina for shopping or business, we spoke Arabic. In our local markets we spoke Massalit. Roanoke, where I live now, reminds me of Al Geneina, where there are smaller towns or villages surrounding it. There is a river similar to the Roanoke River, and there's a valley in the middle of the city filled with lots of trees. But along the river in Al Geneina there are a lot of mango trees and other fruit trees, like guava.

I lived in Gadir until the age of nine. It is located about ten kilometers southeast of Al Geneina city.

I was short and strong, challenging my big brothers at the farm, trying to do the same amount of farmwork; it was all done by hand. In addition, I was funny, talking to older people, pretending I was old too. I liked riding donkeys and horses and taking goats and sheep to the forest; climbing trees in the mountains was my favorite activity.

There is a part of my story that is burned into my memory. The first war in Darfur started near the village where I lived. We lived in a small house. We had our own farm with a lot of land. I had two older brothers and two younger brothers—my sister was born later. I was ten the first time the Janjaweed, the Arab militia, came to our village. It was evening. They killed young boys, so if anyone had boy children, they had to worry about them more than anything else. That day our mother took all of us into the forest, not far away from the village, to hide us. The Janjaweed came to check the forest, looking for us. There was a big hole—a ditch—that looked like it might have been dug by animals. My mother put us inside that ditch and then she covered us with a blanket. The Janjaweed couldn't see us because the forest was big. They never found us. For over two hours we hid, and then when they left, we went back home that night. We knew we had to leave our home—the fighting was too close.

We walked toward Chad on the day the Janjaweed burned our village. They killed an old man and took his camel the same evening that we spent in the forest. That made my mother really frightened because at first, they didn't usually kill women and old men. But then it got worse. They started killing everybody—women, children, and grown men. The Janjaweed used to say to us, "Our president doesn't need any Black people." We are Black, but they are Black too—it was still a racist war. In America, they call us all Black, but it's different in Sudan. I still remember the Janjaweed would say to us in Arabic, "Don't you know that our president doesn't need any Black people in this country?" What they meant was people who weren't Arabs.[1]

Although Sudan is an African country, only 90 percent are Black, and the others are Arabs. Southern and Western Sudan are mostly Black. The other 10 percent are also Black, but they are Arab. They are lighter-skinned, and they mostly live in the east and north. If they went to Saudi Arabia or Dubai, they would still be considered Arab, but they don't treat them as Arab because of their dark skin.

When they came to our villages, they burned everything. I never understood why they did that. They could have just killed us and taken our animals and all our food. We were all farmers and had a lot of food around the villages. They could have helped themselves, but everything was burned—food, animals, everything. Once they found a village, they just attacked it and poured gas on the huts. It's easy to burn them, and after setting them on fire, they stayed around the village. If anyone tried to escape from the fire, they immediately shot and killed the person.

Western Sudan, or Darfur, isn't very far away from the border of Chad. When we first arrived, there weren't any tools to make huts. So we just lived under the trees for some months. But then small nonprofits there gave us some tools so we could make shelter to protect ourselves from the cold. Yet, by the time we arrived, there were so many people, and it was hard for the organizations to help

---

1. Although 90 percent of Sudan is considered Black, the other 10 percent are of Arab descent. The ruling class and government officials are mostly of Arab descent. Most Black Sudanese lived in Western and Southern Sudan, and Arab Sudanese lived in the eastern and northern part of the country. In 2011, South Sudan broke from Sudan and for a time there was peace. However, the roots of the conflict are much more complex and civil unrest continues.

everybody. Some of the local people on Chad's border spoke Massal-it, but they all could speak Arabic. Because we spoke Arabic, too, it was easier to communicate and get some help from the local people. That first place was close to the border, and the Janjaweed could easily get to us.

This went on for four years, from 1999 to 2004, until UNHCR came and opened the first refugee camp, Farchana, about fifty ki-lometers from the border. They filled that area with tents and then they opened the second refugee camp. Over the next several years they built twelve refugee camps, and each had more than thirty thousand people.

We stayed in the camp for eleven years. I don't think that my two younger brothers remember everything about the camp, but they do remember the fire and shooting at our village. Terrible things happened in front of them they couldn't forget. We were all kids.

When I meet Sudanese refugees here in the United States and we speak of when we were in the refugee camps, I learn that all families are missing some people, up to three or four members of their families are dead. Some are parents without kids, and some are kids without parents. This is our history. We thought the Janjaweed would just take what they needed and leave. It has been over twenty years, and it gets worse every day. I don't know when it will end. Everyone thought that. But now I am here in the United States, and I can't ever go back. People are still in the same refugee camps, in the same situation.

When we first escaped to Chad, we all felt the situation was temporary, but when we moved to the Farchana Refugee Camp, it started feeling less so. I remember thinking, *This is not our place and never will be our place.* On our farm we lived in a big hut, and we had land. But in the camp, we just had our tent—there was nothing we could plant or farm. So I thought, *This can't be right, maybe they're keeping us here just for a while, right?*

THE REFUGEE CAMP IS IN MY
MEMORY MORE THAN SUDAN

Even though I don't like it, the refugee camp is in my memory more than Sudan. That's where my life started. The only thing I remember in Sudan is war and farming. But in the refugee camp, school was the best part. I learned how to play soccer, and I was on the team. I can't say it was professional, but it was a big team. So that was part of the entertainment I had there in addition to studying. Going to school and playing soccer were the best parts of the day. I'd get up and have a little breakfast, then walk from our tent to the school. During breaks and after school we'd play soccer. It was a way to pass the time. In the beginning, we did not have soccer balls to play with. We had to make our own balls from worn socks and plastic bags. These balls can be mended with simple materials, but precise measurements are essential for constructing a suitable ball. Later, organizations brought us some balls, but there were never enough because there were always too many players. Farchana Refugee Camp has five zones, each consisting of five blocks. I learned to play soccer with other teens in the C Block. A few years later, I moved to the zone team with some of my block team members. I served as the zone team captain for a few years; it was the highlight of my athletic history. Also, I played defense in the national team of the refugee camp, which played with other nearby refugee camps as well as with local athletes. I never had formal training until I moved to the national team. I also played volleyball and sometimes enjoyed playing it more than soccer.

Before we lived in the camp, I didn't go to school. Several nonprofits or NGOs like the United Nations opened schools, and I started studying there. In the refugee school we were taught in Arabic because most of the tribal languages, including Massalit, were not written languages at the time. It was only after 2010 that Massalit became a written language and books written in it became available. Now it's a subject in school that people can study. A lot of people speak Massalit. I would say close to a million. I have a couple of books in Massalit and studied it for about a year and a half before going to America. My mother learned Arabic in Sudan from going shopping in the big cities—you have to speak Arabic to be able to buy things. In comparison to standard Arabic, how we speak it in Darfur is a bit of a "broken" version of it. My mother would understand someone from Sudan speaking Arabic but not Arabic spoken in other countries.

In the camp school, one classroom could have more than two hundred students, with children of all ages. How could one teacher manage that? It is difficult to even recognize who's paying attention and who isn't.

When I was a student, my favorite subject was the Arabic language. After the teacher finished the class, the other students would say, "Ah, Babikir, you understood. Can you help us understand?" And I tried my best. Then some of my teachers figured out I could help the other students, so they sent me to help other teachers in the elementary school. So I was a teacher and a student at the same time. I went to some of the other camps in Chad to help with teaching and to receive teaching training organized by NGOs.

After I finished as a student, I trained as a teacher. They needed more teachers in the refugee camp, so I signed up with Cord and RET International, the camps' education organizations, for some years.[2] Right before I finished high school, I started volunteering—helping other students and helping my teachers. It's where I met my wife. After I volunteered for some months, they hired me as a regular teacher.

When I taught primary (elementary) school, I began with 108 students in one class, and I taught math and Arabic. I also taught religion. The year after, I stopped teaching religion, and I started teaching science. The year before I came to the United States, I taught in the middle school, and some of my students were around my age. It

---

2. See https://cord.org.uk and https://theret.org for additional information about these educational organizations.

was really hard, but I loved that job. Teaching is amazing. It was my dream. To this day, students from the refugee camps still call me and say, "Hey, we miss you." And though I say, "I didn't do anything," I felt like that was my responsibility. It was the refugee camp, and people need help. I got help, too, and I want to repay that debt.

Before I went to school, I didn't understand why there was a war in Sudan. And I thought, *It's really important to come to the United States to study.* I thought I could be part of the solution. When we got the chance to come to the United States, I was so excited. People told me before I came that it is the best place in the world. You can find a job and study. These two things—work and education—are not available in many places. Out of all the things I have here in the United States, this is what I needed most. That's why I keep working and studying.

WE THOUGHT THAT IT WOULD BE FASTER

My uncle got the resettlement process started for all of us. His son was born sick, and the UN prioritizes sick kids. He pleaded with the UN to take his whole family, including his two sisters and their families—my mom and aunt. My uncle said, "I have a large family, and I am the one who supports everybody here, so please try to process my whole family." So, in his case, our whole family could start the application process together, to travel together, whether to the United States or Europe or Canada.

In 2010, UNHCR took us to Abéché, which is the fourth biggest city in Chad and the nearest city to the Farchana Refugee Camp. They took us there, and then they also told us that we would travel to the US very soon. We met with US immigration services (USCIS), and we felt like we are about to leave.[3] But they also told us, "Be patient. Don't go away. And also, don't think that you are leaving soon." We were told it was going to be difficult, but we thought that

---

3. For more on USCIS, see www.uscis.gov.

it would be faster. Because of the situation in Sudan and agreements with Chad, many of the UN's approvals of emigration were denied by Chad's government.

Initially, locals did not get along with refugees, so finding a job outside the refugee camp was tough. Jobs were mostly in farming, and they were only available in the fall. Circumstances forced people to go outside the refugee camp and look for work to get money or food. About three years later, I went out for agriculture work with my friend to join my older brother. We traveled for a day on foot to reach the work area. We stopped at the Friday market, where farmers get to meet workers. There we met a farmer who took us to his house, and the next day we worked at his farm. My friend was lucky to get work that did not require heavy physical labor—watching a watermelon farm for animals. I had to bend all day pulling peanuts from the ground. The Friday market was the point of all resources: farmers get to meet workers; workers get to find better jobs; friends, families, and familiar faces get to meet and exchange information; workers get to meet those who would return to the refugee camp so they can carry money to families. This market was the meeting point for thirty-plus villages.

Harvest season is organized: pulling peanuts and selling watermelons, cutting millets and maize. Each crop must go through many stages before being harvested. We worked all the stages. The value of my brother's work and mine combined for the entire season was only enough to buy clothes and shoes for our family of six. We returned to the refugee camp with zero money, but we would have had some cash if our boss had paid us fairly; he deceived us and disappeared after failing to pay. Because our schools close at the beginning of each fall and reopen after the harvest, I repeated the cycle for many years.

During those five years we were stuck. The UN would tell people, "Don't leave the refugee camp," but we had to leave to work to get some money, to have some food for ourselves. We received some food from the UN, but it wasn't enough for our big family. Sometimes, there was no internet connection in the camp so we couldn't check to see if the UN or USCIS tried to contact us. If your telephone wasn't working when they need to contact you, they couldn't find you. That's why they didn't want us to go anywhere. At the same time, they didn't know what the true situation was for us. Many people in the camp went to Libya for work, and some people missed their interviews because it's hard traveling to get back.

I volunteered to help get messages between USCIS and the refugees working outside the camp. The representatives would come to me and say, "Hey, go tell this member of the family we need them next month. Find them because they aren't here. Try to bring them in." It was very stressful. I got a motorcycle and went to tell people, "Come back because they need you. You might have an interview next week or next month." People would leave work, quit their jobs, come back to the camp, and then the interview wouldn't happen. Traveling back and forth was very difficult and word got around that once you got back to the camp, you would just still be waiting.

During all this time I was teaching and met Maimouna. She volunteered as a teacher also. Her family had applied for asylum and were waiting like my family. We both came from the same region in Sudan but lived in different areas; she lived in a village called Duroti in southwest Al Geneina. In the refugee camp, we both lived in Zone One but in separate blocks; she lived in B, and I lived in C. We never noticed each other until we participated in the high school students' committee. Although she worked as an information secretary, she was very introverted, while I worked as committee chair and was an extrovert. We were both well respected among the committee and community.

Specially, we treated each other with high respect but never got into a relationship until we finished the term. Our relationship began when we started to volunteer at different schools. Because our traditions did not allow dating, we kept it professional until marriage. We initiated the process of our wedding six months prior, but we did not have any luck. Our marriage occurred in the Block C mosque on a Friday night in 2015. All the community engagement I had done throughout my period in the refugee camp paid off: my brothers and friends told me it was one of the few large marriage gatherings they had ever attended. Our tradition dictates that it is respectful to stay home, not at the mosque, so I remained at my family's home during the marriage hours. Traditionally, we often hold two parties: one on the marriage day and another on the wedding day. A wedding can take months to years to prepare after the marriage; it depends on affordability. Unlike many other traditions, one can get married before preparing a house to live in, which I did too. I could not afford to prepare for our wedding soon after marriage, and we both knew I might travel to the US anytime. So we temporarily occupied my wife's small house without holding the wedding ceremony. It was our best decision because I received my travel notice less than three months after marriage. We wouldn't have my son, Moubarak, if we had waited for the wedding ceremony.

Just a few weeks later, we found out that my family would be going to the United States. Since I was not married when we applied, my new wife could not come with me. But we were sure her family's case would be approved soon, so she allowed me to leave her behind and come by myself. We couldn't make the trip together. It was really hard to leave her. Then, with the immigration ban of seven Muslim countries in 2017, her family's paperwork was delayed, and they could not come to the United States after all. So the UNHCR gave them the option to go to France. She and her family decided to go there since it is safer than the refugee camp. They went in 2019, right before the pandemic. I applied for a travel visa to visit them in Paris and just as I got approval, the pandemic hit, and I couldn't go. That travel visa expired before the pandemic was over.

QUIT MY FULL-TIME JOB

When I first came to the United States, I got a job at a furniture factory—many refugees work there. I was working full time and at the same time going to English as a Second Language (ESL) classes. I worked at several different companies for a while, then in 2019, I quit my full-time job and started going to Virginia Western Community College full time. I became an Uber driver part time and took classes.

American English is very different from the English I learned in the refugee camps. We were taught British English and read from English books. When I first came here, I thought I spoke the same as I was taught, but the pronunciation was different, and I also used the wrong pronouns. And then I said, "Oh, maybe that wasn't English; maybe I studied something else." I was laughing at myself.

Living here is very different. There are more than a hundred tribes in Sudan—different cultures, different languages. When Sudanese people come here, they create a group based on one certain tribe, but the USCIS doesn't bring people here by tribes. People of all different tribes, colors, and religions need to get together to discuss the problems of Sudan. But we are divided and discuss the war in different ways. How to solve Sudan's issues is our own problem. For the ten years I've lived in the United States, I haven't seen a process where Sudanese can work to solve the problems of the country. It's mostly outside organizations.

Even though there are a lot of Sudanese people in Roanoke, outside of my family I don't know anyone who speaks Massalit here. Still, people from Sudan get together. In Sudan, as tribes we might have hated each other, but when we come to the United States, we love each other. All different kinds of tribes and colors. Back in Sudan, some tribes do not get along because of our constant civil wars. One reason is that people in the north did not acknowledge what happened to us in the south and west because they were not exposed to the long civil war. Here in the US, we know exactly what, why, and how it happened. In other words, we know that the long dictatorship in Sudan created hate between the tribes. So it becomes clear that the real problem in Sudan is not tribes but our government. We do have more positive interactions here than we had in Sudan. We communicate via a WhatsApp group in addition to other contact exchanges. Most of the social invitations go through this group. People are very open to engaging in discussions of many different topics. This is only one example in Roanoke, but many similar interactions exist in other US cities.

When you hear someone from Sudan talk, you definitely know if they are from South Sudan. You might not know the specific tribe until you ask. This is partially why my people ask Americans how to tell what region someone is from in this country. In Sudan, when you are introduced, you can ask, "Where were you the last time you were in Sudan?" and they will tell you, "Oh, I was born in that place, but I grew up there and studied there." After that, you can gather if they are Massalit or Zaghawa or Arab or from another tribe.

SURVIVAL AFTER SURVIVAL

All during this time, I took ESL classes and worked and studied very hard. I was motivated to study for citizenship quickly so I could bring my family here. In 2021, I became a citizen. Now that I have a US passport, I can go to France to visit my wife without worrying about the refugee travel visa expiring. I went in August 2021 for three months. I have strong reasons to settle in the Appalachian area. It was so different being in the city, but I was most interested in my family, not the city. I was able to visit again in May 2022, and I met my daughter for the first time. My son was seven when I saw him last. My wife and I have not been able to live in the same place now for more than seven years. I know from our two visits that the children need their father. Moving them will impact their studies and process of education. My son was in pre-Arabic school, now he's in primary school in France. Here he will be in English schools. The main reason to bring them here is the educational opportunity and for all of us to be together. It will be difficult. They will need a place to live and financial support.

My wife's case is pending and in the final stage. We are working with the US embassy in Paris to get them here as soon as possible. I have been working with my attorneys to get my wife and children out of France, to come live here with me. It is such a long, long time—we started the process in 2017. And now that I have citizenship, it should move along more quickly.

I finished my associate degree at Virginia Western earlier this year, and I started the University of Virginia program for bachelor of business administration last spring. I didn't move to Charlottesville, though, because I want my wife and children to live here in Roanoke. I know how hard it is, how difficult, to settle in a new country. Because I have lived here and I know it, I don't want to put my wife and my children in the same situation of not knowing anyone. I decided to take my UVA classes online, something I never thought of doing, but I have to accept this opportunity. I really love and wanted to be on UVA's campus, and online isn't my preferred method of learning. But my life has already been just survival after survival and accepting whatever comes and not letting the opportunity go.

The most different thing for them will be the culture. The children only know France. In our village in Sudan, everybody knows everyone, not just neighbors, but they know everyone in the entire village. And even the children, they know each other as well. When I came into the refugee camp, there were so many people and it was very different, but at least we were of a similar culture. Here it is so different, so many cultures. Also it is very cold here in the winter; in Sudan the coldest it gets is sixty degrees. Even though Roanoke is a city, there are mountains everywhere and lots of big spaces. We had some mountains where I was born in Sudan and also in Chad. They weren't big mountains, but it was pretty much like it is here—many small and connected hills.

I have visited other cities like Virginia Beach, Richmond, Harrisonburg, Lynchburg, all from driving for Uber. So I see the countryside of Virginia. It's very beautiful and it stays green most of the time, more than in my country. All the green, it just makes me feel kind of peaceful. But culturally speaking, it's so different, working in a big factory, trying to find the right ingredients to make our food. Where I grew up, we had a weekly open market, but here the markets are open every day.

I came from a Muslim tradition—99 percent of the population was Muslim; there was no other religion. And then coming here, and not seeing anyone else like me, the way people dress, the way they treat people, the way they act, like everything was different. And for the first two to three months, we said over and over, "Wow, look at that, what amazing holidays"—things like this.

Even though I've been all over the state, I prefer living in Appalachia, particularly here in Virginia. With work opportunities and school, I could have moved, but my extended family is all here, and we just made our decision to just stay here in Virginia for the rest of our lives. I help take care of my mother and father, both of whom are in their sixties. My older two brothers are married and have their children here as well. My sister is the youngest. She's at Virginia Western now as a student.

The situation in France is hard. My wife still lives with her mother and brother and his wife, and also her aunt and grandmother. Her mother had gotten sick. She couldn't handle being in a big city and being separated from the rest of her family. She has mental problems, and it is very hard for my wife and her brother. I am concerned about bringing her and the children here, separating her from her mother.

After all these years praying, working with attorneys, and then doing all the paperwork, sending letters to my senators here in

Virginia and doing whatever I can to bring my wife and children here—but now the big fear is separating my wife from her extended family and leaving her mother's care to the rest of the family. This has been something very difficult for me, separating the only daughter from her mother.

Bringing them here is still good. I don't want my children to grow up without a father. I know my wife is doing everything she can to support them, but from the two visits, I am determined that they need to be here with me.

When I left the refugee camp to come to the US, Moubarak was not yet born. He was born six months after I moved to the US. I met him for the first time in 2021, when he was five. I did not have actual paternal feelings until this moment came. Typically, it would be annoying for a child to call his or her daddy over a hundred times a day, but it was not for me because I desperately wanted to be called Baba. What was more interesting is that he called me "My Baba," which annoyed the rest of the family who say, "We all know he is your Baba, so just call him Baba," but he continued his way. I was secretly saying, "Let the boy enjoy." In fact, I was the one who enjoyed being called Baba; It was great. My daughter Bushra was born in 2022, after my first visit in 2021. I tried my best to be there before her birth, so two of my brothers and I bought our plane tickets for May 14, the day after my college graduation. Instead of waiting for me to arrive on the twenty-second, the estimated due date, she was born early on May 10, so I missed the daddy moment again. However, she made her own record for the city; she was the first baby born in that city at home in twenty-five years. It was crucial in our tradition to honor the newborn after the first week, which I proudly did. She was born on Tuesday, and on the following Tuesday, she was supposed to have the ceremony. My wife attended my graduation ceremony from the hospital via the link I sent her. I asked my wife, teasing her, "Why couldn't you wait for me?" She said, "Your daughter wanted to attend your graduation!" Instead of me attending her ceremony, she attended mine. We both had a long joyful laugh. Oh, that makes me so happy!

Bringing them here will probably have an impact on my studies. There are many tasks for me to handle, working and supporting them while at the same time going to school. I don't know how it will work out, but I will do whatever it takes. I don't want to quit school to support my family—that's a darkness I worry about. These are the fears, but at the same time, I'm excited to have them with me here so I can support my children to get their education.

Babikir's wife and children arrived in the US in May 2023. They are living in Roanoke and his son attends school.

SOHAILA

BORN: 1986, Pakistan
INTERVIEWED IN: Blacksburg, Virginia
Dining Services Worker

Interviewed with Katie Randall

Sohaila offers delicious tea as we meet for the first time. Her daughter is at school, and the balcony door is open, letting in a soft breeze. Quiet yet determined, Sohaila is still learning English. When I needed her address for our meeting, she texted me a photo of a letter with her name and address.

Sohaila is Afghan, but she was born in Pakistan in 1986, after her parents fled their town, Kunduz, in 1984 after the Soviet invasion in Afghanistan. Like nearly one million other Afghans, Sohaila's family fled to Quetta, a town in Pakistan near the border with Afghanistan. Her family arranged for Sohaila, then twenty-five, to marry a sixty-year-old

Afghan businessman with a wife and several adult children, some older than her. As was customary, she lived with her husband's first wife and their extended family. She was forced to do most of the household chores and after her daughter, A, was born, she and her daughter were emotionally and physically abused by multiple members of the family.

Although not formally educated, Sohaila speaks five languages, not counting English. Soon after arriving in the United States in 2017, A was enrolled in elementary school and Sohaila began English classes. She works in dining services at the local university. To protect Sohaila's identity, and per her preference, we use only her first name and her daughter's first initial.

ALL THE KIDS HAVE TO WORK

My name is Sohaila. I speak Farsi, Hindi, a little English, Pashto, Urdu, and a little Arabic. My parents were refugees themselves, during the Soviet war in Afghanistan. They were originally from Kunduz, Afghanistan, and traveled to Pakistan shortly after the Soviets invaded Afghanistan. My parents walked for twenty hours from Kunduz to Quetta. They walked with my brothers, the horses and donkeys, and whatever they could all carry. Quetta is a port city, so they took very small boats across the river to get there. I was born in Quetta, and all my family is in Quetta now. I don't have too many people that I'm related to back in Afghanistan.

I'm the third of four children. Two brothers and one sister. I have one cousin who is like my brother. His mom and dad died, and my mom took him in. My parents married off my younger sister before me. I helped around the house a lot, cooking and cleaning. They needed me because we had a big extended family that was always coming and going. Since I worked, too, it was more beneficial for the family for my younger sister to marry first because she wasn't working much at home yet. I really handled everything for the household in terms of shopping and cooking and cleaning. After she was married, she still lived in Pakistan, and I saw her sometimes.

When I was around twenty-one, my dad got sick. He needed heart surgery, and we didn't have money for it, so he died. After he died, I became the main person taking care of the family. I worked at a sewing company, and I took care of things at home. Not long after that, when she was eighteen, my sister was killed on the streets in Quetta in 2010. She got caught in a gunfire exchange between the police and rebels. Her baby was two months old at the time of her death. My nephew is with the father now. No one in my family can see the boy. We have friends who used to stop by and see him. But his dad and his new wife don't want to be part of our family anymore. My nephew, who's twelve now, told our friends, "I wish I had died with my mom. They treat me like a servant here." They are very poor, and all the kids have to work. And if you don't have a mom, then it's worse. This makes me very sad because I know what it's like.

In 2011, it was arranged for me to marry an Afghan guy in Pakistan. I was his second wife—he was sixty or so. He had kids older than me and had grandkids. He wasn't too mean, but his first wife, Mona, was not nice to me. I became pregnant two months after the wedding. It was the month of fasting at the beginning of my pregnancy, and the first wife forced me to work around the house all the time. I was always very sick and very tired. I threw up all the time. Eventually A was born, but she came two months early and she was so small. The doctor said that she had to stay in the incubator for three to four months. But after only a month, my husband came home with the baby saying, "It's too expensive. She's grown enough. We don't have to keep her at the hospital anymore." I was so scared—she was so small, and the house was very cold. I didn't know how to keep her warm. One of the neighbors told me, "You can boil hot water in big pots, then put them on the floor, and just put the baby in the middle of all the pots of hot water to keep her warm." That's how I kept her warm for some time, until she got a little bit bigger.

My husband was a businessman and we moved to Kandahar, Afghanistan, for his business. I couldn't see my family—my mom and my brothers—even though they had moved back to Kunduz, Afghanistan. It's about a four-hour drive between Kandahar and Kunduz, but I wasn't allowed to go. My husband had money, but he wouldn't allow it. So I couldn't see my mother. I didn't even have a phone; I didn't have anything. Right after A was born, my husband told me my mom had died. I couldn't go to the funeral or anything. He basically said, "Just to let you know, your mom died." I was very sad. And I couldn't grieve—there was no time because I had to do all the work.

My husband didn't really have much power in the house when he wasn't there. He traveled a lot, and whenever he wasn't at home, A and I didn't get anything to eat from his first wife or his adult children who lived with us.

I couldn't breastfeed A because my milk dried up, so I had to get formula for her. The formula was expensive, and the wife wouldn't give me any money to buy it. I had to ask my cousin, who was living in Saudi Arabia, for help. She sent me money through a friend, who would help me buy the formula and other necessities when my husband wasn't around. The other kids and Mona would come and steal things from my room. I had to lock up the formula or whatever I had. Feeding A and keeping her healthy was my first priority, and it was very difficult. I had a little bit of gold jewelry from my mom that I would sell to buy formula and diapers. Whenever my husband was in town, he would buy us what we needed, but if he bought extra there was no way for me to hold on to those things in the house because his kids and grandkids would steal them. I would store them at my friend's house and bring supplies back little by little.

Even though my husband was nice to me, he would still hit me. Whenever there were arguments between his mother and Mona, they would complain about me. Then he would hit me. He told me, "I have to do this because you are young, and they have to see that I am dealing with this. I'm making sure that you are respecting the elders and that you are respecting my mother." But he was never too mean or too hard.

MY LIFE WAS HELL

My husband was threatened by the Taliban many times—because he worked with Americans. He was a businessman—he sold things in the airport and bought things from different places, and some of the people he dealt with were Americans. So the Taliban threatened to kill him. One day when A was about nine months old, he told me, "I might go away for a long time." He told me, "You should never worry because I have talked to one of my very good friends and I have transferred ownership of some land to A." I wasn't part of the picture. He said, "This is for A, okay?" He didn't tell me the name of the friend, and no one ever approached me with deeds or anything. I don't know if that discussion was real or was just something he was intending to do and never got around to.

A few days after that conversation, I was working at home, cleaning, doing regular stuff, and suddenly I heard people screaming. I didn't know what was going on, so I just went toward the sound. I saw everyone standing around crying. Then Mona attacked me. I had no idea what was going on. The other women, the neighbors, they tried to protect me. They said to Mona, "He's dead; why are you hitting her?" Then I realized what had happened. I just fell apart. I didn't love him, but I knew I was doomed because my life was hell when he wasn't around—I was practically a maid. Now I knew it was going to be just completely terrible without him there as a buffer.

I don't remember much of the day after that. Because they knew Mona would beat me, my neighbors took me to their house, and I stayed with them for a little while that day. When I became myself again, I went back to Mona's. They brought in my husband's body, and I begged to see him one last time. One of his brothers, who is affiliated with the Taliban and about the same age as my husband, wouldn't allow me to get close to his body. I found out later that it was him who had my husband killed.

Within a week or two of my husband's death, things got way worse for me and A. I had to work all day and night. The grandkids learned from their parents—they hit A all the time. They pinched her and made her cry.

We all lived together with my late husband's mother. I had one younger brother-in-law who was nice to me. He used to scold everybody: "Why do you hit the baby?" He said, "Why do you hit Sohaila? She's working all day and night doing whatever you ask of her. She's cooking and cleaning. What else do you need from her?" The rest of the family was mean to him too. Another brother-in-law said to him, "Why are you even defending her? You should be like the rest of us."

The beatings became worse and worse. According to Islamic rules, you can't get remarried until three months after your husband is dead. About two or three months after my husband died, the cruel brother-in-law started saying that I should marry *him*. He already had two wives living in that house, so I would just be the third. I said no to him. He would hit me badly—punching and kicking me, throwing dishes at me, sometimes even when I was holding A. I dropped her a few times because he hit me so hard. But I kept saying, "No. No matter what, I am not marrying you."

He tried to rape me many times. Every night I would close the door and block it with chairs and whatever furniture I could find. I slept with the Quran on my chest and A by my side, shuddering and worrying that he would try to get in. He'd hit me so much—bashing my head into the wall—that I was bruised all over my face and body.

One of my eyes was completely swollen and red and bloodshot because he hit me right in the eye—I still have difficulty reading because of the injury. Once when my kind brother-in-law was out of town, the Taliban brother-in-law brought in a mullah to force me to marry. He told the mullah that since I was young and didn't understand what was going on, that I would have to marry him so that he could take care of my child. I showed the mullah the bruises on my arms and my eye. I said to the mullah, "This is my eye, do you see? He has done all that. And I don't want to marry him. I hate him. I am staying in this house so I can take care of my daughter—that's it. But I don't want to marry him." I asked, "What kind of Muslim are you? What kind of human are you that you want me to marry him?" And amazingly, the mullah turned to the brother-in-law and said, "I cannot marry her to you because she really doesn't want to." More and more hitting came after that.

TWO DAYS TO PREPARE

The mullah who had been brought in to marry me off brought his wife to meet A. She was an older woman and didn't have small children. The mullah's wife took A to her home to play a lot. They have a son who lives in the US. When he was back home in Afghanistan to visit, he saw A and asked, "Why does this baby have all these bruises on her?" They told him about me, that I was their neighbor, that the baby was the daughter of the second bride, and it was very typical that I and A were beaten.

The son said to his parents, "Because you are not helping her, you are complicit in all this. She's being hurt. You see her all the time, and you're doing nothing. We should help her escape. I'm willing to give her a ride to Quetta. If she can find somebody over there to take care of her, then I can take her." This would be a big problem for them if they were caught because the brother-in-law is Taliban. At this time, one of my husband's sons was getting married and there was to be a big wedding. The mullah's wife told me in secret, "When there is a wedding party in a few nights, I will help you." She said, "If you want to escape, that's the time." I told her, "For A, I will do it. No matter what, I will do it."

I only had two days to prepare. So on the night of the henna tradition, when all the women gather and paint henna on the bride, there was lots of commotion in our house, a lot of women were coming in and out. The mullah's wife told me to give some medicine to A to make her sleepy. I gave four teaspoons of medicine to A, and she was completely limp. The mullah's wife told me to take as little as possible from the house so that the family wouldn't be suspicious.

I had the clothes I was wearing and my chador. I took a few diapers, a little bit of milk, and left with nothing from the house. The mullah's wife helped me get out of the house with A to meet the mullah's son. I said goodbye to the wife and left with their son in a taxi. It was four in the morning. People were still dancing at the wedding.

We got to the Afghanistan-Pakistan border at nine in the morning. The taxi dropped us off and we walked a little ways to cross the border through the woods, without paperwork. We walked for about an hour until we hit a road. The mullah's son hailed a cab, paid the driver, and said, "Take her to Quetta, wherever she wants to go. No matter what you do, you're not letting her talk to anybody at checkpoints. If anyone asks, just say that she's your sister and she's not allowed to talk. You're talking for her. She doesn't have any paperwork or anything, so try to not have any issues." He gave me ten dollars for food or whatever I needed. He was very sad when he was saying goodbye. He said, "My heart is just bleeding for you. I hope that you go and have a good life." Then he said goodbye and walked back to Afghanistan.

I asked the taxi to take me to a house where friends of mine lived, from when I lived in Quetta before I got married. We got to their house before lunch time. I knocked at the door. The husband opened the door and said, "Hello, what are you doing here?"

FATIGUE FROM THE STRESS

At this point, A was really sick. She'd thrown up a lot and I didn't have enough milk for her, so toward the end of the trip I was just giving her water. She was almost unconscious; she was so sick. I was also completely out of it because of the travel and fatigue from the stress. Even though it was dangerous for them, my friends said, "Okay, stay in the house. We'll take A to the hospital."

They took A to the hospital, and there they gave her an IV and oxygen. She had to stay in the ICU for three nights. She was unconscious for three days, and the doctor said if she didn't wake up, they might have to leave her to die. But then she woke up, and I was so relieved.

My friends paid for everything. I was also very sick myself, very weak. They took me to the doctor, but I couldn't eat anything. I wasn't crying at all. I was just unsure of what was going to happen and waiting. One of the doctors at the hospital took an interest and bought me a lot of formula and diapers and showed me how to take care of A so that she'd get stronger.

For one month we stayed at my friends' house. Their son was married, and his wife said to me, "If you stay here, eventually one of our husbands will want to marry you, and we don't want you to be here." I would purposely not shower, not change clothes, be stinky and looking awful to just show the wives that I didn't want to get married. I tried saying, "You don't have to worry about me." But it was obvious that I wasn't welcome there anymore, and I had to move. So after a month, A and I left, and I found a small room to rent.

I started working, cleaning people's houses, washing clothes, because a lot of people don't have washing machines. When I went to work, I took A with me. With that money I had to pay rent, buy food for myself, and buy A's formula. For one family, I had to be there at six in the morning to do laundry before everybody else was up. I put A on the side of the yard, and I put some blankets on her because it was cold. One morning I was doing the laundry, and the owner of the house came out. He was so upset that A was sitting there in the cold, and he started fighting with his wife, saying to her, "You have to do your own laundry. Why should we bring this lady here that she has to bring her child to sit in the cold?" I said, "Oh, no, no, it's my fault that I have to bring my daughter. I want this job. It's okay." The man's wife said, "No, you're not coming here anymore." So I lost that job.

I was renting a room in a house that belonged to a woman and her two sons, and other people who were renting lived there too. People helped me with some things to live. When one of the women living there heard I was alone, had been beaten, and had escaped, she told me there might be a place that could help me go to the United States. She said, "Let me take you to this place."[1]

She took me to the office of the Women's Commission for Refugee Women and Children. They give me a phone number and a name of someone at the UN. I called that person, and he interviewed me over the phone for a long time. He said, "Tell me your story. What happened to you?" I told him the whole story and after that, he gave me the address for the US consulate in Quetta. Afghan people work there, helping other Afghans apply for refugee status. When I got to the consulate, the man who interviewed me saw that both A and I still had bruises—even almost three months after we escaped.

I lived in Pakistan for almost two years before we left. After about five months, the house where I lived caught on fire, and I lost everything again. Again, people helped me get things like a birth certificate and other paperwork. I had to start over, getting all the paperwork needed for the application process. We refugees are used to this kind of situation where you have no paperwork whatsoever.

The NGO helped me navigate the many, many interviews. They gave me money to go to Islamabad twice. From Islamabad to

---

1. For further information about these organizations, see the World Refugee Commission's blog post, "Afghan Women's Organizations—Key Actors in Rebuilding Afghanistan and Assisting Refugees," at https://reliefweb.int/report/afghanistan/afghan-womens-organizations-key-actors-rebuilding-afghanistan-and-assisting.

Quetta is a fifteen-hour bus ride. The consulate in Quetta can only do so much, so as things progressed in the application, I had to go to Islamabad to do the interviews and come back. The NGO would give me money, but I also depended on neighbors and young men who were not married to come with me—I wasn't allowed to travel alone, plus my husband's brother was looking for me. So many people helped me. We would leave at six in the morning, get there for the interview, and then come back the next day. A would cling to me and wouldn't let go. Sometimes I had to say to her, "Just give me a break." I was so exhausted.

A VERY LOW TIME FOR ME

During this time, my brother-in-law and his sons tried to kidnap me several times. They found me a few times and once they almost succeeded in putting me in a car. I screamed and shouted—the good thing about those places where they found me is that they were always busy, with lots of other people around. The people would gather, and I kept saying, "I don't know these people. They're trying to kidnap me." If it had been in Afghanistan, they would have been able to take me. But because it was in Pakistan, people asked, "What's going on? You guys are not from here." People called the police, and my brother-in-law and his sons had to run.

One time, though, they hit me with a car. A was thrown and she hurt her arm and back. They were hoping that after they hit me, they could take me, but again they had to leave. I took A to the hospital, but I had no money. One of the doctors said he would pay for the X-ray. A's arm was broken, so she had to get a cast. That was a very low time for me. I was injured and tired and right then the US consulate called on the mobile phone my friends gave me to say I had to go to Islamabad again for another interview. I told them I was in the hospital, but the man just repeated, "You have to come for an interview again." I went, but I was very upset. I told them, "I'm done with interviews. This is the last time I'm coming here." They said, "Good thing, because your ticket is ready, and you're leaving in twenty days."

During those last twenty days in Quetta, I was so afraid that word would get out and my brother-in-law would come after me. I would put a hat on A as a disguise and I wore my chador everywhere, really trying not to be seen. One of my friends bought me a suitcase, so we packed as many clothes as I had and flew from Quetta to Islamabad. We'd never been on an airplane before, I was scared to death. I couldn't even talk—I was so scared.

The guy sitting next to me kept talking to me, and asked, "Where are you going?" He added, "You're going to be fine. Don't worry. We do this all the time." Somebody was waiting for us in Islamabad and took us to the hotel. We stayed at the hotel for one night and the next day we got on the plane to come to the US. We flew to Dubai first, then to Washington, DC. In Washington there were other Afghans, but they all went to different places. We were put with a bunch of other refugees who had come from Africa. None of them spoke my language. I thought, *It's just me and A now, and among all these people I don't know any one of them.* I started crying then, and I got really scared. But I thought, *Okay, this is my new reality. I don't know anybody. I can't speak anyone's language. What is going to happen to me?*

I just cried and cried. All the people in the airport were looking at me, but I couldn't stop crying. A man saw me, and I think he asked, "Why are you crying?" I'm not sure. So many people were talking talking talking to me. I was so sad. Someone got help for me, to figure out where to go next. A was crying too. Finally, someone helped us to the minibus.

The minibus at the airport in DC took us to the hotel. At the hotel, nobody understood my language. Nobody gave me any food, no money, nothing. I only had some Pakistani money. I had a hungry child, and when I left the room, I didn't even know how to get downstairs. Finally, I saw some people getting on the elevator, and I followed them. I found somebody who speaks Urdu, and they bought A some cookies and milk. Somebody woke us up at four in the morning to get our next flight to Roanoke, but I didn't understand any of it. They gave me the ticket and left me. I just sat there thinking that somebody would come and get me. Nobody came and eventually I showed someone my ticket. They said, "Your flight is leaving, you have to run to that gate." I ran, holding A, and somehow we made it to the flight. I was wearing a refugee identity card, but my suitcases were gone. I had no idea what to do, so I sat there again, crying. People tried to console me. Somebody brought something for A to eat. We finally arrived in Roanoke, and people helped me get my luggage. My luggage was all opened up and everything was all over the place, and I started crying again. A saw the police and security guards and dogs, and she started crying too.

Finally, a man came up to me speaking Farsi. He said, "I'm Massood, your caseworker." I felt really happy to hear Farsi. I cried again, to celebrate, this time. A, who was three at this time, hadn't spoken the whole time. As we were driving from Roanoke Airport to our rented house, we went past all these trees and mountains—not many houses—and A said, "Mom, you said we were going to the US. This looks like woods here. Nobody lives here." There are many fruit trees in Quetta and mountains on the border of Afghanistan and Pakistan. So when I saw the mountains, I was happy.

We lived for six months in Roanoke. I wasn't working yet. Catholic Charities rented our apartment for us. The first months I was very sick. The doctor told me I had cancer. I was so sad and scared. But I didn't have cancer. I was just sick with allergies and got medicine. I cried all the time. They sent A to school, and I cried all day. My caseworker knew I wasn't happy and wondered if we might like Blacksburg better. There are some other single moms here.

When we came to Blacksburg, it was beautiful. Mr. Scott and Laila helped me. We have a nice apartment, and A likes her friends. We have food and a safe home. Laila asks me, "Sohaila, are you happy?" and I say, "No, I'm not happy. My head is not good." But my daughter is happy here.

It's better, but things are still hard. I went to get my learner's driving permit. But I had to take the bus to get there. The bus didn't come, so we had to walk instead. We had no water and A was crying. I have to take the bus to see my head doctor too. I want to drive a car, but I can't get a car or drive. I take the bus to work. At least there's a stop right here, close to the apartment. A can walk to school, so this is a good place for us.

A is eleven now, but I still have to go to the head doctor. When I go to my appointments, Miss Carrie comes to help A with her homework. We are talking and talking. Everyone says, "Sohaila, you should be happy now. You have an apartment. You have a good job. A is happy in school. Why are you still sad?" But my head is no good. I dream and think about before and it's hard not to.

A wants to go shopping on Saturday, but I say no. She asks, "Why not? It's so boring here." But my head is no good. I wake up at night and look out the door. A says, "What's wrong?" and I cry and cry. Laila says all my crying is no good for A.

When we visited Sohaila again in 2021, the US had just withdrawn from Afghanistan, and Sohaila was very worried about her family there. She explained that the Taliban had been looking for her family since she escaped, but that now she was even more concerned about their safety.

BIG TENSIONS IN MY COUNTRY

I have very bad memories from that time in Pakistan and Afghanistan. And now I am afraid for my brothers and cousin. The Taliban, my brother-in-law, is looking for them. The news says that the Taliban say it will be okay, but it will not be okay. They say no ladies can work; no ladies can talk to each other. If they see more than two ladies together, they shoot them. It has been very difficult these last few days listening to the news about the withdrawal. There is no Wi-Fi for my brothers to call me. I haven't spoken with them in days. I don't know where they are. There's no work in Afghanistan for my brothers, and now there is big fighting. My family is not safe. My husband's brother is looking for my cousin and looking for him to tell him to shoot my brother. They're not safe. The Taliban come and wake up all the kids. They come into houses to look for my cousin.

At this point, Sohaila's eyes water as she describes her fears for her family. As we talk, the birds in a cage on Sohaila's porch sing louder and louder, until we realize that we're talking louder to hear each other over their songs. "A's birds are so loud," Sohaila says. "They want to be part of the conversation." As she continues talking about her life, she smiles and laughs through her tears.

***

When I visited Sohaila a few months later, she explained that the Taliban had kidnapped her brother and killed one of her nieces. As she recounted the story, she moved back and forth between the worry for her family and her hope for A's future. At this visit, A, now twelve, listened quietly, nodding. When I asked her what she liked about school, she said, "I'd have to say math."

We have hard days, but A is happy at school and with her friends. We never had pizza before we came here, and now I love pizza. I work at the university dining hall, and I go to classes for English. In my apartment building, there is another Afghan, and she shared food with us until I started to get the TANF.[2] We are friends now and our families spend time together. I go to work every day. I still take the bus to work, and A takes the bus for school. I get home at five and cook for A. On Saturday and Sunday, we go to the grocery

---

2. TANF is the federally funded program, Temporary Assistance for Needy Families.

store and clean the apartment. A's old enough to go to the store for us; it's just across the street. Then on Monday we start again. Nothing is safe for my family in Afghanistan, but we are safe. A is safe.

I remember the day we moved to Blacksburg, and they took us to see A's school. It was so clean and nice. It's too late for me, but A is going to school, and she can go to college, and she can have a good life here. I have hope for A. I love my job at dining services; they like me. They respect me, and they never say to me, "Oh, why did you take a break now?" Or "Why are you so —?" I'm not used to being respected and contributing. I really, really enjoy that.

PETER LEWIS

BORN: 1943, Washington, DC
INTERVIEWED IN: Roanoke and Apple Ridge Farm,
Copper Hill, Virginia
Retired Educator, Farmer

After driving along a winding road through the woods, the buildings of Apple Ridge Farm appear, a series of cabins and larger buildings. Peter is waiting on his front porch and then together we drive further up the mountain, where we pass by a tennis court, basketball courts, and more trees, a creek, and steep trails.

Peter Lewis grew up in Washington, DC, in the 1950s. He and his brother went to public schools and enjoyed a comfortable life as the sons of a Howard University professor-lawyer and a schoolteacher. During the summers Peter visited his aunt and uncle's farm in Virginia. After attending college at West Virginia State University and working as an

educator in northern Virginia, he bought his own farm in the moun-
tains of southwest Virginia in 1974. In 1978, he turned the farm into
an educational camp, Apple Ridge Farm, where youth who live in cities
can experience life in the country, realizing his long-held dream to have
a farm and help educate children.[1]

MY GRANDFATHERS WERE BORN
AT THE BEGINNING OF THE CIVIL WAR

It's important to know my family's history to know about how I grew up. Both my grandfathers were born at the beginning of the Civil War. My father's father, Peter Simon Lewis, was a very well-known Baptist preacher in North Carolina in the late 1800s, early 1900s. He took a trip to the Holy Land in 1910—he went to Cyprus and Jerusalem. He died in 1920, so I didn't meet him or my grandmother. They were in their forties when they had my dad.

My father, Jesse W. Lewis, was an economics professor at Howard University and also had a small civil law practice. He was born in 1901 in Richmond, Virginia, and he grew up in North Carolina. My father was one of five kids. One of his sisters was a teacher. He went to school in Raleigh and ended up at New York University for his MBA. He was very conservative and stoic. He loved me, but he wasn't a hug-me kind of person. I sat on his lap at night when I was a kid and he read stories, or we listened to Lowell Thomas on the radio or recordings of Louis Armstrong. He was very old-fashioned and very serious. He would take a drink in the evenings and smoke a cigar. I never heard him raise his voice. So one night when my father said to me, "If anything ever happened to you or your brother and I found out who did it, I would see him dead," it shocked me.

We used to take an annual trip to Philadelphia to celebrate my uncle's birthday. One year we left Washington and went up there

---

1. For more on Apple Ridge Farm, see www.appleridge.org/history.

and stopped at a Howard Johnson's in Delaware. We went in and sat down—my mother, brother, dad, and me—and they refused us service. My father told us to get up to go. Then he took a spoon from the cupboard and banged on a glass, *ding, ding, ding, ding,* to get everybody's attention in the restaurant. He said to everyone, "On this special day, with families together here, isn't it a shame that my family is being denied service?" Several people said to us, "You can sit at our table." But he said, "No, we can't do that. Because they won't serve us here." Then we left.

I have intensely fond memories about my father and baseball. He and his good friend, Uncle Jimmy Jones, took me to my first game at old Griffith Stadium to see the Washington Senators play an exhibition game with the visiting New York Giants. My father had played baseball while in college at Shaw University. In his late fifties he could still throw a baseball with either hand. My friend Lawrence, a pretty good high school catcher, tried to catch my dad's drop pitch, a 12-6 curveball that started at Lawrence's head, but when he reached up for the pitch, the ball hit him in the stomach!

We regularly watched the Baltimore Orioles on an old console TV, and when I was old enough, we enjoyed an occasional Miller beer from a seven-ounce pony bottle. He would say, "Son, get us a couple of shorties from the fridge!"

When my father was studying for his doctorate in the 1940s in commercial science and already had his MBA, he applied for a job at a firm on Wall Street in New York City. They told him the only thing they had open was in the mailroom, thinking that would discourage him. But my father had done his homework and knew that's where everyone started. He said, "I'll be glad to start there." But they told him, "Not only would you start there, you will finish there." That broke his heart. So he left New York and moved back to Washington. He took correspondence courses in the law and passed the bar. He became a lawyer and taught economics at Howard University because they needed someone, and he could do it. He started his own finance and investment firm. I didn't know about that Wall Street incident until I heard the story at my father's funeral. I asked my brother, who's six years older than me, why they never told me that story. My brother said, "We didn't want you to have a negative view of the world."

My mother's father was born in Camden, Alabama, in 1861, and he left Camden because he was a really smart kid and his parents felt that he needed to leave the South to thrive. He came to Washington, DC, and finished Howard University Medical School in 1894. Her family lived in a beautiful brownstone in Washington, and her father had his doctor's office on the first floor. The family lived on the second, third, and fourth floors. I remember wonderful wrought-iron steps going to what they called the English basement—it's where the kitchen was. When urban renewal happened in that neighborhood, they took that house from my mother's family.[2]

My mother was a teacher. She finished high school at sixteen. After getting a two-year certification from the normal teachers college, which was what they called a teacher training school and which is now part of the University of the District of Columbia, she started teaching in 1923. She taught for about forty years except for taking time off for my brother's and my birth. She was a very gentle Victorian woman. She was soft-spoken but had a steely gaze.

My mother shared stories with my brother and me about being a teacher. She worked with difficult children and was able to bring out the best in them. I remember a story she told us, that she had an unruly group early in the year and they had gone to the auditorium, and they embarrassed her by being rambunctious and noisy. So the next day during recess she told the class, "We're going to practice walking to the auditorium," and the students did it for the entire recess. They weren't rambunctious after that! So that was the

---

2. In the 1940s and 1950s, many thriving African American neighborhoods were razed or homes taken under eminent domain law under the guise of urban renewal.

world I grew up in. We lived in a segregated world for sure, but we weren't suffering. Both of my parents finished college, and both of my grandparents finished college, so we lived well.

CHILDREN WERE VALUED

I was mischievous as a boy but didn't really get in trouble. I saw my brother receive some hard discipline that I didn't want to get. We took a streetcar every day to go to school in the 1950s. My friends and I had a good time, but we knew how to behave. If the streetcar driver said, "Young man, shut that window," I did, no debate. Once, a few of my friends were walking back from an ice cream place, talking about girls and baseball. Ronnie noticed a woman outside watering her flowers and said to our other friend, "Frank, watch your mouth. There's a lady out here." We self-monitored our conversation so we wouldn't be too loud or have any kind of profanity in front of a woman. And when she said, "Evenin', boys, how are you?" We said, "Nice night, ma'am." Then we finished our ice cream and went back home.

Within the family and neighborhood that I grew up in, children were valued. Our community was insular. I grew up in segregated schools, but my parents were part of the professional class in Washington, and, as it was in most cities at that time, they were adamant about providing opportunities for the children that they came in contact with.

At an early age, people would ask me if I wanted to be like my dad, an attorney. But I had been to his office, and he had all those books to read. It didn't seem like he had fun. I wanted to be like my middle school physical education teacher, Paul Shackleford. He was sharp. He was a teacher, and he was fit, and everybody loved this guy. I respected my father, but Mr. Shackleford was fun loving, a wisecracker. And knowing what I did from my mom about being a teacher, I knew that's what I wanted to do.

ABOUT A HUNDRED ACRES

My mom's sister, Aunt Emma, married Uncle James, who was from Virginia. My aunt was a really neat lady who was trained as a social worker. She took classes to get her educational certificate and ended up teaching for about twenty years as a special education teacher. My uncle was pretty entrepreneurial. He was one of the first private trash haulers in Virginia. He had some rental properties and a chain of taxicabs, but he wanted to buy a farm. He bought three parcels for a total of about a hundred acres. They bought that farm in the 1940s in Fauquier County, Virginia.[3]

At first my aunt told him, "I'm not going to move down there." Then my uncle said, "Well, I guess I'll see you on weekends." But after a year or so she moved down there too. They didn't have a bathroom in the house at first, but they renovated the house to have indoor plumbing. Starting when I was seven or eight, in the 1950s, I went to their dairy farm every summer from June to Labor Day. I had really great times living with them in the country for the summers. We went to church, and I played and worked on the farm. Their land stretched so far. I ran as fast as I could across the fields, with the openness so different from the city where I lived.

"WE DON'T HAVE BLACK PEOPLE WHERE WE COME FROM"

I went to West Virginia State University, an HBCU, from 1961 to 1965, and I was involved in ROTC for two years.[4] I made lifelong

3. Fauquier County is located about sixty miles outside of Washington, DC. At the time Peter was growing up, Fauquier was mostly rural. It now has many suburban neighborhoods and significant numbers of residents commute to work in the Washington, DC, area.

4. West Virginia State University is a historically Black college or university (HBCU), and Peter was involved in the Reserve Officers' Training Corps (ROTC) program. WVSU was originally founded in 1891 as the West Virginia Colored Institute.

friends while I was there. It was a school like Tuskegee, with an army airmen presence because they had trained Black pilots for the Second World War. West Virginia State has a proud history. It has graduated fifteen or twenty Black generals in the army. Many graduates of West Virginia State want to send their kids back here. So there were a few legacy students. Some of my friends were there because of a commitment of Black families to send their kids to an HBCU.

The local white community was aware of the excellent education that people could get at WVSU, so we had a large white commuter presence that interacted with the Black students who lived on campus. The first white students probably came in the late fifties.

I tried out for the football team and made it as a walk-on. I shared a room with a couple of white football players. They were wonderful as roommates. They were kind and funny, and we became good friends. When we first started living together, they told me, "We don't have Black people where we come from." They were from the surrounding counties in West Virginia. So I was the only Black guy they knew.

You might think I would be uncomfortable, but you have to remember where I grew up in Washington, DC, and where I went to school. When I met these guys, I was a sophomore, and they were freshmen. I grew up in northeast Washington, near the Catholic University of America. I lived in a well-integrated neighborhood in DC. The junior high that I went to was probably 40 percent Black when I started there. And when I finished there, it was probably majority Black as a number of white people decided to move out of the city and into the suburbs. One of my dear friends in high school was a guy named Bobby Whitely, who was white. He was just like a brother, and we would hang out. So I was the kind of kid who just got along with everybody. I was around a lot of different people growing up in DC so having those guys as roommates was not awkward for me. With those white roommates at college, I assumed we were equal, and I was confident. And it helped that

I was a sophomore, and they were freshmen—I knew how to get around. I wasn't innocent or naive, but race wasn't an issue for us as roommates.

But there were tensions. When I traveled to get from home to college, I took the Trailways bus from Washington to Charleston, West Virginia, and there were several stops. Somewhere in the mountains of West Virginia, there was a stop at a diner where the local Black people couldn't eat at the lunch counter. We saw the signs, and the locals couldn't eat there. But because I was an interstate passenger on the bus, I could eat there.

A MOB SCENE

In the summer of 1964, I was accepted to an academic program at Benedict College in Columbia, South Carolina. Benedict College had a unique program where kids, mostly Black kids, could come from all over the Northeast and take extra classes to earn academic credits. I stayed for five weeks that summer. That was right when President Johnson signed the public accommodations act in July 1964.[5] While we were there, a friend and I, along with two girls who were also at Benedict, drove to Fort Benning to visit the boyfriend of one of the girls.[6] We drove the five hours from South Carolina to Columbus, Georgia, near the base. On the way, we got lost and some white kids went out of their way to show us where we needed to go.

But on the way back from our visit, we stopped at a gas station in Augusta. On a whim, I bought a postcard that said, "Greetings from

5. Peter is referring to the Civil Rights Act of 1964, which included outlawing racial discrimination in public accommodations, such as schools and other public spaces.

6. As of May 11, 2023, Fort Benning has been renamed as Fort Moore. Alexander Gago and Randy Tisor, "Fort Benning Becomes Fort Moore in Historic Ceremony," 2023, www.army.mil/article/266636/fort_benning_becomes_fort _moore_in_historic_ceremony.

the Peach State," and I mailed it to my parents. Then we stopped at a restaurant. The girls stayed in the car. There was a Black woman at the counter. She says, "I can't serve you. You guys have to go around back to eat." Well, we didn't want to get *her* in trouble. We started to go around back, and all of a sudden, it became a mob scene. A bunch of white guys yelled and cursed at us. So we got back to our car and took off.

Seven or eight cars followed us out of the restaurant and chased us along the road as we headed to the highway. One car kept up with us, coming alongside. People in the other cars were slinging pipes at our car and calling us names and everything else. We kept going and they chased us out of Augusta all the way until finally we got on the highway. One of the cars, I never will forget it—a 1962 Chevrolet Impala—was trying to make us crash. The girls were screaming, and I was yelling at my friend to stop because I didn't want to die in a wreck. I wanted to stop and fight. If I was going to die, I was going to die fighting, not getting chased off the road.

But we kept driving, and we were coming up on the Georgia–South Carolina state line. There's a bridge to cross, and this guy was still trailing us. Just as we were crossing the bridge, we could see a South Carolina state trooper's car. He was turning around in the median to stay in South Carolina. We flashed our lights at him, and he stopped his car in the middle of the highway. We were obviously distressed, and the other seven cars were coming up on us. I ran out of the car and explained that they were chasing us. He said, "I got you." He went back to his car, put his flashers on, got out his rifle, and stood in the middle of the highway with his gun cranked. One by one, these cars came over the bridge and saw that cop standing there. All the cars turned around and went back into Georgia. I still get a bit emotional thinking about that.

It was a close call. I had an inkling of what was happening because these were the Freedom Ride times and violence was building. But we were just college kids. A few days later, after I'd gotten back to my dormitory at WVSU, one of my hallmates knocked on my door and said, "There's a call for Peter Lewis." I thought, *What's going on?* I never got any calls on the pay phone. I'll never forget my father's voice on the phone when he said, "Did you go to Georgia? Are you okay?" He was very concerned. I had forgotten about the postcard, but apparently it had scared my parents to death, because on the same day we were chased, Lieutenant Colonel Lemuel Penn, who was an assistant superintendent at DC public schools and would have been a principal near my neighborhood in DC, was shot and killed by the Klan. He was on the way back from doing his reserve duty at Fort Benning. When it happened, it was international news—"Black Army Officer and Educator Murdered in Georgia." My parents saw the news story the same day they received my "Greetings from the Peach State" postcard. We all realized it was a near miss for me in terms of being in the wrong place at the wrong time. That's why I'll never forget that South Carolina state trooper who helped us.

I knew about the civil rights movement, but I was not really politically aware. Though we did have some marches, West Virginia wasn't a hotbed of civil rights activity. It was somewhat removed from the South, with West Virginia's history with secession and because the mountainous landscape didn't lend itself to the plantations—there weren't as many Blacks living in the state. We certainly had some racism on our campus. When we started having larger numbers of white kids coming to classes, there would be some Confederate flags. West Virginia requires only one license plate on the back of the car, so some kids would put a plate on the front with a rebel flag. There were a number of cars on campus with these plates—and it wasn't Black students who had the rebel flag on their car. We had a graduate student there, who was about thirty years old, who was a veteran of World War II. He would take those rebel flag license plates off the cars with his bare hands and lay them up on the hood. Nobody said anything. They didn't put those plates back on either.

"YOU CAN'T COME *THIS* WAY"

After I finished college, I started teaching in Georgetown at Gordon Junior High School from 1965 to 1968. The student body was very diverse, with kids from forty-nine countries and kids from inner-city DC. There were working-class kids who grew up in Georgetown and middle-class folks too. I was asked to help recruit future teachers, and, in this job, I traveled up and down the Eastern Seaboard north to Maine, New Hampshire, Boston, South Carolina. Then I traveled to the upper Midwest, Minnesota, North Dakota, and Chicago. When I came back to Washington, my principal chose me to become an acting assistant principal at the junior high school. I was an acting assistant principal for the remainder of the year at that school.

During my time teaching, I was also a referee for high school and junior varsity basketball games. Then I got a call from our association to referee tournaments. There was a youth detention center in Quantico, and they had a basketball team, but they couldn't travel, so they hosted a tournament. Nobody wanted the assignment, so I went. After the tournament, they held a banquet. There the recreation director asked if anybody wanted to start a track program at the facility. I raised my hand, and so I started a three-year association with the prison, coaching track and going down there two or three days a week. By then I had my own car, and I drove my Jaguar XE convertible the two hours to get there. They had an old-fashioned track, and I ended up working with a lot of young men in the prison.

One day, Southwest, that was his nickname—they all had nicknames like Soldier, Candy, Rat—asked me if I would visit him on Sunday. At first, I thought he was kidding, and I reacted with a short comment. But something in his eyes told me to back off. He said, "I've been down here thirteen months and I've never had any visitors." So on Sunday I drove down there. When I got there, the guard, who was white, didn't want to let me come in through the front to visit him. I had to kind of raise my voice and be assertive and told the guy, "I'm coming to visit Southwest." He said, "But you can't come *this* way." I said, "I'm coming to visit Southwest, and I'm coming in this way." They finally let me in that way.

I went in and they called Southwest up, and I went to the visitation room with him. The next Sunday, I got his mother and sister and gave them a ride to the prison to visit Southwest. On the way back, I showed them how they could go downtown and get in a ride share. There were a bunch of people who helped each other get down to the prison to visit their loved ones.

Around that time, I found out that two of my former students were in the Fairfax County jail, in Northern Virginia. I went to visit them. When I did, they both asked me to help their younger brothers. "We don't want them to come down here," they said. So I went to meet the boys. They were fourteen and sixteen, and they were streetwise. I thought, *What am I gonna do with them?* What did I do? I took them to the country to visit my aunt and uncle in Fauquier County.

We drove down there. The farm had about a quarter-mile driveway to get up into the house, a beautiful country home, which by this time was all renovated. It sat on a plot in the middle of the farm, with a garden near it and huge maple trees in the front yard. It was really beautiful. My aunt met us at the door. She hugged me and hugged them because they were friends of mine. They couldn't believe it.

Noontime is the dinner meal. So after a meal of roast beef and mashed potatoes and collard beans that only a Southern woman could prepare, we went out on the porch where you could see for miles. One of the boys asked my uncle, "How far does your land go?" My uncle said, "Well, see that ridge over there? You see the road that you came in on? You see way over the hill, way over there? That's 109 acres. See if you can get to the end." These boys started running and their feet didn't touch the ground. We spent the afternoon skipping rocks on the millpond and hanging out, playing in the fields and just running around. It was so great to see these hardened kids so happy. It was an epiphany for me. I realized that I took my uncle's farm for granted and that not everybody's family had a farm that they could visit. I knew I wanted to have a farm myself where I could bring kids. When I think back, that was the genesis of Apple Ridge, watching those boys experiencing the farm.

COUNTRY PROPERTY

After that weekend with the kids on my aunt and uncle's farm, I started looking for country property. I went all over Pennsylvania, West Virginia, and Virginia. In 1973, I found a place listed in the *Washington Post* and loved it. I put a down payment on it, but I couldn't get any financing. No bank would loan me the money, even though I had a good job. They said they didn't want to lend to anybody who wasn't a depositor down here, you know. My home bank wouldn't do it. Then the owner of the place said he would lease it to me with an option to buy. I was elated. I had been trying to get financing for six months. While we were doing the title search, the owner called me and said, "I had to sell it to a realtor because we have to move right away." It was crushing. All that work.

But then in 1974, I found Apple Ridge in Floyd County. It was just stunning. It grabbed me in a way that I couldn't shake loose. And after forty-five years, I'm still in love with the place. You can go online and see parts of it, but the pictures don't do it justice. I love the open space and having the ability to be on the land. When I taught junior high school in DC, I would go golfing once or twice a week. But when I came down here, I didn't need to go golfing anymore because I could just be outside all the time.

When I came to Apple Ridge, there were no Black people. But most people, even those people who are way up north in Chicago, Detroit, and New York, have roots in rural areas. Apple Ridge is a magical place. It has sixty acres of woods, and twenty-five to thirty acres are open fields. There's an apple orchard with thirty different varieties of apples. For about nine years, I worked the orchard, up at three in the morning 'til late at night, putting up apples—picking them, peeling them, drying them. I really enjoyed that work. I worked with the chainsaw to clear limbs and to prune. I liked working in the cold. I got hooked on the country. My first wife, Harriet, and I had two sons here, Peter and John. They loved growing up here. They would run off and get lost in the woods, and we'd have to go find them. After fixing up the place, I later founded the organization Apple Ridge Farm to turn the farm into a youth camp. When I retired in 2016, John took over the farm and he kept it going until 2019. Now our foundation runs the place, but I come back over to talk to the kids and to do some work around the place.

When I brought those boys from the city to my aunt and uncle's farm, I knew I wanted to do that kind of work, to use my knowledge to help youth understand how the system works. And to equip kids going forward. So here at the farm we have some trails that meander through the woods and a little creek. There are opportunities here for some discovery. I want them to know that they can get hold of something, make something of themselves. That's the whole basis of this place and why we've had some success here. I've been an educator since 1965, so I've been in this business for a good long while.

As we sat on Peter's porch talking about Apple Ridge Farm, various campers and counselors passed by, going to activities and the food hall. Looking out over the vast property of trees, rustic buildings, tennis and basketball courts, and mountain views, Peter seemed pleased with the work of Apple Ridge and satisfied with turning over operations to the next generation. His good friend Jordan Bell is now the director of programs.

I live with my second wife, Carla, in Roanoke now, but I still spend time with the kids here on the farm. When college kids on alternative spring break come, the staff wants me as the founder to spend an evening with them. I go around the room and ask them to tell me where they're from and their majors. And then I ask them about their favorite teachers. They often talk about teachers who kept them from falling apart during a tough time in their lives. I think my mother was that kind of person to a lot of kids. As was her mother before her.

Carla, who's also an educator, says, "There are a whole lot of people who have dreams, but you're someone whose dream has come true." Now that I'm retired, I love to drive through the roads of Virginia. One of my favorite trips is driving down Route 29 all the way from DC toward the farm. Or going to Richmond by taking Highway 460. If you take Route 11 all the way through the valley, you can stop at little shops and see mountains the whole way. There are roads that go off to the right, and you can drive down and back up again.

I'm seventy-five now, and the last year has been really hard. I lost my son John—he died unexpectedly—so the last year has been extremely, extremely difficult. I'm trying to make some sense of all of this right now.

All I ever wanted was to be well read and to have an understanding of the world, and I've gotten that done. Together Carla and I enjoy coming to our farm and watching it all happen.

BARTE LANEY

BORN: 1961, Marion, North Carolina
INTERVIEWED IN: Marion, North Carolina
Retired Public School Maintenance Worker

Interviewed by Jordan Laney

*Barte Laney's family was displaced from their home in Hazel Creek,
North Carolina, when the Tennessee Valley Authority took over the
land to build a series of dams to develop southern rural electrification in the early 1940s. Barte's family resettled in McDowell County,
North Carolina, where several new factories offered job opportunities.
A cluster of families from Hazel Creek resettled together, and like many
families displaced because of the dams, they made new homes and communities. Before Barte's family moved, his father worked for the Ritter
Lumber Company. After moving to McDowell County, his father and*

*uncles worked intermittently as loggers, traveling for work. Because his
father and other people like him are no longer around to tell these stories, Barte shares the family's long history of mourning the loss of their
mountain bluff land and returning to the land for Decoration Days,
hunting, and fishing.*

A PLACE IN THE WOODS

My name is Barte Philip Laney, and I live on Goose Creek Road and
was raised on Nix Creek in Marion, North Carolina, in McDowell
County. I'm retired from maintenance work at McDowell County
Public Schools.

I play music a little, more or less the bluegrass type, you know,
that sort of style. I just pick around on the fiddle, mandolin, and
guitar around the house. That's about all I do with COVID going
on right now. I ride horses a little bit and hunt. From October to
March, I deer hunt and I coon hunt and turkey hunt in the spring.
And hopefully I'll get to fish this spring.

As a kid I did what most kids my age did. I tried to get out of
working around the house and going to school. We rode bicycles a
lot and hunted and fished and swam, and stuff like that is mainly
what we done. We rode bicycles all over the place and went swim-
min'. When I got about fifteen, we started staying in the woods
hunting and fishing. It was great, and I thought, *I'm going to have
something like that someday, a place in the woods.*

One time my brother Bobby Jo and Daddy went trout fishin'. I
can't remember anything about first day, but I remember that day.
They were gettin' ready to go and I was standing at the door a-crying,
wanting to go. I thought I should have been able to go. I was only
three or four, I was real little. Then I remember Daddy and Bobby Jo
coming back and having some trout and lettin' me get a picture with
them. I guess they thought that would make me happy. That sticks in
my mind, wantin' to go and be out there with them.

Every morning what would wake me up was the smell of coffee. Mama used to cook breakfast, sometimes bacon but always biscuits and gravy. We'd get up and it'd be cold, but then we'd go in the kitchen, and it'd be warm in there, from the stove.

Since I retired, I still work a little bit, but other than that I just piddle around here a lot. I've been going out in the woods and cuttin' trails. Hopefully I'll get to ride the horse if I ever get the right trail. I'm just cuttin' trails and cuttin' wood and maybe working in the garden here before long.

BARELY LIVING

My daddy's family is from Hazel Creek. He used to work different types of timber. They just grew up barely living. They just did what they had to do. They didn't own a whole lot when they lived in the Smokies, but in those days you didn't have to. They would work and cut timber and acid wood.[1] In their spare time they went fishin' and huntin' and did their own gardening, raisin' something to eat. They did some bear huntin' and coon huntin', whatever they could do to eat.

My daddy and his brothers, they played music too. Now, my grandfather, I don't reckon he played anything, but he did that shape-note singing; they all done that.[2] Somebody down there showed 'em how to sing and play and was there to help them out. They lived in what was called Swain County back then, when Fontana Dam

---

1. The timber industry boomed during the early twentieth century, and many freelance woodcutters provided timber to larger logging companies. "Acid wood" denotes timber that could be used for the chemical processing where logging plants extracted chemicals from wood that became rubber, paint thinner, and so on. See the Northern Woodlands post about the history of the industry and the park at https://northernwoodlands.org/articles/article/the-wood-chemical-industry-in-the-northeast.

2. See the Appalachian Voice blog post about shape singing at https://appvoices.org/2019/12/16/shape-note-singing/.

wasn't there yet, up in Hazel Creek. They lived in a couple different places, the way Daddy was a-tellin' it, he was born in one place
called Sawdust Pile, and they moved up the creek to Bone Valley and
then moved to the top of Sugar Fork Gap—all within ten miles or
so from each other. They moved up another creek near the top, up
Sugar Fork, because that is when Ritter Lumber was a-takin' over in
there.[3] They kept movin' just to get the jobs.

*In the 1940s, the Tennessee Valley Authority (TVA) began a large-scale
development plan to increase access to rural electrification in the southern region of the United States. This process included building a series of
dams, which resulted in the flooding of many towns and family homes,
displacing at least fifteen thousand families throughout the Tennessee
Valley through eminent domain law, the federal right to take land for
public use.[4] Barte's family and their community were forced from their
homes and livelihoods. While landowners were compensated for their
property, family's like Barte's were not landowners and had to start over
on their own.*

When the TVA came through, some of Daddy's family and other
neighbors waited it out. But Daddy and them left out before they
ever flooded their place. They didn't have much to load up. They
didn't know what to expect for jobs, but they heard there was cheap-
er land, and that is what got him to come to McDowell County—
some jobs and some land they could afford to buy.

---

3. Ritter Lumber Company cut all along the ridges and coves on Hazel Creek's
south banks, and then when it got to the top, went across the creek, and headed
down along the creek's north bank, stripping bare the land along the way. Ritter
closed in 1928, and though it employed many, the destructive logging practices
damaged the forest and creek.

4. TVA historian Pat Ezzell estimates that at least 15,000 families were relocated
throughout TVA's domain. Other scholars estimate the number as high as 125,000
residents. See the Tennessee Valley Authority's "Bibliography of TVA History" at
www.tva.com/about-tva/our-history/bibliography-of-tva-history for additional information about the history of TVA.

THE WHOLE CROWD MOVED TOGETHER

In the early forties they started moving to McDowell. At different times different family members went. Some uncles went into Knoxville, Canton, or Waynesville and those areas for a little while, and then some went into the military for World War II, those old enough. Then they was all trying to get here I reckon. The community moved here all at once and eventually everybody made their way here. It wasn't like they moved into a place where they were the new people because all of their family and cousins and distant cousins and some other neighbors who lived over there in Hazel Creek all moved together. It was real kin and not even real kin. And so they weren't really moving to a strange place, except the land was different. So most of 'em come to McDowell County and then the majority wound up on Nix Creek. It's clannish, and I'm sure that wasn't an accident. They found a lot of land they could all buy. I knew most of the people on Nix Creek because we were kin, and they all moved here from the Smokies.

There was a Broyhill Furniture plant and a textile plant and lots of jobs coming on. Somebody said the government guided them this way, but that's just talk. I think somebody they knew come over here, and then with the jobs they all came over.

After they moved here, they went to the Nix Creek Free Will Baptist Church and Zion Hill Baptist. Those churches was close and the same doctrine they were used to, some Free Will, some regular Baptist. Especially Nix Creek, it was within walking distance. My daddy's grandpaw, my great-grandpaw, was a preacher in the Smokies, and sometimes they'd be traveling preachers come through and a big thing every once in a while was brush arbors, just like an outdoor revival. We did homecomings at Zion Hill like the Decoration Days up in Sugar Fork.[5] The families that had all come here together decorated the graves with flowers, and there was

---

5. After the Civil War ended, the Union veterans established Decoration Day as a time for the nation to decorate graves of those who died in the war with flowers. This later became Memorial Day.

lots of food. We'd take snacks and a lot of others would bring a big meal. When I was little, we went back to Bone Valley for Decoration Day. It was three and half miles' walk to the cemetery at Sugar Fork and six and a half to Bone Valley where my daddy's grandpaw's grave is. You can walk to it.

My great-grandpaw worked in timber in Marion a little bit when they first come here. Daddy and my uncles all worked with their uncles a little bit; they was doing the same thing here that they did in the Smokies for a while. They worked for three or four different companies and went to South Carolina to work logging down there. They stayed in a logging camp down there for a while. And then he worked for his uncle and another outfit in McDowell for a while. The last twenty years he worked in a furniture plant. He thought that was the best job ever because it was steady work with benefits, and he'd never had that before. Mama was a homemaker until Daddy retired, then she started to work at Baxter's factory for a while, a solution plant north of Marion.[6] My daddy died when I was fifteen, and at that time the stories about the TVA and the big move wasn't as interesting to me, so I didn't ask a lot of questions. But he told lots of fishin' tales and huntin' stories, stuff like that. I wished I'd asked more questions.

Their lives were different once they moved. The land was different—not in a negative way, it was just flatter than over there, and from a gardening standpoint, it's actually better. Daddy always called it the Glades. It's really Nix Creek. There were doctors over in Hazel Creek, but here they had their first hospital doctors. Over in Hazel Creek it would take a day or two to get to a doctor.

Like I said, the whole crowd moved together, which you wouldn't see happen anymore. Maybe not everyone, but the close family members and the extended family like my grandpaw's family, all the Laneys, and my grandma's side, all the Crispses. Everyone come to Nix Creek and live somewhere along the way. Some of

---

6. The plant she worked for made solution for IVs used in hospitals.

the Crispses married into some of the Cables, and so they moved out there too. Then there was the Brookses too; they was part of the Laney family, their cousins. They come all together and was buying up some land, and then others would come. When they got here, they took care of each other. Like when Daddy was working in South Carolina, and he went down with his uncle—all the men was a-working to cut timber, and the families look out for each other up here. When they got back, Daddy and his brother built on his daddy's house, and one of my uncles gave a cousin money to buy a piece of land out there and put a house on. They all still live there. And they just sort of took care of each other, which you don't see anymore.

Folks got by mainly gardening. None of them had a big farm. I went into work, into "public jobs," is what Daddy called it. Anybody'd rather work outside, but it's hard to raise a family like that anymore. When I was fifteen, I started cutting pulp wood for my cousin, and when I was sixteen, I went up to the Englishes' dairy farm getting building stone out of the hills. We'd shoot it out with dynamite and split it. I didn't really have a whole lot of time for big farming. We would get in hay, have some cornfields just to have feed for the animals. It was mainly just gardening. In the Smokies there wasn't a whole lot of farming because we lived on a bluff of the river, trying to get something to grow just to eat.

Mama and Daddy always had chickens. That's probably one of the mainstays for the eggs and the meat. Paw kept sheep in the Smokies, and they kept pigs, and somebody in the family had a cow but just for milk—there weren't no big pastures for beef cows up there. But sheep can run in them big bluffs. So they got the wool for warm clothing. They didn't bring sheep to McDowell because the land was flatter, but they did bring chickens. Daddy liked having the chickens around. My mama's daddy was more or less a share-cropper. He farmed some big land out there, and lots of the family ran moonshine. He didn't own land. So he didn't get run out by the government exactly, but when he got down here, he quit making moonshine. He wasn't friends with the sheriff down here, so he slipped out of doing that.

Some of Daddy's family played music in Swain County, but then in McDowell, lots of us participated in arts programs and the radio show. Most anything we did before that was church singing or a little quartet or something like that. Now there's a few of us that get together, and I have a couple of 'em to the house. Mostly we just play music around the area, but not many of them got into that. Some would play in a nightclub, but if wasn't church, they didn't do that much.

I started fiddle when I was fifteen, and Daddy was showing me a little bit and that's when he died. I guess I wanted to learn because he would talk about playing for house dances in the Smokies, little community dances. He didn't even have a fiddle when he left over there. I bought a fiddle to learn on at Wilson's music Shop. After Daddy died, I learned listening to records—the Stanley Brothers, Bill Monroe, the Country Gentlemen, the Seldom Scene—and learned from some fiddle players around here. I watched Paul Birchfield, who was from the Smokies, and Pee Wee Davis. Otto Gross was an encourager.

As long as they could, the family went back to hunt and fish on their old grounds, and then eventually they couldn't. At first, we could still go back over until the National Park Service took so much of the Smokies that cut them out of huntin'. You could still go and fish, but you had to have a permit that cost money. The TVA was different than the Great Smoky Mountains National Park. The park wouldn't let people back in to hunt and fish.

THE ROAD TO NOWHERE

I know this is secondhand, but there ain't none of 'em left to tell the stories directly. When the TVA come through, there was a promise of building a road where people who had to move could go to the cemeteries and visit their families. But then the park took over, and they never did build it. And the reason they said was because it would destroy areas where there might be certain wildlife or plants. And if that's right, I can understand that, it being in the park. But the thing was, certain communities got tourism money from the park, like Swain County, so they actually come out better. They became a tourist destination, and they're making money off tourism. But there are more families, or descendants, in McDowell County that was affected by having to move, more than there are in Swain County. The ones that had to move out and went to McDowell, they were more affected by the move. So the way of handling the relocations was political; the politicians from Swain County convinced them where to build things. So anybody who wanted to go to their family's graves, their cemeteries never got a road.

You can go to the cemetery, but you have to go by the lake in the pontoons and at certain times, which I enjoy myself. They haul you across the lake on the ferry, then you either walk or drive. That's a steady cost to the government of doing that, and I understand that, but that's not the point. The point is, they originally told us we'd get a road, and then people didn't get the road and then the county got the money. It was a payoff to try to hush things because most of the people that it affected had to leave that county. There's more people from Hazel Creek in McDowell County than any other county. Most people were convinced to move because they were told they were doing something for the country by moving out. They was told it was patriotic because it would be helping the floods on the Tennessee River. Some people were told it was about the war effort, to do a lot of good for country—the Fontana Dam supplied electricity to an aluminum plant, and as they built it, they played patriotic music 24-7. And the rivers would get in a rage, and the dams were done to keep from flooding in the Tennessee area because that's where the water goes in that part of Tennessee. The Tennessee Valley Authority put to 'em that it was a good thing for them to support the country. But it didn't matter—they didn't have a choice anyhow.

But that's how it was put to them, but then the country didn't back up what they said they was going to do. Then all those people was just left out.

The flooding in Tennessee didn't really affect Hazel Creekers, but they had to move. And where they lived, three to seven miles above the lake, the lake didn't flood them out. The fact that there was no road, they never built that road they promised, that was the reason they had to move—because they didn't have no way in or out, and the government told them they had to move. That had an effect on everybody. Some of the people who lived down in the bottoms on the main river, which is now under the lake—some of them worked on the dam—that's what got flooded back up in the hills were where they lived. But our family didn't get flooded, it was simply they just cut them out from the way.

That's why a lot of my uncles and family was upset about not getting a road at all. I can see not wanting to affect wildlife, but why give Swain County all that tourism money? Plus, they built the road from Gatlinburg, and they didn't seem like they cared if it affected wildlife there. But for Hazel Creek, it was a road to nowhere. Now, they keep the fire road to go to the cemetery gates closed and just open it for Decoration Day.

When I was a kid, we'd go back over there but not into the park. We'd go the country around it, for a family funeral, and then we went to Bryson City. We'd see more distant family who I really didn't know, but I was tickled to go anywhere. As I got older, it meant a little more to go over to the park. We didn't ask questions, but as we got older, we got to figuring out that our family used to live there, that we worked that land, that we loved huntin' and fishin' because of that land. We learned about our heritage going there.

***

I got married to my wife when I was twenty-one. I was real young. I knew Sandra from high school. I was twenty-seven when we had our first kid and twenty-nine when we had our second. I worked in carpentry for myself and for a local company. One day I saw the director of the school maintenance system at the bank, and he told me there was a job opening and it would be six months or so. When the job opened, I went and got the job. I was called "carpenter" for the school system, but there was a lot of things. Carpenter work, pesticides, roofing, and running a little bit of equipment. I was a jack of all trades. I don't guess there was a whole lot in between high school and now, just working.

I'm definitely Appalachian; that land and the area is in our bloodline. We're Scots-Irish and German. They come here and settled here and because of that, because of them a-livin' there. And it's more than that—it's where you live and the culture, the music, everything.

My daddy and the rest of them, they didn't really dwell on being forced out. Now some of the other people in our family was more upset about havin' to leave. I'm sure Daddy was to a certain degree, but they just saw it as a part of life. They didn't complain much about anything. It was fine with them, and they saw it was just living. They had a little more stable money when they come over here and an easier life here. Over there they didn't really need no money, just enough to get some cash to pay their taxes and to buy flour, sugar, and maybe coffee. That's about the only things they ever bought. Salt, maybe. Daddy and Mama didn't go twelve years to school. So for them, when he went into plant work, he was getting paid some cash and getting some insurance, a little bit of vacation and a steady job—for them that was the best thing a-goin'. So their mindset for us kids was, you get a high school diploma and then go get you a good factory job. That seemed like a good thing to them.

SHENG THAO

BORN: 1986, Ban Vinai Refugee Camp, Thailand
INTERVIEWED IN: Nebo, North Carolina
Nail Technician

Interviewed by Jordan Laney

Sheng Thao's family is Hmong, and after the American war in Vietnam, they were forced to leave Laos and go to the Ban Vinai Refugee Camp in Thailand in 1979. She was born in the camp in 1986, and a few years later her family came to the United States through the Refugee Act of 1980. Sheng reflects on her experience of coming to the US as a child, feeling the pressure on her to honor the history and expectations of her family. Her story also shows the long, sustained burden of racism and the intergenerational impacts of displacement and trauma.

Sheng talks with pride about her family's accomplishments and their contributions through a variety of service and business ventures, but she also spotlights how her own and her community's refugee experiences risk being hidden from view.

I COULD SEE THE STARS

I was born at the Ban Vinai Refugee Camp in the Loei region of northern Thailand.[1] I have a bachelor's degree in communications studies from the University of North Carolina. I speak Hmong and English, and I live in Nebo, North Carolina. I'm a nail technician in Marion. We moved to Appalachia when I was in second grade.

My dad's name is Peng Thao, and my mom is Mai Kau Lee Thao. My mom was a Lee. We don't usually change our last names after marriage, but once she obtained US citizenship, she changed her name to Thao. My oldest sister's name is Elizabeth, my older brother's name is Tou Yong. I have three younger brothers as well, Khanthe, Jan, and Ben.

My grandfather's name was Nhiasoua. We were in the camp, and my grandfather's sisters had already moved to the US. When my dad first approached my grandfather about going to the US, Grandfather refused to give his blessing because he was really close with my younger brother Khanthe, who was like *his* child. Khanthe followed my grandfather everywhere. Also, my grandfather didn't really see the opportunities that were available in the US. He forbade my parents from bringing us over here. It was actually my grandma who gave her blessing. My parents decided to go without my grandfather's blessing because they wanted better for our family. A couple years later, my grandma came with my uncles. My dad was the first

---

1. Ban Vinai Refugee Camp (Ban Vinai Holding Center) was located in Thailand from 1975 until 1992. Ban Vinai primarily housed 45,000 Highland people, especially Hmong, who fled communist rule in Laos. Many were resettled in the United States and other countries, and some remained in the camp.

of his brothers to come over. My grandfather stayed behind and re-married. He stayed in the refugee camp until 2007, before he moved over here with his second wife. When he came over there was a big welcoming party for him. There was tension from him not giving his blessing, but no one really showed it. I was in college at that time, so I didn't really get to spend much time with him. Then, a couple years after they moved here, they moved to Alaska, because some of his second wife's children were up there.

My dad was an interpreter in Thailand because he had learned English. So that fast-tracked us on our move to the US. He knew a lady who helped with the process. My family first immigrated to the Twin Cities in Minnesota through a family sponsorship—you had to have a family sponsor to come over.[2] My dad's older sister was already living in St. Paul, Minnesota. So we moved there in the winter of 1991, and it was super cold. There was so much crime, but I was young and didn't know it was dangerous at the time. We moved houses several times. Our car got broken into. Moving to a city with all the traffic and people and being surrounded by so many new types of people—I remember my parents being afraid all the time. My parents kept the incidents quiet. There were so many prejudices within groups that made us more fearful.

There was a large concentration of Hmong people up there in Minnesota. It's an area where Hmong immigrants were resettled by the US government. I had a Hmong teacher for ESL classes at school and I learned English very quickly and started writing stories. I won second place for one I wrote, and there was an ice cream party. The story was called "The Big Flower" about this flower that grew as big as a house.

My dad had another sister who lived down in North Carolina. But you didn't move down here without family. In 1995 Mom and Dad decided to move down here for a quieter life, outside of the city.

---

2. See information about the Refugee Act of 1980 in the timeline.

My aunt, my dad's older sister, had a huge chicken farm that she built herself, and when we moved down from Minnesota, our extended and immediate family helped us to find work and eventually helped my parents purchase some land so they could build a house.

My first impression of North Carolina was that it was very quiet. Because even in Thailand, when we lived in the camp, it was like living in a village with lots of other families. We had neighbors right next door to us. Then, when we lived in the Twin Cities, a huge city, it was very loud and very noisy. The crime was stressful. When we moved down here it was so quiet. I could hear insects at night. I could see the stars. It was very wide and open and quiet.

A LOT OF LAND

My mom worked at Leviton Manufacturing Company. My dad worked at a company called Rexnord, in McDowell. Then he worked at Gerresheimer Glass. It was difficult, physical labor for both of them, manufacturing assembly-line production work. They got the jobs through referrals from family members who were already working at those companies.

As a kid I spent a lot of time outside with my siblings because we had a lot of land. We had some woods behind the house, so we built a treehouse. We would play on tree trunks, too, climbing around on them. We're also a big volleyball family. We went to the park every weekend to play volleyball as a family against other people at the park. It's still fun because as we've grown, so did the people that we played with at the park. Everybody's got their own little families now, and we still play.

I was a good kid. I listened to my parents. I was pretty reserved, kept to myself, was quiet in school, and was very studious. I loved reading. My parents took us to the library, and we'd bring home loads of books to read. I loved school and doing homework. I used to "do" lots of homework to keep from having to do extra chores around the house. I read a lot of books, like The Baby-Sitters Club and Laura Ingalls Wilder's Little House on the Prairie series.

When we moved here, I had to take ESL classes, and I was a year behind in school. I remember kids looking at me. I kind of wanted them to look at me, but I knew they were looking because I was different. It was a good feeling and not a good feeling at the same time. Because of where my parents worked, we had a low income and dealt with poverty. It's not hard to notice that there were differences between my peers at school and myself, things that I lacked, not just being Hmong.

I'm still quiet, pretty introverted, especially in comparison to everyone else where I work, at my brother's salon. The other technicians are all chatting away, and I sit away from the door. I talk to my clients but not if they don't talk back. I don't keep the conversation going. One of my brothers—Jan—is quieter than me. When he was younger, he would talk your ears off. On our road trips up to Minnesota to visit our cousins during the summer, he would talk so much, but then as he grew up, he just stopped talking. He was self-conscious and didn't want to draw attention to himself. We took private Hmong language classes with my auntie over the summer to polish our Hmong language and writing skills. There were at least fifteen of us that went.

I feel like making friends has always been hard unless there were people I just kind of clicked with. I never really had many close friends. It is pretty hard for me to make friends, probably because I felt I was different. Nobody could understand me because of my accent. I was a little embarrassed because we grew up poor. Now looking back, I realize that most of the students in my classes were probably just as poor, but I didn't see it that way then. Our house was too small for friends to come and sleep over because they'd have to sleep in a shared bedroom with my siblings. We didn't have much. There was a little bit of shame in that.

In the sixth grade I danced in the talent show at East Junior High with my cousin Zoovi. We wore traditional Thai dresses and danced to traditional songs.[3] When Zoovi moved here, we danced for fun, and she liked to choreograph our dances.

My mom ordered handmade pieces of cloth from Thailand from an auntie and then sewed them so they fit us. They had beautiful stitching. Everyone talked about it being so different from all the other talent show acts.

We still play traditional Hmong and Thai music at all our family gatherings and parties. Music is a big part of our cultural events and parties. We either have a live band or a DJ. There are several Hmong bands in the community that you can hire for weddings, graduations, or New Year's parties. My brother Jan is a DJ. He throws house parties with lots of traditional music.

A SUITCASE FULL OF PHOTO ALBUMS

When you apply to become a permanent resident of the US, you have to be connected somehow by family or know someone. It is a long process and requires lots of documents. My parents had these bags with the World Health Organization logo on them that we kept our documents in. My mom also had an old square suitcase full of photo albums, and the suitcase and those bags would show up occasionally, when we needed our documents during the immigration process. In the suitcase there are lots of old pictures of all of us, individually, holding up a paper with our alien resident numbers. Like a passport photo but holding our numbers. Those documents are so important. They go back in the WHO bag, placed back in the suitcase with other family photos, and stored in a closet. A lot of the pictures have been moved around to different family members, like when there's a funeral and other family events. The pictures get used to make videos or a slideshow. I remember us as kids looking through all the photos

---

3. See Nengher Vang's "Hmong Dance Transform History" at www.academia.edu/6617337/Hmong_Dance_Transform_History for additional information about the garments used in these dances.

in the suitcase and carefully placing it back in my mother's room. It's now in my brother and sister-in-law's bedroom. It is a special object for our family, and a favorite pastime is going through the pictures.

When we decided to move down here, some close cousins stayed back in Minnesota. I felt like they had so much more opportunity than we did in North Carolina. They had these co-ed scouting programs that allowed them to do extracurricular activities. They were able to get jobs as they were going through school. Down here everything is so spaced out; we couldn't just walk to get anywhere. My parents couldn't drive us, so we'd have to be more independent to be able to work during high school or go to anything after school. There weren't all those programs available to us here anyway. So while my cousins had all these activities and their parents had money so they could travel to France and Thailand, pretty much all we had were some after-school activities and sports.

BACK TO THAILAND

My parents saved enough to take us to visit Thailand in 1997. I went back to Thailand by myself for an internship in 2008 to northeast Thailand. It was a new program that UNC students could apply for, Tar Heels Teaching Fellows. We went to teach English in a rural village, but we also taught family planning. I don't have clear memories from living in the refugee camp, but when I went back to Thailand for the first time, I would have a snack or drink and the memories would come back. My auntie made some food, and I remember sitting there thinking I had eaten the food before, because it felt so familiar. It was mostly dessert. They use the pandan leaf, and tasting it again in the bread from 7-Eleven, it bought back a smell I remembered.[4] 7-Eleven food is a huge thing there.

---

4. *Pandanus amaryllifolius* is a tropical plant known as pandan, whose leaves are fragrant and used in Southeast and South Asian cuisine.

I know this sounds weird, but there was this tree—like a magnolia tree but it didn't have flowers. I don't know if it's from a dream or what, but I remembered it and knew it when I saw it. The traffic, the fruit and veggie stands, and the background noise. . . . It all felt—not really familiar—but like a dream or a memory.

We have a big extended family, so we stayed with family there during our stay. Later, in 2014, I went with my parents to the Chiang Mai area in northern Thailand, a province called Nan where my grandma's sister lives. We don't have any immediate family in Thailand anymore. All of our immediate family are in the US. Some of my mom's side of the family resettled in Australia. We're all spread out now, and that makes my mom sad.

TIGHTLY KNIT COMMUNITY

When I was growing up, there was an elder whom we called *Lotoua Loh*, which means Grandpa. He's from the Loh clan. He was a *punku lotto*; it's like a superintendent or a higher-ranking school personnel position back in Laos. My grandfather knew him, and we just call him Grandpa because that's what you do with anyone older, like calling them Auntie or Uncle, out of respect. He was an educator in Laos, so when he moved here, he was still an important elder for our community.

For us he was like a distant family member, and his was actually one of the first Hmong families to settle here in McDowell County. So it felt like our ancestors were here and we felt close to people here even though we were far from home. That's something that is similar about people who live in this area who aren't Hmong. To me the tight community here, the families here, you don't really find first-generation Hmong folks living out on their own in some random town with no other Hmong people around. The community has to already have established families to move there. If a Hmong family moves to a place, they're following their family. It's only the second-generation young professionals who are living on their own in places like Durham and Raleigh.

We have clan leaders. There are only eighteen last names in Hmong, and we refer to those last names as clans. What your last name is, your clan, impacts who you can marry. Some clan names are considered too close to marry—it's taboo to marry across particular clans. In our community, it's taboo to marry someone with the same last name. The Kue clan is considered a brother clan with the Thao, my clan, so I couldn't marry someone from the Kue clan, even though technically we may not be related—it's the tradition and this history of the clans that's important.

My husband's clan name is Vang, Bee Vang, and it's okay for Thao to marry Vang. His family lives in Syracuse. There is a Hmong community up in Syracuse too. His parents are going to be retiring soon and want to get away from the cold winters. They're thinking of moving down South to either here in North Carolina or Arkansas where they also have family. We met through his cousin who lives in Charlotte and is a friend of mine. His cousin was dating a young aunt of mine. She's actually younger than me. Through her we became friends.

I met his family when we went to Arkansas for his cousin's wedding. When we were getting married, we had so much to do to follow all the cultural wedding proceedings. It was very confusing for us because we didn't know what to do. My sister helped us. She said to contact the president of the Thao clan in our community. She gave me his name and number—I had no clue who he was. But he talked to my husband's family, and then they talked to our fathers who got things together. There are certain people that you have to contact because it's tradition that the parents don't speak directly to each other, at all, until the wedding. The wedding took place over a week, making it an official Hmong ceremony. We wanted to do it this way for our families, but it was very confusing and stressful.

WILL I EVER BE ABLE TO STOP?

After graduating from McDowell County High School, Sheng went to the University of North Carolina and earned a bachelor's degree in communication studies. She had an internship and a job in that field, but her family needed help with their new business. She decided to help the family, and since then has not only worked in the nail salon but also helps with the family's store, making her week very busy.

I work six days a week at my family's nail salon, from Monday through Saturday. My brother, Tou Yong Thao, and sister-in-law, Martina Yang, own it, and I help them out there. Business really picked up after the pandemic times, and we grew clientele pretty fast. I had a steady group of people who came to me. Most of my siblings own businesses, and they work their own schedules. They are successful, and my nieces and nephews have been brought up completely different from us. They have more and there's more to do now. Their parents are loading them up in the car after school to do clubs and sports, stuff that they love to do. My siblings have more time than my parents did and are able to afford to do that.

My sister and my brother-in-law have several rental properties. My brother-in-law owns Phone City, a prepaid phone service business in Hickory. My sister is a real estate agent. And we all got together to help my brother and sister-in-law open up the Bubblys restaurant here in Marion. I help them to manage it. While they're shuttling their kids around, I take care of everything in the salon. My brother Jan co-owns the Bubblys in Hickory.

The salon is a good business for us. We had planned to open in April 2020 but couldn't because of the pandemic. We had the grand opening in June. Business picked up really quickly because people were eager to get back to their normal routines of self-care. It's a supportive community here in Marion. Some people didn't want to wear masks, but if we asked them to, they would. We have clients bring in their business cards and leave them at our salon, so that people can learn about other local businesses.

On my days off, I like to stay at home or go grab a coffee and take a book with me. The quiet is good on those days because so many times I wonder, *Will I ever be able to stop? Will I ever work a normal week? A 9-to-5 schedule with weekends off.* But then I remember that I'm here in the US; I have a job. There's a lot of pressure. There's a spoken and unspoken pressure. You have to earn money. We have to work harder to fulfill our parents' dreams. When I think about being tired or I think it's too much, I feel bad because my parents went through so much more. In those times I tell myself I have to hold it together. I can't fall apart.

THE ONLY THING LEFT

When I was growing up, my dad went to mechanic school at McDowell Tech just so he could fix cars and so he wouldn't have to worry about paying for maintenance on our cars. That was one of the main parts about living in America that was different for us—every family had multiple cars. My parents could never buy a brand-new car, and the ones we had always needed fixing up. So he went to school to learn how. When I was going back and forth from home to college at Chapel Hill, my car died several times on Interstate 40, and I had to call my dad to come rescue me. He would fix the car, and I'd go on to school.

Recently, all my siblings and their spouses gifted my father a car. It brought all of us together, collaborating to make it happen with my mom. My mom and I went to Virginia to pick it up. During that car trip, Mom told me stories I never knew before, like the story of how she and Dad first decided to move us here. My parents got married very young and had children very young. They were in their thirties and had all these dreams. They've accomplished getting all of us through school, and most of us went to university. They built a dream house—the one we're living in now in Nebo. So when she told us that the only thing she wanted for him was a brand-new car, we had to do it. It was a very special thing for us to see that part of their American Dream coming to fruition.

TOTALLY HOME

I wouldn't say that I'm Appalachian if someone asked me. I would say I'm Hmong American. I feel like Appalachian is more of an identity in the western part of the state. We live in the foothills here in this part of Appalachia. We're not in the mountains. I feel like you have to have ancestors from Appalachia to claim that.

But I love being in North Carolina—it's so quiet. After all that chaos getting here, it's totally home to me now. I work downtown and see the growth that Marion's going through. Growing up, we didn't venture downtown. I remember it being a deserted place without many businesses. Now there are restaurants and people walking around shopping, getting ice cream. Even Glenwood doesn't look the same anymore. The entire school is different. Sometimes I have that feeling of missing the old times. But at my home it's still very quiet.

I'd like to stay in this area for my kids, for them to have the same childhood I did but maybe with more opportunities for activities. I can see that my brother's kids are growing up with a much different childhood than we did in terms of sports and things. But they still have that innocence. It's pretty much being able to have options, being able to pick and choose, advance in education if you choose to. Because my parents didn't really have a choice—they could only do factory or farmwork.

I think my family could leave a legacy behind in the Appalachian and Marion areas for people to know that there's a diverse community here too. My legacy is just being. Being Hmong. People have more awareness of who we are. Now, people can say "Oh,

Hmong like Miss Laos and Miss Universe Payengxa Lor (ນາງ ຍ
ເຍົ້ຽງ ລໍ) and Sunisa Lee, the Olympic champion. People know
Hmong is an ethnicity. There are reference points now. People can
know who we are as a people. There is a big Hmong population in
the western part of North Carolina. The museum at the community
center in Hickory shows our contributions to the area. The community is larger now in numbers, but it doesn't seem as close as it was
when I was young. The clans each have their own organizations, and
maybe I feel the disconnect because my parents aren't as active with
the clan organization anymore.[5] I don't see myself taking an active
role, just existing as Hmong and doing the cultural and spiritual
part. But it's important.

I'm preparing for my daughter's Hu Plig ceremony, calling our
souls back. Her name is Aurelia Laim Lias Vang. I have to do it for
my daughter. That is important to me. It gives me peace of mind.
And it's important to have family around me because I have no idea
how to prepare for these rituals. We need to learn it enough to pass it
on to our children. Who will know how to do it in the future? I want
my daughter and nieces and nephews to learn to speak Hmong.[6]

---

5. The United Hmong Association is an international organization meant to provide services and information for this growing diasporic community.

6. There are immersion Hmong language schools in Minnesota, which serve
Hmong food for lunch, but no schools like this in North Carolina.

CINDY SIERRA MORALES

BORN: 1995, Durango, Mexico
INTERVIEWED IN: Marion, North Carolina
Health Care Enrollment Specialist

Interviewed by Jordan Laney

When she was six years old, Cindy's family migrated from Durango, Mexico, to Los Angeles, California, fleeing gang violence. After a short stay with family friends, Cindy's family drove to Marion, North Carolina, where her aunt, uncle, cousins, and older siblings already lived. Her parents held a variety of factory jobs, and Cindy started second grade just a few weeks after arriving. After living in the United States for fifteen years, Cindy and her siblings were able to secure legal documentation through DACA.[1]

---

1. For additional information about Deferred Action for Childhood Arrivals, see the American Immigration Council's 2021 blog post, "The Dream Act: An Overview"

When we met, Cindy talked about how COVID-19 impacted her work as a health care professional. She volunteers much of her time helping multilanguage learners navigate health care services in the area. A leader in her community, Cindy is dedicated to helping people understand what is available to them as they seek services.

I live in Marion, North Carolina, but I used to live in Durango, Mexico, until I was six. My dad ran a lumber company a couple counties over and had to leave for weeks at time. The company was passed down to him from generations of businessmen in the family. We didn't really struggle. We had a nice house in the city. It was a two-story house in a circle of houses. The kitchen had black-and-white tile, and I had my own bedroom. I remember the stairs in the house every single day—they spiraled. My brother taught me to ride my bike and skate on the circle street. We also had a ranch in the country where my grandmother lived. I didn't realize it then, but the rural areas looked very different, with different kinds of houses. We were very fortunate, and our lives were not typical.

Even though we lived in the city, my ancestral roots are very rural. My mom grew up very poor in Mexico. She had ten siblings and they lived in a little house with no electricity or running water. She told us stories about walking a few miles to go to the well for water. My mom was able to go to school, and that's where she met my dad. My dad is the same age as one of my mom's sisters, and she linked my parents together. She was around seventeen when she met my dad, and he was eighteen or nineteen. After she met my dad, things got a little bit better, and they built up the lumber business together. By the time my mom was eighteen, she had my brother, and at nineteen, my sister. Then she had me when she was twenty-eight. My dad studied in college a little, and then they moved.

---

at www.americanimmigrationcouncil.org/research/dream-act-overview.

The mountains outside the city where we had our ranch are very similar to North Carolina. We had mountains, creeks, lots of cows. We called it La Sierra—the mountain range—just because there are literally mountains all in that area. We had to drive for a little while to get there from Durango. We would go to take food and some supplies to my grandmother. I didn't really spend a lot of time at the ranch, but my mom and dad did before they bought the house in the city, which they did so all of us could go to school. We went to a private school, Colegio España, which was kindergarten through twelfth grade. My mother walked with me from our house to the school. There was a pool there where my brother and sister were lifeguards.

My brother and sister, Daniel and Maria, are ten years older than me. When I was really little, in 2000, my aunt, who already lived in the US, came to Mexico to visit us. When she left, she took Daniel and Maria back with her so they could go to school safely and learn English. I remember when they left. It was so weird to go into their rooms and they wouldn't be there.

A year later, we left too, on the last day of school. When my parents picked me up on the last day of school, I got in the car, and it was all packed up. My dad said, "We're going to North Carolina." I knew then that we weren't going back to our house in Durango, but I thought we were going on vacation. I thought this because my teacher had written on my report card, "Have a great vacation." My mom still has that report card.

I didn't realize that we were actually moving. It wasn't until later, when I was fifteen or sixteen, my dad told me, "It wasn't safe to stay in Mexico anymore." Even then my parents wouldn't tell me much—they didn't want to scare me. But it was because we were being threatened. That's why my sister and brother went ahead. Gang members threatened us for money. When my dad would leave our Durango house to go work in the forests, my mom would get calls from people who said, "We have your husband and if you don't give us money, we're going to kill him." My mom was tough, and she's also smart. She and my dad had walkie-talkies. When she would get a call like this, she and Dad had signals to let her know he was okay. Then the threats escalated. They told my dad they were going to "get you where it hurts," meaning they would hurt my mom, me, and my siblings. So that's why we moved to the US; that's why we picked up and left our nice house in Durango.

After we moved to the US and my dad returned to Mexico periodically for his business, these threats continued. He called us from Mexico while he was there and I remember overhearing my mom say to him, "Who's going to be there? Is it safe? Are you taking a guard?" This scared me, and I started asking more questions. Once when I was around fifteen, when he returned from a trip to Mexico, I asked him many questions. But he told me not to worry about it. It was only when I got older that they told me more stories about the threats of violence.

BLURRY MEMORIES OF DRIVING TO THE BORDER

It took us a few days to get to the US border. It's about a two- to three-day drive to cross into California. I was six when we left Mexico, so I only have blurry memories of driving to the border. Our car was piled full of stuff. I couldn't even see out the window, and I was sitting on one little corner of the seat. My mom was on the other side, and between us was all this other stuff. I could barely see my dad in front, driving. I remember when we actually crossed through border control, the officer inspected our car to make sure we didn't have anything bad in there. They took us out of the car and inspected it for drugs and some types of fruits that were illegal to bring in. When we got to California, I remember eating my first McDonald's burger. It was just a cheeseburger and fries, but that was the best cheeseburger I've ever had.

We stopped at a gas station, and when Dad got back in, we thought Mom was there too. The car was so full of stuff my dad really couldn't see the rearview mirror, and I couldn't see the other side of the car. He started to pull away, and I looked out the window and saw my mom running from the gas station, waving her arms. I screamed, "She's coming!" When she got in, she was mad. We kept telling her we thought she was in the car.

We stopped in California because my mom has lots of family there. We were only going to stay for a few days, but then 9/11 happened. It made my mom and dad nervous to drive across the country, not knowing what else would happen. I remember them watching the news replay the images of the towers over and over. So we stayed in California for about a month, then we made our way to North Carolina. We were headed there because that's where my aunt, my mom's sister Pascuela lived, and that's where Daniel and Maria were. Aunt Pascuela and her husband came there for work in 1999. My brother and sister moved with them in 2000. When they left, my parents told me they brought us all to the United States to learn English so that when we went to college in Mexico, we would know English.

When we got to North Carolina, we started unloading all the stuff from the car, and none of my toys were there. My mom had packed only one bag for me with some small toys to play with on the ride. I was really worried about what happened to all my toys at home. In my room at home, I had stuffed animals everywhere. I asked my mom a hundred times, "What happened to all my toys?" She said, "We couldn't bring all of them."

"Fine," I said. "Did you leave them with my cousins at least?"

"They're safe. They're safe. Don't worry," she kept telling me. She had a look on her face, a sad expression when she said, "We'll get you some more here." Now I know they were worried financially, and sadness was all around because we had to leave.

At that point I started to grasp, even though I was young, that things weren't the same, that we weren't going back. We didn't have much money at first because of the big move, and I could tell that everything was hard. Once I asked my mom, "Can we go to Walmart to look at the Barbies? You don't have to buy me anything. I'll just look. I just want to look at them." My mom still remembers that to this day and gets teary-eyed.

I DIDN'T KNOW ANY ENGLISH

When they first arrived in North Carolina, my aunt and uncle worked picking tomatoes. There were a lot of migrant farm laborers in the area. There were some fields out in Pleasant Gardens, which is a town in McDowell County. They started by doing that until they could find a position at one of the furniture plants.[2] My uncle found a job at the Broyhill plant, and he worked there until they shut down. My mom worked there for years too. My uncle had a similar job at Ethan Allen until he retired. They've closed down now too.

My dad got a job spraying for a pesticide company for a while. My dad would be gone all week, come home Friday, spend the weekend, and he'd leave again for a week. He did this for a little while just to get a feel of things. He had to get a little bit of income while we were here, but he was still running his lumber business in Mexico. He went back and forth from Marion to Durango. He would come here and work for a little bit, and then he would go back to Mexico and run the business down there a little bit. Then later he would only come back to visit every few months as he could. That went on for years. He was risking the threats to his life to support us, and because it was a family business, he didn't want to lose it. We all

---

2. North Carolina has several furniture factories, including Broyhill and Ethan Allen, which over the years have provided employment for many in the region. These factories closed in the late 2000s during the economic downturn, impacting many families including Cindy's.

depended on him and the money from the business. We'd only see him at Christmas, sometimes Easter, sometimes during the summer. So it was just really me, my siblings, my mom, and my aunt and uncle, all living in a small house.

When we came to Marion, I went to Eastfield Elementary, which is a great school. They go all year-round for nine weeks at a time, with a couple weeks off in between each nine-week session. We were in Marion only a few weeks before I started school. The first day of school was so vivid to me. My mom dressed me in this navy blue corduroy skirt, little white tights, a red top, and little black shoes. I had a little bag, a sandwich, and a pencil—that was it. As I stood there looking at all the other kids, my parents asked me if I wanted to stay. I did, so they left me there and went back home. I didn't know any English. I didn't understand what the teachers were saying to me. The teachers and the students were all kind. I was in second grade and my teacher's name was Miss Robinson. I still run into her around town. Memories of her will always stick with me— how kind she was.

It was hard for me to make friends at first because of that language barrier. But there was one girl that always stuck by me. Her name was Breanna, and she was really nice to me. She was my friend through school. It was kind of weird for me at first, that she was nice to me. At first, I thought maybe she was drawn to me because I was different. My sister is light-skinned and green-eyed like my dad. My skin is darker, and I have dark eyes. I think some people wondered if we were white, but we were definitely Hispanic. There was one other Hispanic girl in my class. Her name was Tanya, and she sat beside me to help me, especially with the English and Spanish.

My parents didn't speak English at that point, but my older cousins Edwine, Osbal, and Kevin did, and they would sometimes help translate for them. Eastfield Elementary does have a big Latin community, so there were some teachers at school who spoke Spanish and helped me and my parents.

My mom worked at Broyhill for a little while. But in Mexico she was a stay-at-home mom. In Mexico she took me to school. But when she started working at Broyhill, she had to get up at 5 a.m. and take me to a sitter. Then the sitter would drop me off at school. I did not like that because I was so used to having my mom there. At the time I told her that, and she said, "Well, we have to work now." I understood; I just didn't like it. When my dad came home the next time and things were better, they decided she could stay home, so from fourth grade to high school, my mom didn't work outside the home. My dad would send money, and she didn't need to work. In 2013 she went back to work. She actually worked at Yogi Bear Campground, where I was also working. When my siblings graduated from McDowell High School in 2003, they went back to college in Monterrey, Mexico, for a couple years. They couldn't go to college here because we didn't have legal status. They didn't graduate but came back. They were in a different city from where we lived before and didn't tell many people—they knew how to be careful. We didn't have legal status here at first. Then they decided to come back after we got legal status.

I was a happy child. I didn't grow up with smaller kids around because all my cousins and my siblings were older. A lot of times, it was just me and my mom. I did great in school. I learned English that first year of school, and by third grade, I was pretty much fluent. I loved arts and crafts as a kid. I played basketball every year in elementary school. My mom—she's very conscientious, very generous, but she can also be hardheaded about some things. We're a lot alike!

For us it was kind of a backward story: we had a nice house in Durango, a ranch in the country, and we went to private school. But when we got here, we moved into my aunt and uncle's three-bedroom house. All the male cousins would whip out the blankets in the living room, and they would sleep there. I slept in a bedroom with my parents and my sister, and my aunt and uncle were with their younger son in another bedroom. I was just a kid and wondered, *Why are we doing this? Where's our house?* It took about a year before we found a little house to live in across from Spencer's Hardware. My mom still lives there today.

It wasn't the same in Marion as what I had been accustomed to in Durango. My mom stayed home with me. My dad worked; my aunt and my uncle worked. So we didn't really go anywhere. All I knew were the tomato fields and school. When we went on a little field trip for school to the caverns, I realized America was not just this little town where we lived. We weren't able to travel to bigger cities like Asheville or Hickory until my early teens.

SOMETIMES PEOPLE DON'T EVEN KNOW WHAT TO ASK FOR

When we first got here, there weren't a lot of services for people like us who needed financial assistance and language assistance. It was "learn as you go," basically. For example, I needed extensive dental work as a kid. There was a place on Main Street where people without insurance could go. My sister, who was in high school, had to go with my mom to apply for the assistance, and it was embarrassing for my mom, both because of not being able to speak English and because she needed assistance.

Another time, when I was around thirteen, my dad had to go to the Allstate insurance office on Main Street. While I was sitting in the waiting room, another Latino man was there, trying to get help, and the insurance agent couldn't understand him. I knew that he was having trouble, that it was distressing for him. So even though I was a teenager, I asked him, "What do you need? I'll translate for you." He told me he wanted to pay his whole bill, but the agent kept telling him no, he was giving him too much money. I told the agent that the man wanted to pay the bill for the whole year. So then they worked it out. While I waited for my dad, the guy at the desk said, "Thank you. I don't know what I would have done if you hadn't been here to translate." It was hard for people to express what they needed.

These might seem like small things, but they're very distressing. Ever since then, I knew that I wanted to help my community, especially during that transition when you don't know anything that goes on, where things are, or how to get there.

When I was enrolled at McDowell Tech, I had to work during the months I was taking classes, so I applied for a job at the hospital, at McDowell Access to Care and Health.

Even though I was just out of high school, I gave it a shot. I knew being bilingual might help with the growing Latino population. I knew I wanted a job in health care, and being bilingual was my ticket. I got the job and first worked as a registration representative. I worked odd shifts because I was flexible, but then I had my son and needed something more set. I went from the call center to the scheduling center. This is such a small town, so the women in the front office knew to send people who only spoke Spanish to me. They knew I was in the back office, and they'd say, "You go to see Cindy—she speaks Spanish, and she can help you." Everybody knows you who you are here.

Word got out that I could translate, and that's how I got this job. McDowell Access to Care and Health (MATCH) is a nonprofit. We're a resource hub working with people who are uninsured to get them connected to services, mainly primary care and anything related that comes up, like medication assistance, basic vision, dental. As the enrollment specialist I meet with families for an initial overview and health screening. Once we get all that information, get them set up with primary care, we tell them where they need to go, who to be in touch with, to get them on a path toward a good life. We also help folks that are dealing with substance abuse to get them connected to better services for treatment and recovery. We try to find spots for them to go. We provide case management for folks who have chronic conditions such as high blood pressure.

We serve about six hundred people here and there's only three of us. So we're busy all the time. We serve a big population in Marion, which is in McDowell County, and it keeps on growing. During the flooding in 2021, so many people needed help.[3]

I'm also the vice president of Centro Unido (CU).[4] We provide a safe space for people to say what they need, what trouble they're having. Where I work now, sometimes people don't even know what to ask for, so we help them by asking questions about their health, their children's health, what goods they might need, things like that. If we'd had something like that back then, things would have been so much better for my family.

I colocate between the hospital and CU, so that people don't have to drive very far to find me. People might come looking for a doctor, but we ask them, "Do you need help with food? The children? Health screenings?" Like my family, some of the people who are newcomers may have never had health care before, or mental health care. In the Latinx community, mental health is not talked about very much. We try to normalize asking for help for mental health, help them see that mental health disorders are a real thing.

BEING APPALACHIAN IS BEING KIND

People know to come here through family connections. Their family says, "Hey, come live here. You can probably find a job, and you have a built-in support system," because nobody comes here by themselves. There's always somebody else who has already planted roots. I definitely consider myself Appalachian, even though I don't forget where I come from. All of my main memories now are from here in North Carolina. If someone asks me where I'm from, I say I was born in Mexico, but I live in McDowell County; I'm from McDowell. To me, being Appalachian is being kind, Southern hospitality,

---

3. Tropical Storm Fred dropped more than ten inches of rain on Haywood County, North Carolina, washing away bridges and blocking roads with piles of debris.

4. See Centro Unido Latino Americano's website, www.culawnc.org, for additional information about a variety of health care initiatives.

everybody lends a hand to people in need. The county has definitely grown, and there are more people here now, especially Latino communities. It's also grown in terms of service organizations and health care. My sister has three kids. And my brother's got kids too. We all went to the schools here and our kids are going to the same schools. We grew up here, and we'll stay here. We know that our roots are here, so we stay. I don't see us moving anywhere. Marion has everything for us. I have a regular life. After work, I pick up my kids and go home, be a wife and a mom and cook dinner, change diapers, and get them ready for bedtime. Some of the people I work with are really struggling, and I feel guilty at the end of the day. Maybe it's not guilt, but I'm very conscious of things people are dealing with. There's still so much that needs to be done.

My son Donavan is in second grade. He's the same age that I was when I came here. I think it's different for him at school. The school has more Latinx teachers now. They have a dual language program called Splash where they teach Spanish and English to all the children. Donavan's gone to daycare ever since I had him, so when he went to school, he was already used to being brought up with all sorts of children. School really wasn't much different for him. He speaks mostly English. He says he doesn't know Spanish, but he knows Spanish when it's convenient for him. One day we were going to the store with my mom. She and I just talked in Spanish the whole time. My son asked, "Where are we going?" And in Spanish my mom said, "We're going to the store," and he said, "Yeah, so you can get me a toy." So he understands Spanish. He just doesn't know how to speak it very well. For my daughter, Rosalina, who's two years old, we're really going to push for her to learn Spanish better.

My dreams for my children are the same as those my parents had for me. I hope they fulfill their dreams as Americans, but I also want them to know where I came from and what we went through to get here. My son has more privilege than I had as a child, but I want him to be grounded and humble and to give back as well. He's a very kindhearted little boy. He's got a huge heart. Talking about my family reminds me of this quote: "You are the answer to the dreams of your ancestors."[5]

My husband's family migrated, too, but from Veracruz, Mexico, which is not too far from Durango, but we met here in North Carolina. I've actually known my husband since we were like eight or nine, but we didn't start dating until high school. We're high school sweethearts and we've been together ever since. We got married in 2017. There's a lot of people from that area who live here. They all migrated together. My aunt and uncle are actually longtime friends with *his* parents. So they moved to the United States together, which is kind of funny how he and I ended up together. He was born in California and grew up in LA, and his parents had permanent residency, so our stories are very different.

My dad passed a few years ago. But my mom has kept the same car we had when we crossed the border—an old Nissan Pathfinder. It doesn't run anymore, but my mom kept it. She drove that car forever. She drove me to school every day in that car up until high school. She got herself a new car a few years ago, another Nissan Pathfinder, but I think she's holding on to it, even though it doesn't work, because of the memories in that car. It's a memory of my dad because he bought that car for her. It's actually at my house right now. My mom let my husband borrow it for work one day a few years ago, and he was taking the back roads to work. It was storming and a tree fell on top of it while he was driving. He wasn't injured at all, but the car has been sitting by the garage ever since. I look at it every day when I pull up to my house. I was brought here in that vehicle. It's a connection to my father and a reminder of our journey. It's very important to her.

---

5. See Ando Kineret Yardena's "You Are the Answer to the Dreams of Your Ancestors," November 2018, https://zenpeacemakers.org/zpi-publishing/you-are-the-answer-to-the-dreams-of-your-ancestors-by-kineret-ando-yardena-dedicated-to-bernie-glassman/.

I think I've fulfilled my parents' dreams. They wanted us to have good jobs and give back to our community. Even though my dad's no longer here, I know my mom is happy about where I am today. She has said that what I do, she wishes someone would have done that for our family.

GLOSSARY

Note: Although some terms in this glossary do not appear in the text, they are included for a fuller understanding of Appalachia and its people.

absentee land ownership—absentee land ownership in Appalachia refers to the historic pattern of individuals or entities owning land in the region but not actively using the land or living there. Individuals often rent from absentee landowners, making landownership difficult. Further, communities often have little control over land use and development.

Affrilachian—a term coined by former poet laureate of Kentucky Frank X Walker and widely adopted by poets and artists. "Affrilachian" is both a community and a term used to express W. E. B. Du Bois's concept of "double consciousness" for African American Appalachians.

American Native and Indigenous peoples—although fuller pictures of American Native / Indigenous lives precolonization are emerging, in the present day, the Appalachian Regional Commission's recognized regional boundaries include three federally recognized Native American tribal entities (Seneca Nation of Indians of New York, Eastern Band of Cherokee Indians in North Carolina, and the Mississippi Band of Choctaw Indians) and five state-recognized Native American tribal communities (Cherokee Tribe of Northeast Alabama, Echota Cherokee Tribe of Alabama,

Piqua Shawnee Tribe of Alabama, United Cherokee AniYunWiya Nation in Alabama, and the Georgia Tribe of Eastern Cherokee).[1] Several additional tribes, such as the Monacan Indian Nation, although outside of ARC's boundaries, are still considered to be located in and connected to Appalachia. Many tribal communities work to preserve and celebrate cultural traditions from foodways to language.[2]

Appalachian Regional Commission (ARC)—established by the federal government in 1965 to coordinate efforts among federal agencies, state governments, and local communities to improve the region's economic conditions. The ARC's primary goals included reducing poverty, promoting job creation, and enhancing education and health care in Appalachia. It continues to federally define and provide oversight across the region today.

Appalachian Studies—the interdisciplinary study of the region from environmental, economic, social, cultural, and political perspectives with an emphasis on scholar-activism.

Appalachian Studies Association—professional activist-academic association established in 1985 with a mission to "promote and engage dialogue, research, scholarship, education, creative expression, and action among a diverse and inclusive group of scholars, educators, practitioners, grassroots activists, students, individuals, groups, and institutions." In addition to hosting an annual

1. See "Tribal Communities in the Appalachian Region," Appalachian Regional Commission, www.arc.gov/tribal-communities-in-the-appalachian-region, for additional information about the tribal communities in the area.

2. See Barbara Duncan's article, "Native American Traditions in Appalachia," which expands on Cherokee traditions in Appalachia at https://folklife-media.si.edu/docs/festival/program-book-articles/FESTBK2003_12.pdf. To learn more about trail mapping projects in the region, visit https://appalachiantrail.org/official-blog/native-lands.

conference, the membership also published the *Journal of Appala-chian Studies*.[3]

Appalshop—starting as a film workshop in 1969, Appalshop con-tinues to host media archives, a public radio program, media classes, and other storytelling platforms from Whitesburg, Kentucky, high-lighting stories about and from Eastern Kentucky.

asylum seeker, or asylee—a person who has left their country of origin to seek protection from persecution and human rights viola-tion in another country, who has not yet been recognized as a refu-gee and is waiting for a decision on their asylum claim.

Black Appalachian Young & Rising (BAYR)—part of the STAY Project, a youth-led movement and organization that seeks to em-power and uplift Black youth in Appalachian communities through advocacy, leadership, and community-building initiatives.

black lung—also known as coal workers' pneumoconiosis, is a de-bilitating and often fatal lung disease caused by prolonged exposure to coal dust.

caseworker—someone in a social service agency assigned to a fam-ily or individual to help them navigate public assistance programs.

company towns—the coal companies created a closed economic system, where they not only provided employment but also created entire towns to house workers near the mine. The company was the sole provider of goods and services.

---

3. For issues of the journal, visit www.appalachianstudies.org.

corn shucking—a Monacan Indian Nation tradition of harvesting corn.

DACA—Deferred Action for Childhood Arrivals was created under the Obama administration in 2012 and provides temporary relief from deportation for young undocumented immigrants living in the United States.

double consciousness—a concept coined by noted scholar W. E. B. Du Bois in his acclaimed *Souls of Black Folk*, to explain the ways that African Americans face tensions between conforming to dominant/ white society while staying true to African / African American culture.

Eastern Siouan Nations—Virginia Indian nations in the Siouan linguistic group, including the Saponi, the Manahoacs, and the Tutelo-speaking Monacans. They lived mostly in and near the Blue Ridge Mountains, including the valleys between the Blue Ridge and Allegheny Mountain ranges.

Eid al-Fitr—a celebratory time marking the end of Ramadan. Ramadan is a time of fasting in Islam. Muslims fast from sunset to sundown for a month, and the end of that period is celebrated with feasts and presents.

first generation—often refers to the first person in a family to attend a college or university working toward a bachelor's degree.

fracking—the process of injecting liquid at high pressure into subterranean rocks through boreholes to open existing fissures and extract oil or gas.

HBCU—historically Black college or university.

Highlander Research and Education Center—a training and education center since 1932 utilizing popular education practices to address systemic challenges in the US South. Highly active in the civil rights movement (1950s–1960s) and today building leadership opportunities for youth, LGBTQ+, and Black and Brown organizers to dismantle capitalism and extractive industries and make "sure Southern freedom fighters not only have a seat at decision-making tables but are leading national and global efforts to shift systems and structures that all too often have incubated oppression and exploitation in our home communities."[4]

Hillbilly Highway—refers to the outmigration of Appalachians to industrial centers (specifically Detroit, Chicago, Cincinnati, and Baltimore) for work after World War II. The actual routes taken were often US Route 23 / Interstate 75. The individuals who migrated often maintained Appalachian cultural practices in their new communities and continue to maintain regional ties through formal organizations such as the Urban Appalachian Community Coalition.

hot raising—form of gardening developed by Monacan Indian peoples.

HUD—US Department of Housing and Urban Development.

ICE—US Immigration and Customs Enforcement.

immigrant—a person who immigrates and seeks permanent residency in a country other than their country of origin.

internal colonization—a theory or framework to critically examine the socioeconomic dynamics in the region as an area that has been

---

4. For more on Highlander, see www.highlandercenter.org.

colonized (marginalized and controlled for the purpose of resource extraction) by and within the United States. Scholars have pointed out that this framework does not fully account for internal forces implementing positive and negative economic shifts in the region. Further, the framework upholds the misconception of Appalachia as an isolated place.

intersectionality—coined by Kimberlé Crenshaw, a theoretical understanding of the overlapping and complex nature of social categories (such as gender, race, class, and sexuality) in analyzing systems of oppression.

just transition—phrase used to describe a shift toward place-based, inclusive economic and political processes in the aftermath of the loss of extractive industries. It suggests a shift toward a regenerative, diversified economy that centers the well-being of workers and communities.

Massalit—tribal language spoken in Sudan.

Melungeon—people of mixed ancestry and ethnicity in the southern and eastern United States. The term "Melungeon" first appeared in print in the nineteenth century, used to describe people of mixed ancestry in Central Appalachia, notably, Virginia, Tennessee, and North Carolina. Because they did not fit into America's accepted racial categories, Melungeons faced discrimination, and many questions persist about their origins and ancestry.[5] Melungeons have faced challenges in terms of racial identity and acceptance, and their history and heritage continue to be the subject of research and

---

5. For additional information about this complex cultural history, see Melungeon Heritage Association, http://melungeon.org and "For Some People of Appalachia, Complicated Roots," *Tell Me More*, NPR, July 11, 2012, www.npr.org/2012/07/11/156611575/for-some-people-of-appalachia-complicated-roots.

exploration. It's important to note that the experiences and histories of descendants from free people of color in Appalachia extend beyond Melungeons.

Mexilachian—refers to identity, arts, music, foods, and cultures that blend aspects of Mexico, Appalachia, and the Atlantic basin.

mountaintop removal and valley fill—a mining practice where the tops of mountains are removed to access and extract coal. Mountaintop removal can involve removing five hundred feet or more of the summit to get at buried seams of coal. The earth from the exploded mountaintop is then dumped in neighboring valleys.

Native American Graves Protection and Repatriation Act of 1990—federal law that stipulates repatriation and disposition of Native American human remains, funerary objects, sacred objects, and objects of cultural patrimony.

popular education—refers to an educational approach that encourages the participation and collective learning of marginalized or oppressed groups. It is rooted in the belief that education should be a tool for social change and liberation. Paulo Freire's influential book *Pedagogy of the Oppressed* advocated for such practices and was widely used by regional activists and educators.

poverty tours—organized trips or visits to impoverished areas within the Appalachian region, primarily aimed at raising awareness about the persistent poverty and socioeconomic challenges faced by the residents of these communities. These tours provide participants with an opportunity to witness firsthand the conditions and struggles faced by individuals and families living in poverty, as well as to learn about the root causes and potential solutions to address these issues. Controversies and critical conversations about the ethical outcomes of poverty tours are featured in Elizabeth Barret's documentary *Stranger with a Camera*.

resettlement agency—a federal or local agency assisting refugees and immigrants in new communities.

scrip—a form of payment or currency used by coal mining companies to pay their workers rather than offering US currency. "Scrip" was often only accepted at stores owned by the companies (with prices often above market), making personal wealth difficult to establish and leading to economic exploitation and a cycle of debt for workers.

STAY Together Appalachian Youth Project—a network of young people, ages 14–30, who are committed to supporting one another to make Appalachia a place to stay, in terms of social acceptance, safety, and economic opportunity.

Surface Mining Control and Reclamation Act—a 1977 federal law regulating the environmental effects of surface and underground coal mining.

triracial—some scholars understand Appalachia as a triracial contact zone, referring to the early connections between Indigenous peoples, Europeans, and enslaved Africans.

UNHCR—the United Nations High Commissioner for Refugees is a global agency established in 1950 in the aftermath of the Second World War to help the millions of people who were forced to flee persecution of the Nazis.

War on Poverty—in Appalachia refers to the set of initiatives and programs implemented by the United States government as a part of President Lyndon B. Johnson's Great Society domestic agenda in the 1960s to combat poverty and stimulate economic development in the region.

WhatsApp—a communication mobile device application used by many refugees and immigrants because the information is encrypted and thus more secure than regular texting.

WHO—World Health Organization.

TIMELINE

Although what follows is not a comprehensive timeline, the events included here are meant to note some key markers of both Appalachian history and its development and how it converges with immigration, movement, and resettlement regionally and nationally. This timeline includes periods of time and eras, as well as specific dates, to highlight the ongoing movements within history and their relevance to contemporary events.

INDIGENOUS INHABITANTS

The mountain range stretching from northern Georgia to Maine, tracing a line along the East Coast, was first referred to as "Apalachee" or "Apalachi" by Spanish conquistadors and explorers. Previously, the land we now know as Appalachia was cared for by Indigenous populations. We have yet to fully map and understand the complexity of these populations but acknowledge that their respective foodways, artistic, religious, and sociocultural practices have influenced regional and national cultures.

Scholars have confirmed that the following tribes lived in what is now considered the Appalachian region: Massawomeck, Moneton, Tutelo, Abenaki/Abénaquis, Lenni-Lenape, Susquehannock, Pocumtuc, Munsee Lenape, Cherokee, Mohican, Piscataway, Monacan, Nanrantsouak, Paugussett, Manahoac, Penobscot, Wappinger,

Arosaguntacook, Wabanaki Confederacy, Pequawket, S'atsoyaha (Yuchi), and Nipmuc.[1]

COLONIZATION, MAPPING, AND SETTLEMENT, 1540–1860

1540: Most histories of the region begin here, with the recorded exploits of Pardo and de Soto naming the mountain range after Indigenous tribes along the modern Florida-Georgia border.

1830: The Indian Removal Act is passed by Congress to force Native Americans to leave various lands in the east and settle in Indian Territory west of the Mississippi River.

1862: The Homestead Act of 1862 allows for any individual, regardless of gender, ethnicity, or country of origin, over the age of twenty-one or head of household to claim up to 160 acres of free land if they have lived on it for five years and made the required agricultural improvements.

1891: Congress creates the US Immigration Bureau to oversee the admission of immigrants, including those considered "refugees." Because early US immigration laws did not restrict the number of immigrants the US would accept, no separate laws existed for refugee admissions, and refugees could resettle in the US as long as they met the regular requirements for immigrant admissions.

1910–1920: The Mexican Revolution drives thousands of Mexican refugees north across the US–Mexico border. Although some refugees are denied entry under the general immigration laws, most refugees are inspected and admitted for permanent residence by

---

1. See "Looking Forward by Looking Back," special issue, *A.T. Journeys* 18 (Winter 2021), https://journeys.appalachiantrail.org/issue/winter-2021.

Immigration Bureau officers, who allow for "humane considerations" when interpreting these laws.

THE "CREATION" OF APPALACHIA, 1865–1929

Scholars largely agree that the "creation" of Appalachia occurred during the peak of "local color fiction," heavily concentrated on the southern and central Appalachian regions but read by elite and northern audiences. These works portrayed the region as a place rich with (heavily desired) natural resources and "backward" people. The scholar David Walls summarizes this emergence:

> With the geographic nomenclature firmly established, Appalachia began to be defined as a cultural region and a social and economic problem area. Before the Civil War, there was little to distinguish the way of life in the Appalachians from life generally on the American frontier. Local color writers discovered the region in the mid-1870s, and educators and missionaries sought to define the southern Appalachians as a social problem area deserving the attention of church home mission boards and private philanthropic foundations. . . . Since 1965, official designations have followed the Appalachian Regional Development Act and its subsequent amendments. Political considerations have extended the definition from physiographic highlands to lower-lying areas with similar socioeconomic profiles, as in northeastern Mississippi.[2]

INDUSTRIALIZATION AND MINE WARS, 1900–1940s

Although the region is known for its coal production, the radical history of union and labor organizing in the coal fields and textile industries of Appalachia is a lesser-known aspect of US history. Beginning with the Paint Creek–Cabin Creek Strike of 1912 and

---

2. William P. Cumming, *The Southeast in Early Maps* (Princeton, NJ: Princeton University Press, 1958); David S. Walls, "On the Naming of Appalachia," in *An Appalachian Symposium*, ed. J. W. Williamson (Boone, NC: Appalachian Consortium, 1977), 56–76.

ending at the Battle of Blair Mountain in 1921, coal miners and their families worked with union organizers from across the nation to secure safety measures and health care.

1917: The Immigration Act of 1917 requires all immigrants ages sixteen years and older to demonstrate they could read. However, Congress exempts from this new literacy requirement all those seeking admission to the United States to avoid religious persecution.

1921 and 1924: The Emergency Quota Act of 1921 and the Immigration Act of 1924, together known as the "Quota Acts," set specific limits (quotas) on how many immigrants the US would admit from every country each year. These acts make immigration easier for northern and western Europeans and much harder for immigrants from the rest of Europe and other nations. The strict quotas later contribute to the difficulties many Jews and other minoritized groups faced as they sought refuge in the US from persecution overseas before and during World War II and the Holocaust.

1941: Executive Order 8802 is signed by President Roosevelt, forbidding discrimination in federal hiring, job-training programs, and defense industries. The newly created Fair Employment Practices Committee investigates discrimination against Black employees.

TOURISM AND CULTURAL EDUCATION, 1900–1930

With growing populations in the mountains and the emergence of extractive industries, many social and philanthropic organizations, along with faith-based communities and church congregations, worked to not only provide educational opportunities in the Mountain South but preserve and collect cultural practices and heritage that connected to a European ancestry. Efforts resulted in "folk schools" such as Hindman Settlement School in 1902, the John C.

Campbell Folk School in 1925, and the Southern Highland Craft Guild in 1930.

1927: Ralph Peer, a representative for Victor Records, arrives in Bristol, Tennessee, to record local performers. Peer had been a key figure in the development of "race" and "hillbilly records." These sessions capture numerous musicians, most notably Jimmie Rodgers and the Carter Family, the latter of whom are credited with being the forebearers of county music, leading many to refer to the event as "the Big Bang of Country Music."[3]

THE GREAT DEPRESSION, 1929–1939

During this time Roosevelt instituted the New Deal, which provided job opportunities in Appalachia including the Civilian Conservation Corps that built roads in Smoky Mountain National Park and Shenandoah National Park. The Works Progress Administration also built schools during this time.

1932: Highlander Folk School is founded by Myles Horton and Don West as an educational center for social activism, civil rights, and labor rights, using popular education practices. In the mid-1950s it becomes one of the leading entities in the civil rights movement.

1940: Frank Smith moves from John C. Campbell Folk School to Berea, Kentucky, and founds the Country Dancers.

---

3. Charles K. Wolfe, "The Legend That Peer Built: Reappraising the Bristol Sessions," in *The Bristol Sessions: Writings about the Big Bang of Country Music*, eds. Charles K. Wolfe and Ted Olson (Jefferson, NC: McFarland, 2005); Beth Harrington, *The Winding Stream: An Oral History of the Carter and Cash Family* (Georgetown, MA: PFP, 2014).

1943: Cratis Williams teaches "Appalachian Ballads and Songs" course at Appalachian State Teachers College.

ROUTE 23 / HILLBILLY HIGHWAY, 1940s–PRESENT

1940: Beginning in the early 1940s, this highway is the route along which the outmigration of Appalachians from the mountainous areas of Appalachia to industrial cities in northern, midwestern, and western states occurred. Metaphorically, it represents the Appalachian migration that saw those formerly employed by a declining coal mining industry moving in search of better-paying jobs in urban spaces. Route 23, which stretches from Florida to Michigan (now Interstate 75), is one of several highways traversed during this period of outmigration.

1945: At President Truman's request, the commissioner of immigration and naturalization travels to Europe to investigate conditions and develop a plan to process displaced persons. Ultimately, the Immigration and Naturalization Service collaborates with the US military, the US Public Health Service, the Department of State, and numerous charitable organizations on a plan that allows over 40,000 displaced persons to enter the US under the existing quota regulations. The United Nations is conceived during this time.

1948: The Displaced Persons Act of 1948 allows refugees to enter the US within the existing quota system, and the US admits more than 350,000 displaced persons before the act expired in 1952.

1950: In response to the refugee crisis after World War II, the United Nations creates the United Nations High Commissioner for Refugees (UNHCR). UNHCR provides legal protections for refugees. The US does not sign the 1951 Refugee Convention but later signs the 1967 Protocol Relating to the Status of Refugees.

1952: The Immigration and Nationality Act allows individuals to be eligible for US naturalization. The act also reaffirms the national origins quota system, limiting immigration from the Eastern Hemisphere and leaving the Western Hemisphere unrestricted; establishes preferences for skilled workers and relatives of US citizens and permanent resident aliens; and tightens security and screening standards and procedures.

1953: The Refugee Relief Act of 1953 allows for 200,000 nonquota immigrant visas for refugees and escapees from communist countries, particularly China.

1954: Harriette Arnow publishes *The Dollmaker*, highlighting the challenges of rural to urban migration and subsequential stereotypes that emerged.

1956: Cratis Williams and Beulah Campbell organize the workshop on Living Folk Arts of the Southern Mountain People.

1957: Tom and Pat Gish buy and begin publishing *The Mountain Eagle* in Whitesburg, Kentucky; Ford Foundation grants $250,000 to Berea College to fund an Appalachian regional survey. The survey is organized under the name of "Southern Appalachian Studies."

1960: Conference of Appalachian Governors is formed (precursor to the Appalachian Regional Commission).

1962: The Ford Foundation report *Southern Appalachian Region: A Survey* is published. That same year, the Migration and Refugee Assistance Act of 1962 provides monetary assistance to refugees, particularly those fleeing from Cold War communist countries. It also revises the Fair Share Refugee Act of 1960 and allows nearly 20,000 refugees to enter the US between 1960 and 1965.

1963: Harry Caudill publishes *Night Comes to the Cumberlands*; Appalachian Volunteers forms at Berea College and Eastern Kentucky University; Council of Southern Mountains opens office in Uptown Chicago.

1964–1965: Appalachian Regional Commission is established by the federal government to coordinate efforts among federal agencies, state governments, and local communities to improve the region's economic conditions.

1965: American War in Vietnam begins. The military draft disproportionately impacts working-class populations, like those in Appalachia.[4]

1966: The publication of the *Foxfire* series begins, the classic folklore books that document arts, folkways, gardening, and botanical practices of Appalachia.

1967: The 1967 United Nations High Commissioner for Refugees (UNHCR) Refugee Protocol removes "geographical and temporal limits" of the 1951 United Nations Convention Relating to the Status of Refugees.

1968: W. L. Eury Appalachian Collection at Appalachian State University is founded; Urban Appalachian Council (UAC) is founded, now known as the Urban Appalachian Community Coalition (UACC).

1970: Appalachian People's Old Timey Folk-Rock Camp Meeting Music Fair, High Knob Recreation Area in Norton, Virginia, takes place.

1970: Appalachian Consortium is founded; Appalachian March for Survival Against Unfulfilled Promises (Welfare March on Washington)

---

4. See, for example, Christian Appy, *Working-Class War: American Combat Soldiers and Vietnam* (University of North Carolina Press, 1993).

occurs; *Appalachian People's History Book*, People's Hearing on Strip Mining is held in Wise, Virginia.

1972: *Appalachian Journal* begins publication; Our Common Heritage is founded in Dayton and immediately begins to sponsor a Mountain Days festival.

1973: *Appalachian Heritage* is published by Alice Lloyd College from 1973 to 1982.

1974: Appalshop begins publication of *Mountain Review*.

1975: At the end of the American War in Vietnam, Congress passes the Indochina Immigration and Refugee Assistance Act to fund the 130,000 Southeast Asian refugees allowed to enter the US. Roughly 300,000 Southeast Asians enter the US between 1975 and 1980.

1978: First Appalachian Studies Conference is held at Berea; Center for Appalachian Studies developed at Appalachian State University.

1980: The 1980 Refugee Act, a more comprehensive policy, creates the Federal Refugee Resettlement Program (Office of Refugee Resettlement) to provide for the effective resettlement of refugees and to assist them to achieve economic self-sufficiency as quickly as possible after arrival in the US.

1998: Congress passes the Haitian Refugee Immigration Fairness Act to provide the same provisions for asylees to seek lawful permanent residence, similar to the 1997 Nicaraguan Adjustment and Central American Relief Act that granted provisions to certain Central Americans.

2006: The Sago Mine disaster in Sago, West Virginia, occurs. The coal mine explosion causes the mine to collapse and traps thirteen miners, of whom only one survives. Like other disasters, such as the Walter Resources Mine disaster in Alabama in 2001 and the Farmington Mine disaster in 1968, Sago causes a resurgence of safety regulations against exploitative practices by the coal industry.

2010: The Upper Big Branch Mine disaster kills twenty-nine miners and similarly stirs local response to industry safety standards.

2018: Beth Macy publishes *Dopesick: Dealers, Doctors, and the Drug Company That Addicted America,* in which the opioid epidemic is examined.

2020: The Trump administration institutes Title 42 of the Public Health Services Act of 1944, which authorizes the Centers for Disease Control and Prevention (CDC) to suspend entry of individuals into the US to protect public health. It is implemented in March 2020 in response to the COVID-19 pandemic, and it allows for the quick expulsion of migrants, including asylum seekers seeking entry into the US at the land borders. The Biden administration lifts the order authorizing Title 42 on May 11, 2023, when the federal government officially ends the COVID-19 public health emergency, but not before invoking the order several times for immigrant expulsion.

2022: *Another Appalachia: Coming Up Queer and Indian in a Mountain Place*, by Neema Avashia, is published by West Virginia University Press.

2023: Barbara Kingsolver's *Demon Copperhead* is corecipient for the Pulitzer Prize for fiction. Kingsolver's novel provides an example of a counternarrative to dominant narratives told about Appalachia.

APPALACHIA: A REAL AND IMAGINED PLACE

By Jordan Laney and Katrina M. Powell,
with Savannah Murray, Janet Hanks, and Katie Beth Brooks

You cannot know a place without loving it and hating it and feeling everything in between. You cannot understand a complex people by only looking at data—something inside you has to crack to let in the light so your eyes and brain and heart can adjust properly.

—Silas House, "The Matter Is You Don't Know
What You're Talking About"

The word "Appalachia" (commonly pronounced *ap-pa-LATCH-a* in the central and southern mountains and *ap-pa-LAY-cha* by northern Appalachians, and much of the US), invokes strong images in people's minds. A quick search of the term "Appalachia" or "Appalachian people" online yields pages of black-and-white photographs, a place seemingly lost in the past. Even recently made images are edited to appear aged or premodern with black-and-white or sepia, tone filters. Common responses to "What do you picture when you hear the word 'Appalachia'?" are stereotypical images that are split into two distinct categories: overly romanticized pastoral landscapes and "barbaric" or "peculiar" people—two drastically different sides of the same conceptual coin; a place different from dominant representations of popular American culture. That tension between beauty and otherness is wrought with political, economic, and cultural meaning that reflects national, middle-class, capitalist desires, and within those desires the violence used to obtain them. Although those desires are important to understanding the context for the creation of Appalachia as a social construct, the complex realities of Appalachia, a real *and* imagined place, allow for a deeper understanding of life in a place that is dynamic and ever-changing despite all attempts to portray it as a monolithic and isolated place. As the map in the introduction indicates, the porous and shifting boundaries of a place like Appalachia, like any other geopolitical region, are critical to understand as the people living there are represented and understood.[1]

Appalachia is a physical place, mapped and explored and with unique sociocultural traditions and specific challenges, *and* Appalachia is an imagined place, constructed within the national imagination. Representing Appalachia is what scholar Barbara Ellen Smith calls the "impossible necessity of Appalachian Studies."[2] Even the term "Appalachia" generalizes a massive area, rich with unique foodways, musical communities, religious practices, and industries, to a singular place with common challenges and assets. The term and physical definition are more accurately understood as federally created and scholarly adopted sociopolitical, economic, and geographically informed boundaries. These boundaries creating the "Appalachian region" are used to consolidate and better understand the concentrated needs and assets of thirteen states and over 420 counties. The boundaries used to create this definition are founded on the idea of overwhelming poverty and the connection between poverty and place, emerging out of the War on Poverty and efforts to address (white, rural) poverty in the US. This context is important, because

---

1. Scales, Satterwhite, and August, "Mapping Appalachia's Boundaries."

2. See Smith's "Representing Appalachia: The Impossible Necessity of Appalachian Studies," in *Studying Appalachian Studies: Making the Path by Walking*, eds. Chad Berry, Phillip J. Obermiller, Shaunna L. Scott (University of Illinois Press, 2015), 42–61, www.jstor.org/stable/10.5406/j.ctt1hd18n2.6.

as scholar Gregory H. Nobles observes, "We must also realize that much of the information conveyed by a map is the product of human history, and therefore subject to significant change over time."[3]

APPALACHIA AS A SOCIAL CONSTRUCT

In colleges and universities where classes are taught in Appalachian Studies, many teachers and students discuss five major generalizations or "myths" that dominate discourse about the region. These generalizations include:

- The notion of total poverty and that the region is the poorest place in the United States
- Assumptions of uniform rurality
- The idea that the region and all Appalachians are racially white
- The misconception that the region is simply a homogenous mountain range, and
- Premodernity, or the idea that the entire region is full of people who live as if it were a hundred years ago

Although Appalachia does have rural areas (technically, 42 percent of the Appalachian region is considered rural by the Appalachian Regional Commission [ARC]), locations with predominantly white populations, some sites of persistent poverty, and a notable mountain range, the reality of Appalachia in the US psyche is much more complex.[4] And, although often and easily flattened to a "hillbilly" image, the *Appalachian experience is diverse*. Indeed, it's not possible to understand Appalachia without examining race, class,

---

3. Gregory H. Nobles, "Straight Lines and Stability: Mapping the Political Order of the Anglo-American Frontier," *Journal of American History* 80, no. 1 (June 1993), 9–35.

4. See the ARC's blog post, "Rural Appalachia Compared to the Rest of Rural America" at www.arc.gov/about-the-appalachian-region/the-chartbook/rural-appalachia/.

gender, and ethnicity in an intersectional way, without attending to Appalachia in all its complexities. However, narratives of diversity are often hidden, especially in national narratives about Appalachia.

The region's history is often shared as a story that begins in the 1500s and with the arrival of Spanish explorers; however, knowledge of the region prior to European colonization is emerging. A collaborative project of the Virginia Tech College of Natural Resources and Environment, Appalachian Studies professors, historians, and members of Virginia tribal communities is working to create a tangible vision of what the region looked like. This includes recognizing and tracing the spread of Eastern Siouan Speaking Peoples throughout the area. Virginia Tech sociology professor Sam Cook shares, "It's very difficult, especially for contemporary audiences used to modes of binary thinking, to understand that there weren't absolute boundaries that defined territories. There were multicultural and multilingual settlements everywhere, and they endured through systems based on mutual understandings."[5]

And although the Eastern Siouan languages being mapped by this project are no longer spoken, the connections between those who once occupied the region remain. Victoria Ferguson, director of Solitude-Fraction Site at Virginia Tech and member of the Monacan Indian Nation, notes these connections: "We don't have a reservation, but we have a community. We don't have our language anymore, but we have idiosyncrasies in how we speak. We have traditions of gardening and gathering that have helped us survive. And we have family: because we're in this tight-knit group our families are huge. All that factors into the community we are."[6] Similarly, in

---

5. For additional information, see David Fleming's *VT News* article about a new map developed by a team of Virginia Tech scholars at https://vtx.vt.edu/articles/2021/11/cnre-eastern-siouan-map0.html.

6. Victoria Ferguson, together with a team from Virginia Tech. See https://vtx.vt.edu/articles/2021/11/cnre-eastern-siouan-map0.html for additional information about these political boundaries.

Cherokee, North Carolina, the Eastern Band of Cherokee Indians members are working to preserve and rekindle their language, which has seen active speaker usage decline. Through the New Kituwah Academy, kindergarten to sixth-grade students participate in an elementary immersion school.

Since the early 1970s, Appalachian Studies scholars have criticized the persistent pejorative accounts of Appalachia. Henry D. Shapiro, in *Appalachia on Our Mind*, suggests that since the "discovery" of Appalachia in the decades following the American Civil War, the US Mountain South has been understood by most as "a strange land and a peculiar people."[7] Appalachia's "strangeness" was, according to Shapiro, no accident but instead the rhetorical product of sensationalist local color writers, who, after briefly passing through the region, composed hyperbolic depictions of the "exotic" in Appalachia.[8] Further, Shapiro argues that these local color texts did not circulate passively among the popular magazines of the postwar US bourgeois class, but that instead, US readers were "hit on the head" with the confusing and puzzling reality of the Appalachian region's "otherness."[9] Combatting stereotypes of Appalachians as white, poor, and illiterate, among other pejorative traits, has been the focus of a large body of work within rhetoric and composition as well as Appalachian studies.

Popular narratives about Appalachia often obscure and erase realities and experiences in the region. For example, the stereotypical "hillbilly" is a white male, confirmed by mascots, cartoons, and marketing campaigns. All other experiences become doubly difficult—for example, to be Black and Appalachian, or a Black woman in Appalachia, queer in Appalachia, or Indigenous in Appalachia.

---

7. See Henry D. Shapiro's *Appalachia on Our Mind: The Southern Mountains and Mountaineers in the American Consciousness, 1870–1920* (Chapel Hill: University of North Carolina Press, 1986), ix.

8. Shapiro, *Appalachia on Our Mind*, x.

9. Shapiro, *Appalachia on Our Mind*, x.

Existences that challenge a white (masculine) Appalachian identity continue to lack representation in mainstream media and to a large extent, academia. This is one reason why the work of Affrilachian poets and of musical groups such as the Lua Project, Che Apalache, and Cornbread & Tortillas are so powerful—they reveal the intersectional nuances of an Appalachian identity. Intersectionality (a term coined by law professor Kimberlé Crenshaw in 1989) as a framework or tool can help to understand how an individual's social, political, economic, and cultural identities create different modes of discrimination and privilege. It is not a framework to "blame" anyone for inherent sociocultural privilege but rather a lens for understanding the various challenges people face.

The earliest descriptions of the Appalachian region and its perceived otherness focused on how the inhabitants of the US Mountain South lived in extreme geographic isolation, one that shaped their culture and way of life. That meant that "Appalachian" could be interpreted as the "solid, white, pioneer culture that had first settled the eastern seaboard and contributed to the building of early American institutional life." This depiction of "Appalachian Americans" as the offspring of strong, fiercely independent people with Anglo-Saxon roots produced a "compelling trope" that, no matter how misleading and inaccurate it was, "would prove highly serviceable for popular and scholarly accounts of Appalachia written throughout the next 100 years."[10]

The isolation of Appalachia, according to Shapiro, is not strictly referring to a literal, geographic sense, but in fact "isolation has meant a state of mind, an undesirable provincialism resulting from the lack of contact between the mountaineers and outsiders."[11] Although this description of Appalachian people as Caucasian and

---

10. See *Appalachia in the Making: The Mountain South in the Nineteenth Century*, ed. Dwight B. Billings, Mary Beth Pudup, and Altina L. Waller (Chapel Hill: University of North Carolina Press, 1995), 2.

11. Shapiro, *Appalachia on Our Mind*, 77.

"peculiar" can still be found today, the geographic isolation model is not the most accurate to explain changes, or the lack thereof, in the region over time. Indeed, mountaineers had access to markets and trade systems, suggesting they were not completely isolated from the outside world. This model also fails to fully acknowledge that Appalachia is not now and has never been a completely white region.

Although not completely accurate, the geographic isolation model persisted for decades as the primary explanation for the perceived static nature of the Appalachian region. In the 1960s, a variety of events resulted in the widespread rediscovery of and reawakening to impoverished conditions in the Appalachian region including John F. Kennedy's campaign visit to West Virginia and the ensuing media exposure of the state's poverty, as well as the publication of Michael Harrington's *The Other America*, which examined poverty in a variety of US communities. During the Johnson administration, the federal government perpetuated the culture-of-poverty model as a means of "educating" the numerous VISTA (Volunteers in Service to America) and other volunteers who flooded into the region hoping to uplift Appalachia and its people from their impoverished conditions. Similarly, a "lack of progress" trope was perpetuated about the region. At this time, Appalachia's history of protracted absentee land ownership, political corruption, and lack of economic opportunity were not understood as reasons for the region's persistent problems. Rather than placing blame on the structural inequalities present in the modern, capitalist United States, negative portrayals of Appalachian people in the culture-of-poverty thesis made it easy to blame Appalachians themselves.

In the 1970s, Appalachia was studied as an internal colony within the United States, which discredited the culture-of-poverty thesis and also generated critical investigation of the region. The understanding of coal towns, and hence company towns, as products of colonization meant investigating them as "artificial communities that restricted rather than induced economic growth . . . company towns effectively blocked the growth of local retail enterprises and diversified or supporting industries that might have accompanied coal mining." For historian Ronald Eller, company towns manifest as a symptom of the internal colonization of Appalachia because just as the coal flows out of the mountains, "the profits from mining went to nonresident owners . . . and flowed largely out of the mountains."[12]

However, seeing Appalachia as a colony can reduce its inhabitants to victimhood, subject to exploitation and without agency.[13] In contrast, a worlds-system analysis explains an early capitalistic impulse within the region, one that extends all the way back to the North American fur trade of the 1500s. Rather than depicting Appalachians as being incorporated into the modern capitalist economy as a colony and quickly drained of natural resources, worlds-systems analysis understands the region as a peripheral economic entity with capitalist impulses that were required to fulfill the raw material demands of the core. This includes the development of the timber industry in West Virginia from 1880 to 1920. This industry transitioned from local and small-scale operations controlled by Appalachian residents to a large-scale endeavor controlled from afar by absentee landowners. The entrepreneurial activities do not situate Appalachia as an internal colony of the broader United States but pose Appalachians as capable economic actors participating in a global system.[14] Relatedly, changes in agricultural practices and the splitting of land holdings to descendants left some individual owners open to

12. See Ronald D. Eller, chapter 5, "Coal, Culture, and Community: Life in the Company Towns," in *Miners, Millhands, and Mountaineers: Industrialization of the Appalachian South, 1880–1930* (Knoxville: University of Tennessee Press, 1982), 161–98.

13. See Crandall Shifflett, *Coal Towns: Life, Work, and Culture in Company Towns of Southern Appalachia, 1880–1960* (Knoxville: University of Tennessee Press, 2001).

14. See Helen Lewis, Linda Johnson, and Donald Askins, eds., *Colonialism in Modern America: The Appalachian Case* (Boone, NC: Appalachian Consortium Press, 1978).

industrial farming purchases from families.[15] The variety of nonagricultural practices that utilized enslaved labor in the Appalachian region resulted in "mountain masters," individuals looking to increase their own wealth in a variety of ways, including running hotels, stores, and taverns and leasing out enslaved labor when profitable.[16]

Although the worlds-system model for understanding Appalachia does provide residents with more agency as economic actors than the internal colony model, the intense focus on economics seems limiting and unable to address the social and historical components that have also impacted change in Appalachia. The innovation and leadership of Indigenous communities, together with fierce defense of territories and treaties, are critical to understand the "persistence and change, conservatism and adaptation, tragedy and survival" of the original inhabitants of Appalachia.[17]

This very abbreviated context, then, dispels common notions that the region is premodern or static; in fact, *Appalachia is in production*. We create and re-create Appalachia with each story published about the region, foodway preserved, song archived, image tagged, and film viewed. Appalachia is being built, redefined, and experienced by new people every day. And, with new understandings of historic erasure and efforts to better reflect the realities of the region, work is done to produce a truer story about Appalachia. For example, Appalachian State University professor emeritus Fred Hay successfully petitioned the Library of Congress to change the definition of "Appalachians" from "Mountain Whites" to "Appalachians (People)."

15. See Dwight B. Billings and Kathleen M. Blee's *The Road to Poverty: The Making of Wealth and Hardship in Appalachia* (Cambridge: Cambridge University Press, 2000).

16. See John C. Inscoe's *Mountain Masters: Slavery Sectional Crisis Western North Carolina* (Knoxville: University of Tennessee Press, 1996).

17. See Theda Perdue's *Cherokee Women: Gender and Culture Change, 1700–1835* (Lincoln: University of Nebraska Press, 1999), 195.

APPALACHIA AS A PLACE OF MOBILITY, MOVEMENT, AND RESETTLEMENT

Like many parts of the United States, Appalachia as a place, particularly for immigrants, whether refugees or asylum seekers, has complicated ways of resettling new Americans. This is in part because the federal government has no coordinated integration policies and states often have differing or conflicting policies. Refugees, asylees, immigrants, and the people working with them rely on community networks, service providers, faith-based organizations, and volunteers during the resettlement process, which can mean for refugees, asylees, and immigrants many long years of waiting for assistance, paperwork, case management, court decisions, and citizenship tests. Developing understandings of how things work in a particular place, whether in Appalachia specifically, or the US more generally, is a long process and requires working with nonimmigrants. Language access, education, transportation, employment, childcare, assistance programs, insurance, and medical care are among the top concerns for recently resettled families. Depending on the place, resources can vary, and navigating those resources can be difficult. In addition, being able to comply with certain policies and laws can be burdensome, especially if resources necessary for compliance are not readily accessible. Because much of Appalachia is rural, some resources are difficult to find, and again, community networks have developed as people seek assistance during resettlement. Because US federal policy is not comprehensive, places within Appalachia, and indeed across the United States, have collectively managed resettlement within their own communities in ways that often reflect the community's values, perceptions, and goals. Most other countries resettling immigrants have more comprehensive educational, medical, and employment programs than the US. As a result, many refugees and immigrants live in or near urban areas with more resources. However, not everyone wants to live in an urban or suburban environment, and some prefer to live in rural spaces.

Legal protections for immigrants have a long international history, but as the timeline in this collection shows, US immigration policy generally lags behind international law and has always been embroiled in controversy. The history of citizenship in the US has deeply informed the complex workings of citizenship today. Citizenry, slavery, territory, and state boundaries were inextricably linked and came to a head during the Civil War. Since the writing of the Constitution, citizenship and who counts as a citizen have been contested and fiercely debated. The drafters of the US Constitution were interested in what negatively became known as "popular sovereignty," where property rights and individual rights were seen as equally important. As a reaction against the abuses of King George regarding indiscriminate land taking by a single sovereign, the framers of the Constitution sought to avoid such abuse in the US. However, because "popular" at the time did not include African Americans, women, or Indigenous people, this approach became subject to the same abuses of land takings and denial of citizenship. A series of amendments and ordinances (Northwest Ordinance of 1787, Indian Removal Act of 1830, the Louisiana Purchase, the Kansas-Nebraska Act of 1854, and the Dred Scott decision in relation to the Kansas-Nebraska Act) created many individual cases of citizenry versus states' rights and territory sovereignty. Relatedly, the Naturalization Act of 1906 included a requirement for speaking English. At various other times requirements for reading, writing, and understanding English were proposed (see, for example the Internal Security Act of 1950), but requiring literacy (in any language) is a higher bar. The Naturalization Act of 1906 was repealed and replaced by the Nationality Act of 1940, which was later modified by the Immigration Act of 1990. Each modification is politically and racially wrought, contexts that are critical to understanding the US resettlement and citizenship processes and to understanding the roles and responsibilities related to being a citizen more generally. This country was founded on displacement, the denial of citizenship, and a particular definition of citizenship. That history deeply informs contemporary debates and perceptions around immigration more broadly. Indeed, rhetorical renderings of asylum seekers and immigrants (among others) as "aliens," "illegals," and other derogatory terms have criminalized the very act of seeking refuge.

While migration and citizenship have been a part of US history since the early days of colonial activity, a major moment in resettlement law occurred when the United Nations hosted the Geneva Convention in 1951. The convention established the UN High Commissioner for Refugees (UNHCR) in response to the mass exodus of refugees during World War II. Between 1951 and 1980, more than one billion refugees have been resettled to the US through a variety of refugee resettlement and immigration laws. In 1980, the US passed the act that established the resettlement program, which is now the US Refugee Admissions Program (URAP). Since then, more than three million people have resettled in the US, with most arriving from Myanmar, Somalia, Iraq, Bhutan, and Republic of the Congo. Although the top resettlement states are New York, Texas, California, Michigan, and Arizona, with the recent Afghan evacuation, states within Appalachia have also seen record numbers of refugees arriving. Refugee resettlement, asylum adjudication, and the path to citizenship can take years, sometimes decades. All go through an arduous process, and the US, like many other hosting countries, is constantly refiguring services and processes.[18] The UN predicts that by 2050 there will be 1.2 billion climate refugees; therefore, streamlining resettlement processes will continue to be a top priority for local, state, and federal governments. The stories in this collection identify just a few of the many reasons, including climate disasters, that people seek refuge.

***

---

18. See UNHCR, "Figures at a Glance," www.unhcr.org/us/about-unhcr/who-we -are/figures-glance.

For some, Appalachia is a romanticized rural place of nostalgia. For others, it is a place of violence and ruin. And for still others, it is a place of welcoming and homemaking. It is perhaps most true to cite Helen Lewis's assertion that Appalachia is both real and imagined. It is a place with unique challenges—from extractive industries and the rurally targeted opioid crisis to the lack of transportation infrastructure and often unequitable access to resources—one with a history of economic growth without sustainable development driven by outside industrialists. The responses to these challenges have etched out a cultural, environmental, and economic landscape against the region's real and imagined history that make Appalachia a truly unique and complex place in which to live.

NINE ACTIONS FOR JUSTICE
IN APPALACHIA

In an area as vast and expansive as Appalachia, efforts to welcome displaced populations require multidimensional, reflective, and adaptable efforts. Activists, organizers, faith communities, and others emphasize that there is no single objective or answer to the troubles that communities in Appalachia face. Likewise, the narratives in this collection reveal that different approaches and paths to creating communities of belonging are needed, in addition to negotiating the unique challenges of the region. Appalachian scholars often look to Helen Lewis's twelve steps for community revitalization as a guide for asset-based, community-directed growth.[1] Here, these approaches and tools have been synthesized and presented with the hopes that they can be utilized in Appalachia, and other communities, to welcome displaced populations.

Many of these practices are rooted in the understanding that solutions come from the people directly impacted by harm. Although the sources of harm and challenges across the region vary from locality to locality, some systemic issues persist across county and subregional borders. These include but are not limited to availability of fresh and healthy food options, access to transportation and health care, the influx of opioids, and infrastructural challenges such as clean water and safe roads and buildings.

---

1. Helen M. Lewis, "Rebuilding Communities: A 12-Step Recovery Program," *Appalachian Journal* 34, no. 3/4 (2007): 316–25.

The following relies on Lewis's twelve steps as a foundation for creating intentional communities of care and belonging in Appalachia (and beyond) as we seek justice in Appalachia, especially for displaced individuals and communities. Additionally, the list is inspired by power-mapping activities created for the 2016 "It's Good to Be Young in the Mountains" gathering hosted by the STAY Project, with help from the Highlander Center, Kentuckians for the Commonwealth, Strategic Concepts in Organizing and Policy Education (SCOPE), Project South, and Advocates for Youth.

Resources specific to refugees and immigrants include resettlement agencies such as International Rescue Committee, Commonwealth Catholic Charities, and Church World Service, together with hundreds of nonprofits and local, regional, and national volunteer groups that support people as they transition to new homes.

Progressive education practices teach us to "meet people where they are" and since community organizing encourages relationship building as a foundational step, there is no specific order in which these actions can or should occur. Learning about where you are and asking, "What is my place in this place?" is a question we can all return to again and again.

Jordan Laney

1. LEARN THE HISTORY OF THE PLACE YOU INHABIT.

Whether accessing local genealogy records and newspapers, tracing the history of the land you live on, or identifying native plants and trees, learning about the place you live can take many forms. Not only does uncovering a place's history reveal overlooked or forgotten stories that push back against common homogenized narratives, it also allows you to reimagine the *future* of a place.

2. UNDERSTAND OPPORTUNITIES IN YOUR COMMUNITY.

Learning about a place also means understanding the power dynamics of its communities. Find out about available services (who offers meals, classes, and other resources?) and ways for you to contribute to your community.

3. UNDERSTAND YOUR PERSPECTIVE AND POWER.

Assess your resources and the opportunities you have access to as ways to support community members. For example, if you are a landlord, your property can be temporarily donated to recently displaced families. If you are an employee, you can advocate for collective organizing and supportive policies in your workplace.

4. CELEBRATE TOGETHER.

Relationships that celebrate our similarities and differences can help create a community of belonging. Consider not only sharing your cultural practices but learning about others' as well. Sharing meals, learning about hobbies, engaging in collaborative art projects, making music together, and celebrating holidays and milestones are a few possible gestures of friendship and solidarity.

5. EDUCATE YOUR COMMUNITIES.

Learn the facts about employment, mobility, and housing opportunities and share them widely. Letters to the editor, social media posts, and speaking with clubs, churches, and civic organizations can make a difference in addressing inequities across communities. Think about ways that community members' access to resources might be impacted by racial, ethnic, and citizenship status inequities.

6. DEVELOP LOCAL PROJECTS.

If there are no programs in place to support newcomers in your community, develop projects on a local scale to respond to the needs around you. Greeting and welcoming families, providing food, assisting with transportation, translation services, and employment opportunities are all challenges that can be addressed on the local level. You can volunteer your time with a specific skill set (cooking, gardening, resumé writing, or childcare, for example).

7. SUPPORT EFFORTS BEYOND YOUR HOME.

Understanding displacement and resettlement in Appalachia is connected to understanding displacement in international contexts. Donating, sharing information on social media and in your immediate circles, and volunteering for remote/online tasks are all ways to support global organizations and to support US policy that facilitates migration. For instance, the Afghan Adjustment Act is proposed legislation that would allow for persons with Special Immigration Visas who were evacuated at the end of the war in Afghanistan to obtain a green card in the United States.

Another way to support displaced populations is to donate to national organizations. The UNHCR (www.unhcr.org) and International Rescue Committee (www.rescue.org) accept donations, as do many faith-based organizations that provide support services. Consider supporting BIPOC (Black, Indigenous, and people of color) organizations that focus specifically on BIPOC communities.[2] You can sign up for a monthly reoccurring gift or material donations such as furniture, clothes, and toiletries.

---

2. For additional information about supporting BIPOC communities, see www. thebipocproject.org.

8. TAKE (POLITICAL) ACTION.

Writing letters to politicians, phone-banking, petitioning for funds and scholarships for displaced people, and attending public gatherings in support of refugees and marginalized people are all ways to take political action. In Appalachia, environment justice efforts such as Mountain Justice work to resist the practice of mountaintop removal, Stop MVP works to end the construction of the Mountain Valley Pipeline, and No Hate in My Holler seeks to ensure social justice through community art.

9. ASSESS EMERGENT OPPORTUNITIES FOR CONTINUED LEARNING.

Commit to learning about challenges new neighbors face and how to support those around you by actively listening to those who share their stories. Caring for community members and being open to connection can build and strengthen a community. For instance, mental health challenges are present in all communities, and challenges that relocated and displaced people face are diverse and do not have a "one size fits all" solution. For those interested in training in mental health services, Mental Health First Aid and Trauma Informed Care trainings are two certification programs offered online and in person to support community mental health and well-being.

ACKNOWLEDGMENTS

This project has been a massive collective and collaborative effort. This work began while I was directing the Center for Rhetoric in Society in the Department of English at Virginia Tech. I appreciate the department's support and the support of the College of Liberal Arts and Human Sciences. Thanks to research assistants Tarryn Abrahams, Ke Hu, Katie Randall, Kelly Scarff, Katie Beth Brooks, Savannah Paige Murray, Jenni Hall, Katherine Brazas, and Michelle Kim. I also thank Janet Hanks, Babikir Harane, and Deidre Hand for their work on the curriculum. Thanks to Ren Harman for providing oral history training workshops for students and community members. Thanks also to the Jon Catherwood-Ginn and the Moss Arts Center for partnering on workshops and events.

Funding from Voice of Witness, the National Endowment of the Arts, and the Center for Refugee, Migrant, and Displacement Studies helped make this work possible. Special thanks to Rebecca Hester, Brett Shadle, Marianne Hawthorne, and Deirdre Hand for your commitment to the Center. Thanks also to Laura Murphy, Katie Randall, Jessica Taylor, and Jordan Laney for interviewing and for lending your insights to this project. Thank you to Lacy Hale for the wonderful illustrations. Dina Fathi Ali, Leyla Nazhandali, and Joseph Scarpaci provided translation services that were critical. I'd also like to thank fellow oral historians Jessica Taylor, Ricia Chansky, and Rae Garringer for their support, guidance, and insights. Thanks to Nikki Giovanni and Ginney Fowler for always supporting me, in this and other projects. As always, thanks to my family for the encouragement and support.

Lastly, I'd like to thank Cliff Mayotte, Rebecca McCarthy, Kathleen Brennan, Erin Vong Limoges, Jessica Fagen, Mimi Lok, Ela Banerjee, Annaick Miller, and Kate Garrett at Voice of Witness, and Rory Fanning and Rachel Cohen at Haymarket Books. The effort of this team has been amazing. I am especially grateful to Đào X. Trần for her commitment to this project and to oral history. Thank you, Đào, for everything.

And finally, thank you to the narrators for their stories. I appreciate the time you took to help us understand your lives in Appalachia.

ABOUT VOICE OF WITNESS

Voice of Witness (VOW) is an award-winning nonprofit that advances human rights by amplifying the voices of people impacted by—and fighting against—injustice. VOW's work is driven by the transformative power of the story, and by a strong belief that an understanding of systemic injustice is incomplete without deep listening and learning from people with firsthand experience. Through two key programs—our oral history book series and education program—we amplify these voices, teach ethics-driven storytelling, and partner with advocates to:

- support and build agency within marginalized communities;
- raise awareness and foster thoughtful, empathy-based critical inquiry and understanding of injustices;
- and inform long-term efforts to protect and advance human rights.

STAFF

EXECUTIVE DIRECTOR: Natasha Johnson
EDITORIAL DIRECTOR: Đào X. Trần
EDUCATION PROGRAM DIRECTOR: Erin Vong Limoges
EDUCATION SPECIALIST & PROGRAM COORDINATOR:
Jessica Fagen
COMMUNITY PARTNERSHIP MANAGER: Ela Banerjee
COMMUNICATIONS & OUTREACH DIRECTOR:
Annaick Miller
DEVELOPMENT DIRECTOR: Kathleen Brennan
INDIVIDUAL GIVING MANAGER: Kate Garrett

THE VOICE OF WITNESS
BOOK SERIES

The VOW Book Series depicts human rights issues through the edited oral histories of people—VOW narrators—who are most deeply impacted and at the heart of solutions to address injustice. The VOW Education Program connects over 20,000 educators, students, and advocates each year with these stories and issues through oral history–based curricula, trainings, and holistic educational support. *Beginning Again: Stories of Movement and Migration in Appalachia* is the twenty-first book in the series. Other titles include:

MI MARÍA: SURVIVING THE STORM
Voices from Puerto Rico
Edited by Ricia Anne Chansky and Marci Denesiuk
"A crucial oral history by Puerto Ricans surviving the twin disasters of Hurricane María and colonialism." —Molly Crabapple

HOW WE GO HOME
Voices of Indigenous North America
Edited by Sara Sinclair
"A chorus of love and belonging alongside the heat of resistance."
—Leanne Betamosake Simpson

SOLITO, SOLITA
Crossing Borders with Youth Refugees from Central America
Edited by Steven Mayers and Jonathan Freedman
"Intense testimonies that leave one . . . astonished at the bravery of the human spirit." —Sandra Cisneros

SAY IT FORWARD
A Guide to Social Justice Storytelling
Edited by Cliff Mayotte and Claire Kiefer
"Reminds us the process through which we document a story is as important and powerful as the story itself." —Lauren Markham

SIX BY TEN
Stories from Solitary
Edited by Mateo Hoke and Taylor Pendergrass
"Deeply moving and profoundly unsettling." —Heather Ann Thompson

CHASING THE HARVEST
Migrant Workers in California Agriculture
Edited by Gabriel Thompson
"The voices are defiant and nuanced, aware of the human complexities that spill across bureaucratic categories and arbitrary borders." —*The Baffler*

LAVIL
Life, Love, and Death in Port-Au-Prince
Edited by Peter Orner and Evan Lyon
Foreword by Edwidge Danticat
"*Lavil* is a powerful collection of testimonies, which include tales of violence, poverty, and instability but also joy, hustle, and the indomitable will to survive." —*Vice*

THE POWER OF THE STORY
The Voice of Witness Teacher's Guide to Oral History
Compiled and edited by Cliff Mayotte
Foreword by William Ayers and Richard Ayers
"A rich source of provocations to engage with human dramas throughout the world." —*Rethinking Schools Magazine*

THE VOICE OF WITNESS READER
Ten Years of Amplifying Unheard Voices
Edited and with an introduction by Dave Eggers

PALESTINE SPEAKS
Narratives of Life under Occupation
Compiled and edited by Cate Malek and Mateo Hoke
"Heartrending stories." —*New York Review of Books*

INVISIBLE HANDS
Voices from the Global Economy
Compiled and edited by Corinne Goria
Foreword by Kalpona Akter
"Powerful and revealing testimony." —*Kirkus*

HIGH RISE STORIES
Voices from Chicago Public Housing
Compiled and edited by Audrey Petty
Foreword by Alex Kotlowitz
"Gripping, and nuanced and unexpectedly moving." —Roxane Gay

REFUGEE HOTEL
Photographed by Gabriele Stabile and edited by Juliet Linderman
"There is no other book like *Refugee Hotel* on your shelf." —*SF Weekly*

THROWING STONES AT THE MOON
Narratives from Colombians Displaced by Violence
Compiled and edited by Sibylla Brodzinsky and Max Schoening
Foreword by Íngrid Betancourt
"Both sad and inspiring." —*Publishers Weekly*

INSIDE THIS PLACE, NOT OF IT
Narratives from Women's Prisons
Compiled and edited by Ayelet Waldman and Robin Levi
Foreword by Michelle Alexander
"Essential reading." —Piper Kerman

PATRIOT ACTS
Narratives of Post-9/11 Injustice
Compiled and edited by Alia Malek
Foreword by Karen Korematsu
"Important and timely." —Reza Aslan

NOWHERE TO BE HOME
Narratives from Survivors of Burma's Military Regime
Compiled and edited by Maggie Lemere and Zoë West
Foreword by Mary Robinson
"Extraordinary." —Asia Society

HOPE DEFERRED
Narratives of Zimbabwean Lives
Compiled and edited by Peter Orner and Annie Holmes
Foreword by Brian Chikwava
"*Hope Deferred* might be the most important publication to have come out of Zimbabwe in the last thirty years." —*Harper's Magazine*

OUT OF EXILE
Narratives from the Abducted and Displaced People of Sudan
Compiled and edited by Craig Walzer
Additional interviews and an introduction by Dave Eggers and Valentino Achak Deng
"Riveting." —*School Library Journal*

UNDERGROUND AMERICA
Narratives of Undocumented Lives
Compiled and edited by Peter Orner
Foreword by Luis Alberto Urrea
"No less than revelatory." —*Publishers Weekly*

VOICES FROM THE STORM
The People of New Orleans on Hurricane Katrina and Its Aftermath
Compiled and edited by Chris Ying and Lola Vollen
"*Voices from the Storm* uses oral history to let those who survived the hurricane tell their (sometimes surprising) stories." —*Independent* UK

SURVIVING JUSTICE
America's Wrongfully Convicted and Exonerated
Compiled and edited by Lola Vollen and Dave Eggers
Foreword by Scott Turow
"Real, raw, terrifying tales of 'justice.'" —*Star Tribune*

ABOUT HAYMARKET BOOKS

Haymarket Books is a radical, independent, nonprofit book publisher based in Chicago. Our mission is to publish books that contribute to struggles for social and economic justice. We strive to make our books a vibrant and organic part of social movements and the education and development of a critical, engaged, and internationalist Left.

We take inspiration and courage from our namesakes, the Haymarket Martyrs, who gave their lives fighting for a better world. Their 1886 struggle for the eight-hour day—which gave us May Day, the international workers' holiday—reminds workers around the world that ordinary people can organize and struggle for their own liberation. These struggles—against oppression, exploitation, environmental devastation, and war—continue today across the globe.

Since our founding in 2001, Haymarket has published more than nine hundred titles. Radically independent, we seek to drive a wedge into the risk-averse world of corporate book publishing. Our authors include Angela Y. Davis, Arundhati Roy, Keeanga-Yamahtta Taylor, Eve L. Ewing, Aja Monet, Mariame Kaba, Naomi Klein, Rebecca Solnit, Olúfẹ́mi O. Táíwò, Mohammed El-Kurd, José Olivarez, Noam Chomsky, Winona LaDuke, Robyn Maynard, Leanne Betasamosake Simpson, Howard Zinn, Mike Davis, Marc Lamont Hill, Dave Zirin, Astra Taylor, and Amy Goodman, among many other leading writers of our time. We are also the trade publishers of the acclaimed Historical Materialism Book Series.

Haymarket also manages a vibrant community organizing and event space in Chicago, Haymarket House, the popular Haymarket Books Live event series and podcast, and the annual Socialism Conference.

ALSO AVAILABLE FROM HAYMARKET BOOKS

Border and Rule
Global Migration, Capitalism, and the Rise of Racist Nationalism
Harsha Walia, foreword by Robin D. G. Kelley,
afterword by Nick Estes

The Case for Open Borders
John Washington

Digging Our Own Graves
Coal Miners and the Struggle over Black Lung Disease
Barbara Ellen Smith, photography by Earl Dotter

Going for Broke
Living on the Edge in the World's Richest Country
Edited by Alissa Quart and David Wallis

No One Is Illegal (Updated Edition)
Fighting Racism and State Violence on the U.S.–Mexico Border
Justin Akers Chacón and Mike Davis

Resisting Borders and Technologies of Violence
Edited by Mizue Aizeki, Matt Mahmoudi, and Coline Schupfer,
foreword by Ruha Benjamin

RX Appalachia
Stories of Treatment and Survival in Rural Kentucky
Lesly-Marie Buer

ABOUT THE EDITOR

Katrina M. Powell is Professor of Rhetoric and Writing and founding director of the Center for Refugee, Migrant, and Displacement Studies at Virginia Tech. Her research focuses on displacement narratives, and her books include: *The Anguish of Displacement: The Politics of Literacy in the Letters of Mountain Families in Shenandoah National Park* (University of Virginia Press, 2007), *Practicing Research in Writing Studies: Reflexive and Ethically Responsible Research* (co-edited, Hampton Inc. Press, 2012), *Identity and Power in Narratives of Displacement* (Routledge, 2015), and *Performing Autobiography: Narrating a Life as Activism* (Palgrave, 2021). She is cofounder of the digital-born oral history initiative VT Stories, a board member of the VT Center for Oral History, founding editor of the journal *Roots and Resettlement*, and codirector of Monuments Across Appalachian Virginia, funded by the Mellon Foundation.